Truman and MacArthur

Adversaries for a Common Cause

Donald J. Farinacci

MERRIAM PRESS

HOOSICK FALLS, NEW YORK

2017

First published in 2010 by the Merriam Press

Second Edition (2017)

Copyright © 2010 by Donald J. Farinacci
Book design by Ray Merriam
Additional material copyright of named contributors.

ISBN 9781576386286
Merriam Press #MM119-P

This work was designed, produced, and published in
the United States of America by the

Merriam Press
489 South Street
Hoosick Falls NY 12090

E-mail: ray@merriam-press.com
Web site: merriam-press.com

The Merriam Press publishes new manuscripts on historical subjects, especially military history and with an emphasis on World War II, as well as reprinting previously published works, including reports, documents, manuals, articles and other materials on historical topics.

Contents

Foreword

MY purpose in writing this book was to tell a story of events which occurred during a brief but momentous period in American history, involving two extraordinary men, President Harry S. Truman and General of the Army, Douglas MacArthur. The story tells of their interaction during a time of grave national crisis, how they veered badly off course and ultimately collided head-on. It was a collision which both altered the course of history and irreparably changed their personal destinies.

What is related here is first and foremost a human story, but one that plays out against the panorama of the Korean War—a nasty, brutish and fearsome slice of hell where what was at stake was nothing less than the determination of whether the Communist Sino-Soviet alliance would gain dominion by force over large regions of the continent of Asia or be contained and held in check by a coalition of United Nations Forces led by the United States.

As the drama unfolded during a critical period of approximately ten months in 1950 and 1951, the all-pervasive tension holding the principal players in its grip was the ever-present threat of nuclear war looming over all of humankind.

Other larger-than-life personalities also emerge in this epic tale and are interspersed with the two main characters. They include Eighth Army Commander Matthew B. Ridgway, Secretary of State Dean Acheson, Secretary of Defense George C. Marshall, South Korean President Syngman Rhee, NATO Commander Dwight D. Eisenhower, Ambassador Averell Harriman, Army General Walton W. Walker, Marine General O.P. Smith, Army Chief of Staff J. Lawton Collins, Chairman of the Joint Chiefs of Staff Omar Bradley, and Marine Colonel "Chesty" Puller. Every one of them played an integral role in the drama and some of them such as Ridgway, Acheson, Marshall and Eisenhower actually changed the course of history. But, the overarching giants of this tale are Truman and MacArthur. Their saga of 1950-1951 underscores the fact that no matter what the magnitude of events, history is still primarily a collection of stories about people.

This is one of those stories—one that is part of the larger framework of the forty-five year-long Cold War, but one that is surpassed in importance by none other in that singularly perilous epoch of world history.

"I never give them hell. I just tell
the truth, and they think it is hell."
—Harry S. Truman

"It is fatal to enter any war
without the will to win it."
—Douglas MacArthur

Korea: Pre-Invasion, June 1950

TRUMAN AND MACARTHUR

Chapter 1

The Invasion

War is nothing but the continuation of politics with the admixture of other means.

—Karl Von Clausewitz

The only excuse for war is that we may live in peace unharmed.

—Cicero.

T HE President's spirits on that early summer day, June 24, 1950, were as high as they had been at any time during his five years on the job. His reversal of fortune since his unsought ascension to the Presidency upon the sudden death of Franklin D. Roosevelt in 1945, was complete.

Those early days of Harry S. Truman's on-the-job training, of being the object of derision as he labored to fill the shoes of F. D. R.—of scathing criticism by his detractors of his qualifications to be chief executive—were beginning to retreat into the distant regions of memory. True, he still bore the mental scars of wounds inflicted upon him by so-called friends and unquestioned foes alike—gibes such as "To err is Truman," the "Truman Merry-Go-Round," and "the Pendergast errand boy." But less and less frequently were those cruel allusions heard in the darkly elegant saloons of downtown Washington where the professional pols and lobbyists conducted much of the real business of government; or in the hallowed corridors and cloak rooms of Congress; or even where the Washington beat reporters gathered for their late afternoon martinis and scotch on the rocks.

By mid-1950 it was no longer fashionable to belittle the man from Missouri. How does one credibly deride the man who probably did more than any other to shape and mold the post-war world? And this was after first ending World War II with a minimum of American casualties by dropping the "A"-bomb on Japan. Then in 1947 he saved Greece and Turkey from Soviet domination by sending them military aid under the Truman Doctrine. He also went on to help save West Berlin with the Berlin Airlift and partnered with his Secretary of State, George C. Marshall, in engineering the economic revival of war-torn

Western Europe under the Marshall Plan. After Western Europe's economic renaissance, Truman then transformed it into a bulwark against Soviet aggression by forging a great Military Alliance called NATO.[1]

And how did one disparage the man who ran probably the greatest presidential campaign in history while pulling off an astounding upset over his Republican rival, the estimable Thomas E. Dewey, in the 1948 presidential election? The cognoscente who in 1945 had ridiculed Harry Truman's fighting words, delivered in flat Midwestern cadences, were now—in 1950—far more likely to exclaim, "Give 'em hell, Harry."

The War in the Pacific against Japan, the Potsdam summit conference and almost five years of cold war had seasoned Harry S. Truman. The resounding endorsement of the electorate in 1948 had raised his confidence level to its all-time high. He was now his own man. His emergence from the giant shadow of Roosevelt was complete.

Freed from the clouds of doubt in which Truman had been enshrouded for much of the almost four years of Roosevelt's unexpired term, the lighter, more upbeat, side of Truman's personality had been liberated from the shackles of worry and care. He was finally able to enjoy his family and friends without the insistent interference of the preoccupations of office.

It was against this backdrop that Harry Truman cheerfully wrote his friend, Stanley Woodward, the United States Ambassador to Canada, on the morning of June 24, 1950. In the letter Truman chided Woodward good-naturedly, reminding him that just because he was now an important ambassador didn't mean he was so high and mighty that he could be excused from Truman's persistent efforts to get him to visit his old friend, the President. Truman then extended a warm invitation to Woodward and his wife, who Truman jocularly referred to as "Mrs. Ambassador," to come to the vacation White House in Key West, Florida in the winter of 1951 to spend time with the President and Mrs. Truman.[2] In extending the invitation, Truman could not possibly have foreseen that the Nation would be engulfed by one of its worst crises ever during the winter of 1951.

---

[1]   North Atlantic Treaty Organization.
[2]   *Harry S. Truman* by Margaret Truman (William Monroe & Co., Inc.: N.Y. 1973).

Many thoughts rumbled around in Truman's hyperactive mind on that fateful day, June 24, 1950, but few of them had to do with war and death.

Of course, he had been aware that North Korea had made many hostile incursions across the border into South Korea, but most in the defense establishment thought that they were no more than border skirmishes or probes conducted to test the strength of South Korea's border forces. He was also acutely aware that Stalin had installed his hand-picked strong-man, Kim Il Sung, as premier of communist North Korea in 1945, after Russia first wrested North Korea from Japan. He also knew that Soviet Russia had designs on Japan and that Mao Tse Tung, the Red Chinese leader, wanted to oust U.S. ally, Chiang Kai-shek, and his nationalist forces, from Formosa and unify all Chinese people under one rule. What he could not know was that Stalin had given Kim Il Sung the go-ahead to invade South Korea but had skillfully insulated the Soviet Union from direct involvement, by eliciting the promise of Mao Tse Tung and Red China to back North Korea's military with the Chinese Army should the invasion falter. Mao in return was looking for Russian support and aid should communist China go to war with the Nationalist forces of Chiang Kai-shek over Formosa, Nationalist China's island redoubt.[3]

On the domestic front, Harry Truman still had formidable political enemies to deal with—constant thorns in his side such as Republican Senators Joseph McCarthy of Wisconsin and William E. Jenner of Indiana. Their unrelenting attacks on his foreign policy, his anti-communist credentials and his key cabinet secretaries, Dean Acheson at State and George C. Marshall at Defense, were to his mind galling and unjust. Nothing irritated Harry Truman more than what he perceived as baseless criticism—especially of the scornful and personal variety—that which made not the slightest concession to the patriotism, dedication and toughness of men like Acheson and Marshall.

Nevertheless, Harry Truman felt so good on the morning of June 24, 1950 that he wasn't even going to let the demagoguery of Joe McCarthy and those of his ilk, get his goat. He was Harry S. Truman and he could handle anything they could dish out.

Anyway, he would think about that some other time. Right then he had to get up to Baltimore to give a speech dedicating its newest airport. He hastily finished the letter to Woodward and buzzed his administrative aides to have them contact the White House contingent

---

[3]   Now known as Taiwan.

of the Secret Service so that arrangements could be made for the short trip North to Baltimore, about thirty miles up U.S. Route 1 from Washington.

The presidential helicopter gently lifted the President of the United States and his party into the brilliant skies above the nation's capital for the short flight to Baltimore. A wave of pleasant anticipation wafted over the President as he thought about the weekend ahead. His wife, Bess, and daughter, Margaret, who together formed the center of his world, were already at their family home in Independence, Missouri. Never mind that the house was actually owned by Madge Gates Wallace, Bess Truman's mother, who fancied herself an aristocrat and far above her son-in-law and his people on the social scale. It was still the place Harry Truman enjoyed more than any other. It was home. It was also the home of the aforementioned Madge Gates Wallace and never for an instant did she consider herself to be living with her daughter and son-in-law. To the contrary, they lived with her.

Immediately upon finishing his speech in Baltimore, Truman would fly directly to Missouri on the presidential airplane, *The Independence*, to join Bess and Margaret who had been there all week. Truman ruminated over his agenda for the weekend. Most importantly, he would spend enjoyable time with his wife and daughter. They were a very close-knit family who enjoyed each other's company enormously.

He also looked forward to spending some time with his sister, Mary, and his brother, Vivian. Together the three of them had inherited the Truman family farm from their parents; and upon Vivian fell the primary responsibility for seeing to the proper management of the farm. Harry always enjoyed Vivian's company but there were important business matters to be discussed as well. The fences were badly in need of repair and the farmhouse needed a new roof. A drive out to the farm from Independence was a top priority of the weekend. The Trumans were not wealthy people and personal financial matters often intruded upon affairs of state.

The speech at the Baltimore Airport was a rousing success. Truman enjoyed making speeches. For that matter he enjoyed most things about the vortex of high-end political action and intrigue, which was indigenous to official Washington, D.C. He just wished that Bess enjoyed life in Washington more. She did tolerate it and certainly carried out all her official duties as First Lady conscientiously, albeit without much relish. But Bess did not really like the topsy-turvy Washington political and social scenes. Running the Trumans' home in Independence suited her far more. She was too private a person to thrive in the Washington fish bowl.

Bess and Margaret usually met Harry's plane when it landed in Independence but on this particular languid summer afternoon, they succumbed to laziness and decided to skip it. Instead, Truman's sister, Mary and a group of his friends were on hand to meet the President when he landed. But even the non-appearance of Bess and Margaret at the airport were not enough to spoil Truman's mood on this fine day. He knew that Margaret's singing career was beginning to take off and that she was undoubtedly preoccupied with rehearsal or arranging dates and travel schedules. Harry was thrilled by Margaret's burgeoning career and his heart swelled with pride at the thought of it.

There was little doubt that Margaret was her father's daughter. She was smart, tough and determined. Her admiration for her famous father approached hero-worship at times but such was a daughter's prerogative. She was interested in affairs of state but was probably born a generation or two too early to pursue a political career of her own. She was, however, multi-talented. In addition to music, she had a real talent for writing. After her singing career ended, she became a successful author of murder mysteries and also wrote non-fiction, including a critically acclaimed biography of her father, simply titled *Harry S. Truman*.

After enjoying a quiet and relaxed dinner at home that evening, The President, First Lady and First Daughter repaired to the library for some family small-talk.[4]

The break-neck whistle-stop tour that the President, accompanied by Bess and Margaret, had conducted during the 1948 campaign had cemented the threesome into a political partnership, in addition to being a tight family unit. Running far behind Dewey, Truman had made a daring gambit by placing all of his hopes for a come-back on a cross-country train trip, stopping at scores of towns and cities along the way, with Bess and Margaret gallantly at his side as he delivered one stemwinder after another from the back of the train. Dewey was running way ahead and basically sitting on his lead by playing it safe. His speeches included few details of what he would do if elected president. Truman skillfully exploited Dewey's passivity by pounding over and over again on the same themes—Truman's record of accomplishment in keeping the country peaceful and prosperous, contrasted by Dewey's offering essentially no clue as to what he intended to accomplish if

---

[4]   *Harry S. Truman*, op.cit., pp. 454--455.

elected president. Truman's strategy and its execution turned out to be phenomenally successful. The upset victory was seen by most pundits as one of the most impressive accomplishments in American political history; and fond reminiscences of it often crept into the intimate three-way conversations among the President, his wife and his daughter.

But, many more mundane topics were also part of their discourse on that particular evening—the needed repairs and improvements to the family farm, Margaret's career, Harry's Baltimore speech and the appearance of Joseph McCarthy before the Senate Foreign Relations Committee, chaired by Democratic Senator Millard Tydings of Maryland, then in progress back in Washington.

Their interlude of private, family time was suddenly and rudely interrupted when the phone rang at about 9:00 p.m. It was Secretary of State Dean Acheson. "Mr. President," intoned Acheson "I have very serious news. The North Koreans have invaded South Korea." At that instant, everything changed. Euphoria at once gave way to alarm. The President considered what Acheson had just told him to be grave news—possibly the opening round of World War III.[5]

In the meantime, on the other side of the globe in Tokyo it was shortly after 4:00 a.m. on June 25, 1950,[6] when the telephone rang in the bedroom of the Supreme Commander of American Forces in the Far East, General of the Army, Douglas MacArthur. Being the early recipient of earth-shaking news had been a constant in MacArthur's long military career but a call in the early morning darkness was particularly ominous. With a sense of foreboding MacArthur picked up the phone and on the line was the duty officer at headquarters. "General, we have just received a dispatch from Seoul, advising that the North Koreans have struck in great strength south across the 38th Parallel at four o'clock this morning."[7] Years later, MacArthur wrote that "Thousands of Red Korean troops had poured over the border, overwhelming the South Korean advance posts and were moving southward with a speed and power that was sweeping aside all opposition."[8]

MacArthur's first perception on that early Sunday morning upon hearing such startling news was a chilling sense of déjà vu. It was nine

---

[5] *Harry S. Truman*, op.cit., p. 455.

[6] There was a seven hour time difference.

[7] *Reminiscences* by Douglas MacArthur (McGraw-Hill Book Company, 1964) page 327.

[8] Ibid.

years before, also on a Sunday morning at about the same hour, when he received a similar urgent phone call in Manila, where he commanded American and Filipino forces, informing him of Japan's surprise attack on Pearl Harbor.

"Not again—not again" he said to himself upon hearing the news about Korea. "It couldn't be... How could the United States have allowed such a deplorable situation to develop?"[9]

Only six days earlier John Foster Dulles, the personal representative of Secretary of State, Dean Acheson, in the Far East, had visited MacArthur in Tokyo to discuss a possible U.S.-Japan peace treaty. In an address to the South Korean Legislature, Dulles had stated unequivocally that the United States would defend South Korea if it were attacked. This seemed to be a radical departure from a major foreign policy address previously given by Secretary Acheson in which he had stated that Korea was not within the U.S. defense perimeter and the U.S. would not "unilaterally" defend it. Understandably, MacArthur had cause to wonder just what U.S. foreign policy was as to Korea.

Consistent with his life-long view of himself as a lone voice crying in the wilderness, the five-star general believed that his attempts to warn Washington of the growing Communist threat in the Far East had been "in vain".[10] What was worse, thought MacArthur, was the incompetence of the civilians who came over to assess the situation in Korea for the current Administration. On his visit of the previous week, Dulles had even traveled by automobile from the South Korean capital, Seoul, up to the 38th Parallel, the line of demarcation between the North and the South, and assessed the South Korean forces guarding the border—approximately one hundred thousand troops, but without tanks, artillery or other heavy weaponry. According to MacArthur, Dulles expressed no alarm over the vulnerability of the South Korean position in noting that "the South Korean forces appeared quite ready if any attack should come from north of the border."[11]

MacArthur's conclusion was that Dulles "with his tactical inexperience and possible lack of accurate information,...did not realize the inferiority in both troop strength and material of the [South Korean] forces...when compared to those north of the 38th Parallel."[12] MacArthur described the North Korean forces as "Combat" troops number-

---

9   Ibid, p. 324.
10   Ibid.
11   Ibid.
12   Ibid.

ing about two hundred thousand as opposed to the South Korean forces whom he referred to as merely "constabulary".[13]

A constant in Douglas MacArthur's criticism of United States policy towards Asia, dating back to Washington's firm policy when MacArthur commanded American forces in the World War II Southern Pacific Theater of Operations, was that America considered the defense of Europe as its first priority, with Asia second. MacArthur was basically correct in his assessment. What he did not clearly articulate, however, was why he believed this was incorrect global policy. Army Chief of Staff George C. Marshall had admitted to him during World War II that there was an imbalance between the men, arms and matériel allotted to the European theater and that provided to our forces in the Pacific. Hitler was considered a much greater threat than Tojo.[14] The way MacArthur saw the situation in 1950, five years after the end of World War II, was that the creation of NATO, the enunciation of the Truman Doctrine for Greece and Turkey and the implementation of the Marshall Plan for Western Europe, served to make the imbalance even worse.

MacArthur believed that the greater threat to the free world was posed by Russia and Red China in the Pacific—a threat to Korea, Japan, Formosa, Indochina and the Philippines. He was convinced that the victory of the Communists on the mainland of China and the build-up of North Korea's military forces foreshadowed the ultimate and decisive conflict to come—between the forces of democracy and the forces of communism—and the venue for that final test would be the Far East, not Europe.

"The all important difference," said MacArthur, "was that while during World War II we had been fighting in Europe, now we were not. And it could not fail to be obvious even to the non-military mind that Soviet military dispositions in eastern Europe were defensive rather than offensive."[15]

Truman's view was diametrically opposed to MacArthur's on this issue. While he clearly had evolved in his own thinking to formulate an extension of the Truman Doctrine to the defense of non-communist Asia, he couldn't have disagreed more with MacArthur's characterization of "Soviet military dispositions in eastern Europe as defensive rather than offensive."

---

[13] Ibid, p. 330.
[14] Prime Minister of Japan.
[15] Ibid, p. 337.

As North Korean forces smashed across the border on June 25, 1950, in Europe Soviet-controlled Bulgarian and Rumanian armies stood in great force on the border of Yugoslavia, whose dynamic leader, Marshal Tito, had broken with Stalin in 1949 and now sought U.S. aid. There was also a huge Russian garrison in East Germany and the sealing off of West Berlin from the rest of West Germany in 1948 in an attempt to starve it into submission, could hardly have been described as a "defensive disposition." Simultaneously, the Russian Army and surrogate guerilla forces directly across the border from Iran and Turkey posed a major threat to those U.S. allies. [16] Even MacArthur agreed with Truman that the next big Soviet offensive would be in Iran.

After absorbing the news of the North Korean invasion and coming to a full consideration of its possible consequences, MacArthur initially had relatively little to do. He, of course, was fully occupied, beginning immediately, with an ongoing assessment of the situation in Korea as it unfolded, but at least for the first twenty four hours he was in a type of limbo, awaiting action by the United Nations and orders from his commander-in-chief, a title MacArthur almost never used when referring to President Truman. The President upon contacting MacArthur concerning the North Korean action on June 25, 1950, asked the general if he required any orders. MacArthur replied that he did not.

In his memoirs, MacArthur described his initial situation as follows:

> The only immediate military obligation involving my own forces had to do with the evacuation of 2,000 American and United Nations personnel from the area of the Korean Republic. Late on Sunday (June 25, 1950), the American Ambassador to Korea, John Muccio, asked that they be brought out. I acted immediately. Within minutes, flights of transport planes were rising off runways in Japan and ships were swinging about and heading full draft toward Korean ports. When enemy aircraft began to threaten, I sent in our war planes from Japan. The operation was successfully concluded without the loss of a single man, woman or child." [17]

---

[16] *Harry S. Truman*, op.cit., p. 455.
[17] *Reminiscences*, op.cit., p. 328.

Clearly the main drama on Sunday, June 25, 1950 was taking place in Washington and at United Nations headquarters at Lake Success, Long Island. President Truman requested that United Nations Secretary-General Trygve Lie call the Security Council into special session.

The United States proposed a resolution for consideration by the Security Council condemning the action taken by North Korea. It also contained the following main elements:

1.) The immediate cessation of hostilities coupled with the immediate withdrawal by North Korea of its forces to their former position at the 38th Parallel;

2.) That compliance by North Korea of withdrawal be monitored by the United Nations Temporary Commission on Korea, which would also provide the Council with its fully considered recommendations on the Korean situation;

3.) That all members render every assistance to the United Nations in the execution of the resolution and refrain from assisting North Korea in its illegal action.

In a quirk of history, Russia which had previously walked out of the Security Council in protest over its failure to seat Communist China as a permanent member of the Council in place of original member Nationalist China, was not present for the vote on the resolution. Russia, which had encouraged, trained and supplied the North Korean Army and was a full, though secret supporter of its aggressive action, would surely have vetoed the resolution. In its absence the resolution passed without protest on June 26, 1950.

There was no mistaking what Truman and his policy advisors, Dean Acheson, George C. Marshall, Averell Harriman and Dean Rusk meant by the language "render every assistance". They meant full military assistance to South Korea in repelling the aggressive action taken by the North. On June 27, 1950, only a day later, the Security Council expanded upon the general language of the first resolution in a second resolution which removed any remaining doubt as to its intent, by stating that "urgent military measures are required to restore international peace and security...and that the United Nations furnish such assistance to the Republic of Korea as may be necessary to repel the armed attack." By telecom from the Pentagon, General MacArthur was directed to take any and all such action.

MacArthur's criticism of his civilian commanders did not stop just because he was directed to take decisive military action to counter

North Korea's offensive. In his memoirs he makes the following observation suggesting a lack of resolve on the part of the leadership in Washington: "No one in Washington was quite ready to commit the United States completely, so by 'telecom' I was directed to use the Navy and Air Force [to evacuate U.S. civilians from Korea]."[18] Yet, further down the page MacArthur appears to lapse into a contradiction when he criticizes the President, not for his indecisiveness or timidity but rather for an excess of zeal in taking the momentous step of committing U.S. forces to war without first seeking the consent of Congress and without even consulting with the field commander, namely, General Douglas MacArthur himself.

Nevertheless, MacArthur and Truman at this early stage of the Korean War seemed to be of one mind as to what initially had to be done—stop the North Korean assault and drive them back across the 38th Parallel and out of the Republic of South Korea. MacArthur provided a vivid and sobering depiction of what the United Nations Forces faced, in describing the North Korean thrust across the border:

> The North Koreans had advanced across the 38th parallel in an estimated strength of six infantry divisions and three constabulary brigades, spearheaded by nearly 200 Soviet tanks, with supporting units of heavy artillery, all under cover of an air umbrella. The main attack was along the central corridor, with simultaneous attacks to the west and down the east-coast road and amphibious landings at various South Korea coastal points. They crossed the Han River, and South Korean resistance became increasingly unsuccessful.[19]

MacArthur was faced with the daunting challenge of getting enough U.S. combat troops from Japan to South Korea to make an effective stand and keep South Korea from being completely overrun. The main effort would fall to the U.S. Eighth Army under the command of General Walton Walker, a tough and courageous fighting general, if not a brilliant strategist. Compounding the problem was the fact that there had been a stand-down by U.S. military forces in general, following World War II, and many of the troops in Japan were green, and far from combat-ready. But there was no time to ponder

---

[18] *Reminiscences*, op.cit., p. 331.
[19] Ibid.

these difficulties in the middle of the dire emergency confronting the President and Joint Chiefs in Washington and MacArthur in Japan.

The invading North Korean People's Army (NKPA) was a Russian-trained and equipped force numbering about 135,000 and spearheaded by Russian-made T-34 tanks. The defending South Korean Army (ROK) was lightly armed by the U.S. and consisted of about 110,000 troops, only 65,000 of whom were combat-trained. The remaining 45,000 were essentially policemen patrolling the border at the 38th Parallel. Added to the overall force were 500 American military advisors comprising the Korean Military Assistance Group (KMAG).

One of those American Advisors, Captain Joseph R. Darrigo, U.S. Army, was assigned to the 38th Parallel where he was quartered in a house on the northeast edge of Kaesong, located almost directly on the parallel. On the morning of June 25, 1950, he was rudely awakened by the booming noises of artillery. In the midst of his confusion and surprise, he dressed rapidly and headed for the front door as "shell fragments and small arms fire were striking his house..."[20] Darrigo drove into the center of Kaesong where NKPA troops were being off-loaded from railroad cars.

Darrigo was the only U.S. officer on the 38th Parallel and logically one would assume that he had been warned of imminent invasion. But despite literally hundreds of border clashes between the North and the South, the attack was still unexpected due mainly to the fact that it was the rainy season. The NKPA had gone against conventional military stratagems in ignoring climate and in so doing, had caught the South Korean defenders completely by surprise.

The NKPA moved with lightning speed to the Han River which they began crossing without difficulty. In a desperate move to slow their progress, the ROK Army blew up the bridge over the river resulting in stranding many of its own units north of the Han River. Most either fled the onslaught, were killed or were captured.

Despite MacArthur's complaints that he had on many occasions issued a clarion call of warning to the Pentagon and the White House concerning the serious threat that the Soviet and Red Chinese communists posed to Korea and other Asian nations, when the massive attack occurred he seemed to have been caught by surprise just like everyone else. Clearly, his own intelligence group, his G-2, had failed to properly gauge the seriousness of North Korean intentions and the imminence of the invasion. MacArthur's forces in Japan were woefully

---

[20]   *A Brief Account of the Korean War* by Jack D. Walker.

inadequate to repel a major North Korean attack and there does not appear to have been any urgent pre-war requests by MacArthur to Washington to beef up those forces, especially given that his primary responsibility before June 25, 1950 was the defense of Japan, which was placed at considerable risk by the North Korean action in Korea.

Of course, the White House and the Pentagon were also caught completely by surprise—but most of the accusations of lack of foresight and general unpreparedness were directed by MacArthur against Washington and not the other way around.

Regardless of who might have been to blame, there can be no criticism of the speed with which MacArthur mobilized and moved U.S. Army and Marine Divisions into key strategic defensive positions in South Korea. Given the quality and size of the forces MacArthur had to work with, it would have been all but impossible to immediately staunch the flow of the fast moving and powerful North Korean troops, tanks and artillery. All he could really do was buy time until more substantial, better equipped and better trained units could be introduced into Korea from the United States and other theaters of operation.

To buy time, MacArthur needed to slow down the pace of the North Korean juggernaut lest the entire country be overrun. He swiftly put into play every available plane, train, truck and ship in order to move troops from Japan to South Korea at a break-neck pace. Whatever divisions or regiments could get there first were injected piece meal into the battle, even if it meant that they were without artillery and air support, deprived of adequate means of supply and reinforcement and without the proper clothing, equipment and ammunition. Once there, the American units needed to slow down the flow of the North Korean Army on the main south-bound roads. They hastily established road blocks and set up barricades—anything to obstruct and interfere with the forward progress of the invading army. Many of the inexperienced, poorly-trained and out-numbered South Korean units had simply broken and run in the face of the onslaught from the North, leaving clear paths in the central corridor of the country for the enemy's advance. U.S. forces desperately needed to plug the holes and put up some sort of meaningful resistance. As MacArthur had calculated, the mere injection of American troops into the battle areas gave the North Korean commanders some incentive to pause. They had no real way of gauging the full strength and depth of the UN forces they were now encountering, and more importantly, those that were on the way. Many of the fastest moving North Korean units, lacking adequate intelligence, and facing uncertainty over what strategies the U.S. might employ, paused and fell-back temporarily to regroup and re-assess their situations. MacArthur's plan to slow down the North Korean offensive was meeting with a measure of success in some areas and General Walton Walker, a tenacious bulldog of a man, was doing his best to move his undermanned 8th Army battalions and regiments from one collapsing defensive position to another, trying to plug a leak at one location at the cost of weakening the defenses of another; and only to have new leaks spring up at yet other places.

Through June and much of July there was serious doubt both in Tokyo and Washington that the UN forces would be able to stem the tide of their determined foe, whose forward momentum was inexorably pushing the U.S. Eighth Army and the Republic of Korea forces in a southeasterly direction to the Pusan Peninsula, where their backs would be to the Sea of Japan.

MacArthur had also inserted Task Forth Smith composed mainly of the Army's 24th Infantry Division into South Korea but it was soundly defeated by North Korean forces at Osan, with very heavy casualties suffered by the American troops.

Even MacArthur, who in his memoirs tried to put the best face possible on the U.S. set-backs and staggering defeats during the early weeks of the war, admitted that "The enemy...aided by this preponderance of numbers and weapons...was able simultaneously to exert heavy pressure against General Walker's men in the center and flow around them on both sides."[21]

Indeed, by the beginning of August, the U.S. Eighth Army under General Walker and the ROK (i.e. Republic of Korea) forces had been driven back into a small region in the southeast corner of the Korean Peninsula around the city of Pusan. By September the UN coalition forces held only about ten percent of the Korean Peninsula—the area at and around Pusan. But massive American troops, supplies, air and naval support and reinforcements poured in to the port of Pusan from the United States, and allowed General Walker to establish and maintain a defensive perimeter along the Naktong River, which became known as the "Pusan Perimeter".[22] The desperate rearguard action was working but only to the extent of providing MacArthur with the invaluable time he needed to plan and execute his next move. The UN

---

[21]   Ibid, p. 336.
[22]   Eventually UN troops in Korea numbered approximately 348,000, the vast majority of whom were American.

forces, however, were sustaining staggering losses—6,886 casualties by August 25th and almost 14,000 by mid-September.

President Truman had returned to Washington from Missouri on *The Independence* the afternoon of June 25, 1950. The last remnants of his euphoric mood of the previous day were long-gone. They had been replaced by a combination of anger and hard resolve. American prestige had been put to a severe test by the invasion and needed to be preserved during this time of cold war at all costs. The eloquent words of Dean Acheson said it best: "Prestige is the shadow cast by power, which is of great deterrent importance." [23] After five years of the Cold War, Truman needed no convincing. He "was already a hard-liner." [24] He knew with an unassailable certainty as he alighted from the plane at Andrews Air Force Base that the United States was going to go to war in Korea. And it would happen under the command of General MacArthur, a man "whom he did not like, and who in turn did not respect him." [25] Truman viewed MacArthur as a pompous prima donna who put his own public image ahead of the country. MacArthur considered Truman a light weight—a woefully inadequate commander in chief. How could he, MacArthur, the greatest military mind of the 20th Century, be expected to take orders from a former national guard captain? Dwight D. Eisenhower, having served directly under MacArthur before World War II in both Manila and Washington, was acutely aware of the potentially corrosive relationship between the two men. Even after allied forces under Eisenhower had liberated Europe and defeated Nazi Germany, MacArthur still referred to Eisenhower as "the best clerk" he had ever had. Shortly after hostilities broke out in Korea, Eisenhower told General Matthew B. Ridgway that they badly needed a younger general for Korea, rather than "an untouchable whose actions you cannot predict and who will himself decide what information he wants Washington to have and what he will withhold." [26]

Truman, however, had enough problems to deal with in late June of 1950 and would not add to them the domestic uproar and international fall-out which would ensue were he to replace an icon—one of the most revered military men in the world, who was practically a God to millions of Americans. No, General of the Army Douglas

---

[23] *The Coldest Winter*, by David Halberstam (Hyperion, New York) p. 91.

[24] Ibid.

[25] Ibid.

[26] Ibid, p. 102.

MacArthur would be the supreme commander of all United Nations forces in Korea. Truman had made up his mind that MacArthur it would be, notwithstanding the fact that John Foster Dulles had advised Truman on Dulles's return from Korea and Japan "to bring MacArthur home and retire him before he caused trouble."[27] Dulles considered MacArthur to be "well past his prime and a potential liability."[28] Such advice coming from Dulles, "the most prominent Republican spokesman on foreign policy,"[29] carried special weight for Truman. Still, he could not accept it. To recall MacArthur, a man with national heroic status, in this time of strife, would set off such a reaction of outrage among his countrymen that Truman would be crippled in his ability to lead the nation to war.

Privately, Truman's view of MacArthur was far worse than that of either Dulles or Eisenhower. He had penned his own colorful sobriquet for MacArthur in his journal in 1945, calling MacArthur "Mr. Prima Donna, Brass Hat"—"play actor and bunko man."[30]

None of this, however, reflected Truman's opinion of MacArthur as a military leader. On June 25, 1950, Truman had no doubts about MacArthur's ability. Truman may have considered MacArthur to be a stuffed shirt but the man from Independence was no fool. MacArthur had had nothing short of a brilliant career as a wartime leader, strategist and tactician in both World War I and World War II. His nation, personified in its President, was turning to him once more to reverse the tide against an implacable and extremely dangerous foe—the monolithic axis of Russia and Red China and its junior partner, North Korea.

---

[27] *Truman* by David McCullough (Simon and Schuster, 1992), p. 793.
[28] Ibid.
[29] Ibid.
[30] Ibid.

"The official flag of the United Nations, now flying with national banners over the U.N. armed forces in action to restore the peace in Korea, is shown in this photograph. The background color of the flag is the light blue associated with the U.N. since its early days, while the official United Nations seal in its center is in white." (Quoted from the original caption). Photograph is datelined New York, 1950.

Russian-built North Korean SU-76 self-propelled gun is examined by U.S. personnel, including a Navy Commander, after it was disabled by United Nations' forces during early fighting in the Korean War. This 1943-44 vintage vehicle had a crew of four and mounted a 76.2mm gun with 62 rounds of ammunition. The hole in the angle of the bow glacis plate may have been made by the projectile that knocked it out of action. Other damage is visible just above the gun barrel.

Senior U.S. and British naval officers confer on board USS Rochester (CA-124), flagship of the U.S. Seventh Fleet, during the early days of the Korean War. The original photograph is dated 1 July 1950. Those present are (from left to right): Captain A.D. Torlesse, RN, Commanding Officer of HMS Triumph; Rear Admiral John M. Hoskins, USN, Commander, Carrier Group, Seventh Fleet; Vice Admiral Arthur D. Struble, USN, Commander, Seventh Fleet; and Rear Admiral Sir William G. Andrewes, RN, Commander, British Commonwealth Forces.

First Korean War carrier air strikes, 3-4 July 1950. A North Korean rail-road train is attacked just south of Pyongyang by planes from the joint U.S.-British Task Force 77, 4 July 1950. The carriers involved were USS Valley Forge (CV-45) and HMS Triumph.

USS Juneau (CLAA-119) receives ammunition and fuel at Sasebo, Japan, on 6 July 1950. Flagship of Rear Admiral John M. Higgins, Commander, Task Group 96.5, Juneau actively patrolled and bombarded along the Korean east coast from 28 June to 5 July 1950. She was the first U.S. Navy cruiser to see combat action during the Korean War. Note Japanese floating crane alongside.

Wonsan Oil Refinery, Wonsan, North Korea, under attack by aircraft from Valley Forge (CV-45) on 18 July 1950. Smoke from this attack, which reportedly destroyed some 12,000 tons of refined petroleum products and much of the plant, could be seen sixty miles out at sea.

Grumman F9F-3 "Panther" of Fighter Squadron 52 (VF-52) taxies forward on USS Valley Forge (CV-45) to be catapulted for strikes on targets along the east coast of Korea, 19 July 1950. Note details of the ship's island, including scoreboard at left.

A Vought F4U-4B fighter is fueled and armed with 5-inch rockets on board the USS Valley Forge (CV-45), prior to strikes against targets on the Korean east coast, 19 July 1950.

TRUMAN AND MACARTHUR

*Lieutenant (Junior Grade) W. Boyd Muncie disembarks from a HO3S heli-
copter, upon his return to USS Valley Forge (CV-45) on 19 July 1950, following his rescue from the Sea of Japan by an amphibian "Sea Otter" from
HMS Triumph. The first Naval Aviator to be shot down by North Korean
anti-aircraft fire, he spent two and a half hours in the water.*

Captain David Booker, USMC (left), "mans his aerial reconnaissance plane on flight deck of a U.S. Navy aircraft carrier with the Seventh Fleet." Quoted caption was released with this photo on 19 July 1950. If the view was taken at about that time, the carrier would be USS Valley Forge (CV-45), then the only Seventh Fleet carrier, which was engaged in early Korean War operations. Capt. Booker's plane is a Vought F4U-5P "Corsair". Note its camera hatch low on the fuselage behind the cockpit.

Flight deck crewmen wheel carts of rockets past a Vought F4U-4B fighter on board the USS Valley Forge (CV-45), while arming planes for strikes against North Korean targets in July 1950. This plane is Bureau Number 97503.

Flight deck tractors tow Grumman F9F "Panther" fighters forward on the flight deck of the USS Valley Forge (CV-45), in preparation for catapulting them off to attack North Korean targets, July 1950. This photograph was released for publication on 21 July 1950. Valley Forge had launched air strikes on 3-4 July and 18-19 July.

TRUMAN AND MACARTHUR

A fuel or ammunition train burns near Kumchon, North Korea, after being hit by planes from USS Valley Forge (CV-45). Photographed on the morning of 22 July 1950.

Admiral Forrest P. Sherman, Chief of Naval Operations (left), talks with Admiral Arthur W. Radford, USN, Commander in Chief, Pacific and Pacific Fleet, during a press conference at Naval Air Station North Island, San Diego, California, in July 1950.

Admiral Forrest P. Sherman, Chief of Naval Operations (center), and Admiral Arthur W. Radford, USN, Commander in Chief, Pacific and Pacific Fleet, at a press conference at Naval Air Station North Island, San Diego, California, in July 1950. Note electronic gear on and near the table, including a case in lower left labeled "Columbia Broadcasting System".

Rear Admiral Edward C. Ewen, USN, Commander Carrier Division One (left), Vice Admiral Arthur D. Struble, USN, Commander Seventh Fleet (center) and Rear Admiral John M. Hoskins, USN, Commander Carrier Division Three, pose with a World globe, while conferring aboard a Seventh Fleet ship, circa August-December 1950.

Chapter 2

The General

Action is eloquence.
—Coriolanus by William Shakespeare

The greater the power, the more dangerous the abuse.
—Edmund Burke, Speech, 1771

GENERAL Douglas MacArthur was a man of many talents and it may be fairly stated, with opposition from some quarters, that the man was far greater than the sum of his parts. He was also a man of many contradictions.

MacArthur was a devoted American patriot but an inveterate self-aggrandizer. He was a brilliant military strategist but almost never willing to admit a mistake and, therefore, a flawed leader. He was brave and resourceful in combat but, on occasion, blindly exposed his troops to unnecessary risk.

He was loyal to his country but sometimes contemptuous of the chain of command. His love for America often did not include its leaders and on more than one occasion, he treated both his military and civilian superiors in Washington with a lack of respect. In certain instances, his lack of respect rose to the level of insubordination. He had poor relationships with Roosevelt, Truman, Eisenhower, Marshall and Bradley, his top civilian and military superiors during the momentous last 15 years of his career.

He was an erudite man—eloquent of speech with the capacity to communicate the most intricate plan of action with total clarity. In conversation, he could be courtly and charming. He could also be dismissive and condescending.

MacArthur began his career as an apolitical professional soldier but wound up being the most political of men, with his own private constituency. He imposed absolute control over the flow of information from his headquarters, took the sole credit for positive developments; and none of the blame when things went wrong. All successes were credited to MacArthur and his subordinate officers were not permitted to share in the glory.

Those officers who advanced in MacArthur's chain of command were often sycophants who subordinated themselves to MacArthur and were subsumed within his all-powerful aura. This almost monarchical culture did not breed the most talented and enterprising officer corps and many of those in his high command were known more for their fierce loyalty than for their competence.

MacArthur was flamboyant and charismatic, which often masked the flaws in his decision-making. When it came to the subject of his own successes and failures, he was frequently self-deluded by egotism.

All that said, however, MacArthur's successes were among the most monumental in American history. He cut a bigger than life figure—the product of the sheer dramatic nature of his victories and his skill at always being out in front of everyone else in the spin of the war publicity machine.

While other generals were self-promoters, none were as successful in elevating themselves to cult status—a lofty Mt. Olympus—type perch where the rules and standards governing ordinary men did not apply.

MacArthur was not a soldier's soldier in the manner of General William Tecumseh Sherman of Civil War fame ("Uncle Billy") or General Omar Bradley of World War II renown. He essentially lived and operated within the confines of his own exalted self-image where, nonetheless, driven by his enormous talent—some would say genius— he performed many prodigious military feats, usually preceded by grandiose plans.

In the final analysis, MacArthur was unique in the annals of American military history—a shameless self-promoter—but a true legend, icon and hero nonetheless, who fought fiercely and skillfully for his country in three major wars of the twentieth century; and governed the defeated Japanese nation after World War II with wisdom, skill and humanity, enabling it to reform and eventually re-join the community of nations.

The multiple forces which ultimately caused the Truman-MacArthur fission to attain critical mass and implode on April 10, 1951, during a critical period of the Korean War, could be reduced to a sort of power-point presentation with bullet points for the well-known historical facts of the oft-chronicled events occurring between August of 1945 and April of 1951. But this would provide about as thorough an understanding of the cause and significance of the debacle as, for instance, one would comprehend about the origins of World War I if told only that it resulted from the assassination of Archduke Ferdinand of Austria-Hungary by Serbian terrorists. In both instances the precipitating events would be clearly depicted but we would have no real understanding of the meaning of those events.

Any exegesis of the causes and significance of the Truman-MacArthur crisis requires a far-reaching, but not necessarily exhaustive, recitation of the key facts of each man's background. In those backgrounds are found the seeds of the final confrontation.

MacArthur was among the aristocracy of the U.S. military firmament. He was born to it. His father, Arthur MacArthur, Jr., was also a celebrated national military hero—awarded the Congressional Medal of Honor during the Civil War for his daring charge up Missionary Ridge in Tennessee, as a very young Captain, serving under General Philip Sheridan of the Union Army.

Douglas MacArthur was born into military life in 1880 at a desolate New Mexico outpost where his father commanded an infantry company with a mission to counter the "Indian menace". He claimed that his earliest childhood memory was the sound of bugles. MacArthur was immersed in military lore as a boy of tender years—taught to ride and shoot before he could even read or write. In his memoirs, *Reminiscences*, he laid claim to a rich ancestry of grand and noble fighting men, all descendants of Clan Campbell of Scotland. With a grandiose flourish he wrote that "the traditions of the family are linked with heroic lore of King Arthur and the Knights of the Round Table."[31] And if this weren't enough to imbue Douglas MacArthur with a deep sense of reverence for his roots, there was the presence in his life of the towering figure of his grandfather, Arthur MacArthur, who was brought to America by his widowed mother from Scotland in 1825. Eventually Arthur settled in Wisconsin and there elevated himself from ordinary beginnings to become the Milwaukee City Attorney, Judge of the Second Judicial Circuit and eventually was appointed by President Ulysses S. Grant as Justice of the Supreme Court of the District of Columbia. Arthur MacArthur was one of the leading jurists of his day and passed on to his grandson a reverence for law and liberty which held the latter in good stead more than half a century later when he served as military governor of Japan.

Always with a flair for the dramatic, Douglas MacArthur, referring to his father, Arthur, relates in *Reminiscences* that hearing the drums of the Old Clan Campbell war cry, "Listen, O Listen", Lt. Arthur Mac-Arthur, Jr. volunteered and entered the Union Army on August 4,

---

[31] *Reminiscences*, op.cit., p. 3.

1862 at the age of 17.[32] Whether Douglas MacArthur allowed himself a bit of dramatic license in positing that as the precipitating cause for his father's entry into military service is beside the point. Like the "King Arthur and Knights of the Round Table" reference, it demonstrates a key facet of MacArthur's personality—his sense of grandiosity combined with drama in assessing the accomplishments of his distinguished forefathers, as well as his own.

MacArthur achieved academic distinction at West Texas Military Academy and in 1898 entered the United States Military Academy at West Point, where he graduated number one in his class in 1903 with one of the most outstanding academic records in the history of the Academy. He was honored with the title of First Captain of the Corps of Cadets. Already he was beginning to view himself as among the elite of the elite of America's young corps of academy-trained military officers, a group of men who were part of an exclusive caste system, a gentlemen's club. This fact often rankled plain-mannered men like Harry Truman, who had a visceral dislike for those he judged as putting on airs and too full of themselves. The contrast presents an anomaly which in some ways is uniquely American. While the very top U.S. wartime generals usually were and are West Point graduates and, therefore, at the pinnacle of the military's rigid hierarchy (e.g. Eisenhower, MacArthur, Marshall, Pershing, Patton, Bradley, Ridgway, Schwarzkopf), their commander-in-chief, the President, isn't required under the U.S. Constitution to have any particular military training and, in fact, need not have even served in the military at all. This reflects the wisdom of the founding fathers in enhancing the Constitution's system of checks and balances through civilian control over the military. But the system also created a natural tension between the nation's military and civilian leaderships. That Harry S. Truman, a man of little formal education and service only in the Missouri National Guard, could give orders to the great MacArthur was a bitter pill for the latter to swallow. Had the man in the White House from June 25, 1950 to April 11, 1951 been Dwight David Eisenhower, one of MacArthur's peers, it is unlikely that he would have pushed the envelope as far as he did; and the historic confrontation between a five-star general and a sitting president is unlikely to have occurred. Truman and MacArthur were like oil and water. Their interpersonal dynamic was similar to many others since the beginning of recorded time, which affected the course of history. Of course, as MacArthur eventually learned, Harry S. Truman

---

[32] Ibid.

may have been plain and simple in dress, speech and manner, but he was no ordinary man.

Upon being commissioned as a second lieutenant upon his graduation from West Point, MacArthur's first assignment was as an aide-de-camp to his father in the Philippines. This was followed by service as an aide-de-camp to President Theodore Roosevelt. MacArthur demonstrated his bravery in action for the first time during the Vera Cruz Expedition of 1914. By the time the United States entered World War I in 1917, MacArthur had steadily ascended the promotion ladder to the rank of full colonel.

World War I gave MacArthur his first real taste of fame. Even before the war he helped create what would later become the famed "Rainbow Division," cobbled together from various National Guard units. It was a natural fit when MacArthur was sent to France in 1917 as chief of staff of the 42nd ("Rainbow") Division. Anyone who thought MacArthur would be content to lead from a rear echelon position back at Division Headquarters did not know the man. Almost from the beginning he entered the thick of the fighting, consistent with his conviction that a real commander leads from the front. To him it was a case of "no guts—no glory." MacArthur was all the things you could ask for from a combat leader—courageous, skillful, highly intelligent and dedicated. He was also out to make a name for himself. His personal ambition, however, in no way diminishes or detracts from his achievements.

The Rainbow Division's first major attack on the Germans came in early March of 1918. Under heavy German artillery fire, MacArthur "decided to walk the line, hoping that my presence might comfort the men."[33] Then MacArthur went "over the top" and led his men into battle and routed the German salient. On March 21st, in the face of a huge German offensive against the British and French Armies in an attempt by the Germans to end the war, and aimed ultimately at the Marne and Paris, the "Rainbow" under MacArthur was left on its own to guard the entire Baccarat section on the Lorraine front. After eighty two days of almost constant combat, the Rainbow was cited by the French general command, under whose umbrella it served, for its "offensive ardor, the spirit of method, the discipline shown by all its officers and men." MacArthur had left his distinctive stamp on the Division. In many battles over the ensuing months—including offensives under first, the French Fourth, and later Sixth Armies, MacArthur and

---

[33]   Ibid, p. 55.

the Rainbow distinguished themselves repeatedly. MacArthur himself was awarded six Silver Stars, and France made him a Commander in the Legion of Honor, while twice awarding him the Croix de Guerre. He was promoted to Brigadier General and given command of the 84th Infantry Brigade of the Division. In an attempt to break the Hindenburg Line at its pivotal point MacArthur led his brigade in a daring attack against the German City of Metz, won a great victory and was awarded his sixth Silver Star. He also won two Distinguished Service Crosses. General Black Jack Pershing, the Commanding General of all American Forces in Europe during World War I, in response to criticism of some of MacArthur's methods in combat, which had led to an investigation, responded with the command to "Stop all this nonsense. MacArthur is the greatest leader of troops we have, and I intend to make him a division commander."[34] The criticism had been mainly of his failure to wear a helmet in battle, to carry a gas mask, to carry a weapon (he carried a riding crop only) and his refusal to lead from the command post. In typical fashion, MacArthur dismissed the charges as "specious". He defended himself by stating that, "I wore no iron helmet because it hurt my head. I carried no gas mask because it hampered my movements. I went unarmed because it was not my purpose to engage in personal combat, but to direct others. I used a riding crop out of long habit on the plains. I fought from the front as I could not effectively manipulate my troops from the rear."[35]

MacArthur's stated reason for not carrying a gas mask made little sense and he paid the price for his vanity. Shortly after the Armistice on November 11, 1918 he fell gravely ill with a throat infection from being gassed so many times in combat. He managed to pull through, however, and returned to the States as America's most celebrated and decorated officer of World War I. Pershing's response to the criticism and investigation of MacArthur's methods was to promote him shortly before the Armistice to command the 42nd Division.

As a result of his refusal to wear a gas mask, MacArthur would suffer from respiratory problems for the rest of his life.

MacArthur's exploits in France and Germany during World War I made him a national figure. In 1919 at the age of 39 he was named superintendent of the U.S. Military Academy at West Point. The Academy had in many respects become outmoded and in dire need of modernization. MacArthur took a scalpel to its various curricula and forced

---

[34] Ibid, p. 70.
[35] Ibid.

dramatic changes. He reformed its tactical, athletic and disciplinary systems; added liberal arts, government and economics to its curriculum and in 1922 took the groundbreaking step of forming the Cadet Honor Committee to review all allegations of violations of the Cadet Honor Code.

In 1922, MacArthur left West Point to serve two tours of duty in the Philippines after his first marriage to socialite, Louise Cromwell Brooks, ended in divorce.

MacArthur was promoted to the rank of Major General in 1925 and his climb to the top of the military pyramid was proceeding in a smooth and seamless fashion. But, one of the most controversial and revealing episodes in MacArthur's professional life would occur in 1932 and would deeply stain his previously unsullied reputation.

By July of 1932, MacArthur had ascended to the lofty position of Chief of Staff of the Army. The world-wide economic depression was at its zenith, however, rending the financial and social tissue of American life by exposing deep and ugly wounds in the body politic. The wounds were chiefly the result of a vast chasm which had opened between rich and poor, ownership and working classes and immigrants and native-born Americans. MacArthur was largely oblivious to the currents of unrest surging outside the cloistered sanctuary of the Army's upper echelon.

In June of 1932, a rag-tag "army" composed mainly of destitute World War I veterans marched upon Washington, D.C. to conduct a massive demonstration protesting the failure of the federal government to provide them with a long-promised bonus for their war service.

The demonstration was peaceable but approximately twenty thousand veterans, their wives and children set up a crude and flimsy encampment in the Anacostia Flats section of Washington, on the other side of the Anacostia River from the Capitol. Their sprawling camp was composed of tents, make-shift shacks, huts and other crude forms of shelter. The crowded, cramped and unsanitary conditions constituted a health, safety and fire hazard, but certainly no threat to the Republic. The deplorable state of the many thousands of veterans who had descended upon the capital and their pitiful shantytown were a public relations nightmare for the administration of President Herbert Hoover. The saturation press coverage was giving the Hoover Administration a black eye before the whole world, and it was getting worse each day of the camp's continued existence. Herbert Hoover was already reeling from the Depression and faced a tough re-election battle against the formidable governor of New York, Franklin D. Roosevelt.

Things went from bad to ludicrous for the besieged President when into the fray stepped the politically tone-deaf General Douglas MacArthur. Hoover ordered MacArthur to make a show of military force to the demonstrators sufficient to evacuate them from their encampment, and cause them to disperse and leave the city. Hoover wanted the exercise to be as quiet, peaceful and orderly as possible. Any impression that the public received, either through the press or with their own eyes and ears, that veterans who had risked their lives for their country in a foreign war were being treated like a common rabble—like law breakers—at a time when poor people everywhere were suffering great hardships—would be a public relations disaster and a political fiasco, just when Hoover needed every bit of good press he could muster if he stood any chance of being re-elected.

MacArthur's top aide when the situation reached a crisis on July 28, 1932 was Major Dwight D. Eisenhower. With his razor-sharp political instincts, Eisenhower knew that any confrontation between the Army and the demonstrators, named the "Bonus Army" by the media, had the potential for political disaster unless handled with great finesse. Eisenhower reported for duty in civilian clothes on the fateful day and strongly argued that MacArthur should do the same in order to downplay the spectacle of American Armed forces taking military action against its own indigent war veterans. He also urged MacArthur to stay in the background and assign the operational control of the exercise to a subordinate officer.

MacArthur, unwilling to pay even lip service to the sensitive nature of the situation, ordered that his uniform be brought to headquarters and ordered Eisenhower to go home and change into his uniform as well. Then MacArthur, referring to the thousands of war veterans as "communists and pacifists," appeared in full uniform replete with seven rows of ribbons on his left chest. And rather than falling back to a rear echelon position, he ostentatiously proceeded to the head of the column in full view of the reporters and cameras. There he assumed personal command of the operation.

At some point on July 28th, Hoover finally realized the potential damage the explosive situation could cause to his image in an election year and sent orders to MacArthur that no troops were to cross the Anacostia River or enter the Veterans' squalid village. MacArthur refused to acknowledge receiving the orders and instead led his forces across the bridge to the Anacostia Flats. Then a heavy tank and infantry contingent under the command of Major George S. Patton, of World War II fame, entered the large encampment and routed the

"Bonus Marchers". They fired tear gas canisters into the village resulting in the deaths of two infant children from asphyxiation. Suddenly, the camp became engulfed in flames and burned to the ground. It has never been known for certain who set the camp on fire. The Army said it was the veterans and the veterans said it was the invading troops. Eisenhower was appalled at the way things turned out and recognized it immediately for what it was—a dark stain on the reputations of both the U.S. Army and the Hoover Administration. He knew that it would be recorded as one of the most shameful episodes in American history. MacArthur on the other hand blithely adopted the public posture that things had gone extremely well. He even held a press conference during which he credited President Hoover with having saved America from a serious anti-American insurrection. By cannily, though none too subtly, shifting the responsibility for the decisions to Hoover, he trapped Hoover in a corner from which he could not escape because if he were to decry the incident, he would contradict MacArthur's claim that the president had won a great victory against domestic enemies of the United States. When it came to blaming others for his mistakes, MacArthur had no rivals. Three months later Hoover was decisively defeated by Franklin Delano Roosevelt in the presidential election.

MacArthur admitted no mistakes at all in the episode and mounted a spirited defense of his actions, as may be seen by his uncompromising statements.

MacArthur's description of the military action taken by the U.S. Army against a crudely-armed assemblage—though huge in number—of its own veterans, made an ugly and dangerous confrontation sound almost innocuous:

> In accordance with the President's request, I accompanied General Miles and brought with me two officers who later wrote their names on world history: Major Dwight D. Eisenhower and Major George S. Patton. Not a shot was fired. The sticks, clubs and stones of the rioters were met only by tear gas and steady pressure. No one was killed and there were no serious injuries on either side....The show of force, the excellent discipline of the troops and the proper use of tear gas had turned the trick without serious bloodshed. [36]

---

[36]   Ibid, p. 95.

In providing what he saw as the larger context, MacArthur wrote:

> During the Bonus March communist threats continued to be made against responsible figures. I was to be publicly hanged on the steps of the Capital. It was the beginning of a definite and ceaseless campaign that set me apart as a man to be destroyed...[37]

About six or seven weeks before the Bonus March reached a crescendo, MacArthur warned in a speech that "Pacifism and its bedfellow, Communism are all about us."[38] In *Reminiscences* he decried the personal crisis with which he was faced:

> I was roundly denounced not only by pacifists and Communists but even on the floor of Congress itself...I was harassed ceaselessly in the effort to force me into acceptance of their appeasement views. I was slandered and smeared almost daily in the press. The propaganda spared neither my professional attributes nor my personal character. It was bitter as gall and I knew that something of the gall would always be with me.[39]

As a counterpoint to the MacArthur view of things, David Halberstam, in *The Coldest Winter* wrote:

> To MacArthur they [the Bonus Marchers] were nothing but a dangerous anti-American rabble. The Veteran Administration, which kept close records, later reported that 94 percent of them were actual veterans, 67 percent of whom had served the United States overseas. Dwight Eisenhower, then a major and MacArthur's talented young aide, thought the marchers might be mistaken in what they were attempting, but felt there was a poignant quality to them and their demands—'They were ragged, ill-fed and felt themselves badly abused.'[40]

---

[37] Ibid, p. 97.
[38] Ibid, p. 90.
[39] Ibid.
[40] *The Coldest Winter*, op.cit., p. 125.

Years later in relating his attempts to prevent MacArthur in full regalia from personally leading the operation against the veterans, Eisenhower reportedly said, "I told that dumb son of a bitch that he had no business going down there. I told him it was no place for a chief of staff."[41]

"For millions of ordinary Americans," wrote Halberstam, "who in hard times sympathized with the marchers, it was a defining moment; MacArthur became forever in their minds the kind of military man who abused the rights of ordinary people, a man who was never to be trusted politically and was too militaristic."[42]

MacArthur, on the other hand, had crystallized the exact political image he was seeking to create—that of a champion of total victory by the U.S.A. over all enemies—foreign and domestic. He seemed to have no sense of just how callous, extreme and paranoid he had come across during the incident.

Part of MacArthur's unique persona was his unpredictability. He never lost his capacity for surprise. It was no secret that MacArthur and Franklin D. Roosevelt neither trusted nor liked each other. Washington insiders were shocked, therefore, when MacArthur openly supported Roosevelt's "New Deal" and even accepted the assignment to head up the Civilian Conservation Corps. (CCC). But soon MacArthur began to clash with the Roosevelt Administration over the issue of pacifism and quickly wore out his welcome in official Washington.

In 1937 when Manuel L. Quezon, President of the Commonwealth of the Philippines, which had achieved semi-independent status in 1935, invited MacArthur to supervise the creation and growth of a Philippine Army, he gladly accepted and was even willing to revert to the lower, but permanent grade, of major general. Clearly less enthused about joining MacArthur in the Philippines as one of his assistants was Dwight D. Eisenhower, ordered to report there by the Army's high command. Years later when Eisenhower was asked if he knew MacArthur he replied, "Know him? I studied dramatics under him for seven years!"[43]

The five years MacArthur spent in Manila prior to America's involvement in World War II were both happy and productive. He fell in love with and married thirty seven year old Jean Marie Faircloth

---

[41]   Ibid.

[42]   Ibid, p. 126.

[43]   *Washington Post*, Review of *George Marshall and Dwight Eisenhower in War and Peace* by Mark Perry, June 15, 2007.

from Tennessee. A son was born to the MacArthurs in the Philippines and without hesitation they named him Arthur MacArthur IV (Douglas MacArthur's brother was Arthur MacArthur III). Arthur IV was the pride and joy of Douglas MacArthur's life and the 58-year old general doted upon him constantly. With Eisenhower's invaluable assistance, MacArthur created and built an efficient and well-disciplined Filipino Army. His fledgling army and air force, however, would be no match for the powerful and relentless forces of Imperial Japan, and by early 1942, MacArthur would be enmeshed in one of the most perilous and dramatic crises of his life.

On December 7, 1941, the Japanese launched a massive surprise attack by air upon the U.S. Naval Base at Pearl Harbor in Hawaii. With the exception of its aircraft carriers, which were out to sea on maneuvers at the time of the attack, the United States Pacific Fleet was largely destroyed. General George C. Marshall, the U.S. Army Chief of Staff, gave MacArthur notice of the next expected attack—upon the Philippines, nine hours before Japanese Zeros first appeared over Clark Air Force Base at Luzon Island, on December 8, 1941.

MacArthur was ordered by Marshall to immediately take action to defend the Philippine Islands. Instead of quickly acting on those orders, MacArthur committed the twin errors of underestimating the capabilities of the Japanese[44] while overestimating the competence of his air commander of only two months, General Lewis H. Brereton. Brereton failed to configure his aircraft on the ground at Clark Air Force Base in a proper defensive alignment. Like the commanders at Hickam Field at Pearl Harbor, he left his fleet of planes out in the open and close together on the ground, where they were fully exposed to Japanese bombs. Brereton failed to take even the most rudimentary action to protect his aircraft, of placing them in camouflaged revetments. Most of the aircraft were destroyed before they could even get off the ground.

Of course, MacArthur, as the Commanding General of Allied Forces in the Philippines, has to shoulder most of the responsibility by reason of his failure to promptly order Brereton to deploy the planes for combat.

In a display of bravado and over-confidence, MacArthur insisted that he would have no problem holding the Philippines and other key points in the Pacific because of "the inability of our enemy to launch

---

[44] *Douglas MacArthur and Defeat in the Philippines* by Richard Connaughton (Overlook Press: 2001).

his air attacks on our islands."[45] MacArthur defended his actions by asserting that he was given no details as to what transpired at Pearl Harbor and his "first impression was that the Japanese might well have suffered a serious setback."[46]

Whatever may have been the case, by 11:45 a.m. on December 8, 1941, MacArthur had become aware of a huge enemy formation closing in on Clark Field. Attempts by General Brereton to engage and interdict the Japanese formation in the air before they reached their target were too little and too late.

On December 10, 1941, the Japanese invaded Luzon, the largest of the Philippine Islands, by amphibious landing.

MacArthur wrote in his memoirs that it was by these landings, three days after the attack on Pearl Harbor, and mass landings closer to Manila two days later, that "the strategy of General Homma (Japanese Commanding General) became immediately apparent." "It was obvious," wrote MacArthur, that he sought to swing shut the jaws of a great military pincer."[47] The objective of the Japanese was to divide MacArthur's forces on Luzon and annihilate them. They would split MacArthur's South Luzon Force under General Jones from the North Luzon Force under General Wainwright and destroy both of them on the central plain of Luzon.

MacArthur countered with his own strategy of having General Wainwright fight a delaying action along the central plain while General Jones's forces were removed, under cover of Wainwright's delaying action, to the Bataan Peninsula.

MacArthur explained his reasoning as follows: "By retiring into the peninsula, I could exploit the maneuverability of my full forces to the limit and gain our only chance of survival."[48] "The imminent menace of encirclement by superior forces," wrote MacArthur, "forced me to act instantly." The viability of MacArthur's strategy was predicated upon massive relief being ordered by Roosevelt and the Pentagon for the defense of the Philippines. MacArthur seemed to be sure that he would receive heavy reinforcements of troops, ships and planes, although there was little evidence to support that belief. Roosevelt, Marshall and the Joint Chiefs appear to have decided early-on that they had no such massive relief to give to MacArthur; and that MacArthur's

---

[45] *The Coldest Winter*, op.cit., p. 128.
[46] *Reminiscences*, op.cit., p. 117.
[47] Ibid, p. 124.
[48] Ibid.

true mission was simply to hold out for as long as he could, thereby tying the Japanese offensive forces down until the U.S. could solidify its position in the Pacific. The U.S. could not provide the level of support MacArthur needed to survive without weakening its position in Australia and exposing Australia to conquest by Japan. Australia was America's anchor in the Pacific—the location which would serve as the staging area for the eventual U.S. counter offensive against the enemy. It is doubtful, however, that the sometimes devious Roosevelt took MacArthur into his confidence concerning his true plans.

MacArthur also decided in mid-December 1941 that the island of Corregidor, separated from Bataan by two miles of water, would serve as the supply base for the defense of the Bataan Peninsula as well as MacArthur's headquarters.

With the assistance of Generals Jones and Wainwright, MacArthur implemented his strategy with dispatch. His vivid description of his tactics are succinctly stated in the following passage from *Reminiscences*: "Stand and fight, slip back and dynamite (roads and bridges). It was savage and bloody but it won time." [49]

MacArthur did the best he could with the resources available to him but it would be only a matter of time before his out-manned provincial army would fall before the onslaught on the mighty forces of Japan.

As usual he displayed remarkable courage mixed with a measure of recklessness.

MacArthur set up his new headquarters in an arm of the Malinto Tunnel on the Island of Corregidor, a location vulnerable to Japanese bombs, artillery shells and land invasion. The tunnel was carved deep into the rock and its civilian function was to serve as the terminal point of a street car line. The danger of being trapped inside the tunnel by bomb-created blockages at both tunnel openings was ever-present.

In his memoirs, MacArthur disclaimed any special bravery on his part in offering the explanation that "there was nothing of bravado in this. It was simply my duty." [50]

In January 1942, the Japanese struck with full force against Bataan and Corregidor. MacArthur's combined U.S. and Filipino forces fought a stubborn and valiant holding action. As the battle wore on through January, February and into March, his ragged but resilient battalions endured great suffering. Still they fought on with skill and

---

[49] Ibid, p. 125.
[50] Ibid, p. 131.

determination. "Our troops were approaching exhaustion," recalled MacArthur, "My heart ached as I saw my men slowly wasting away. Their clothes hung on them like tattered rags. Their bare feet stuck out in silent protest." [51]

General Marshall did make some attempts to get relief to MacArthur's beleaguered army by air, but all U.S. Pacific forces were still reeling from the devastating losses they had suffered at Pearl Harbor; and he was forced to renege on early promises. In a dispatch to MacArthur, Marshall wrote, "It now appears that the plans for reaching you quickly with pursuit plane support are jeopardized." In a passage in his memoirs, MacArthur exposed his life-long tendency to become self-absorbed and shortsighted at key times, when he wrote the following about the Pentagon's inability to provide him with the support he needed. "No one will ever know how much could have been done to aid the Philippines if there had been a determined will to win." [52] Such a statement revealed a total lack of appreciation for the grave crisis the U.S. was facing all across the globe. On the day after Pearl Harbor was bombed, Hitler joined Japan in declaring war on the United States. The stakes were now America's very survival and that of Europe as well, not just the Philippines.

Although Roosevelt and MacArthur did not like each other, the President was not about to sacrifice one of his greatest generals to the Japanese. In April of 1942, FDR ordered MacArthur to leave the Philippines. He, his wife and son were evacuated by PT boat to Australia, where MacArthur would plan a massive counter-offensive against the Japanese.

MacArthur, prior to his evacuation had declared forcefully, "I have not the slightest intention of surrendering and/or capitulating the Filipino forces of my command." [53] By ordering him to leave the Philippines, Roosevelt spared MacArthur the agony of having to make that decision, and may have saved his life as well.

After safely arriving in Australia and seeing that his forces left behind on Bataan and Corregidor were faring worse each day against the Japanese onslaught, MacArthur contacted General Marshall and told him he would be glad to temporarily rejoin his prior command in the Philippines and take charge of the Filipino guerrilla effort against the Japanese. Marshall and Roosevelt, however, believed MacArthur

---

[51] Ibid, p. 135.
[52] Ibid, p. 128.
[53] Ibid, p. 139.

would be far more valuable to the overall war effort, in Australia, and they rejected his offer. Their decision strategically placed MacArthur in a position from which he would launch one of the greatest offensives of his military career, one that would make him both an icon and a household name in America.

However, in a monumental display of presumptuousness mixed with ingratitude, MacArthur wrote the following concerning the denial of his request to return temporarily to the Philippines:

> But Washington failed to approve. Had it done so, the dreadful Death March which followed the surrender (of the allied forces in the Philippines), with its estimated 25,000 casualties would never have taken place. [54]

But as unfair as MacArthur was to his superiors at the White House and Pentagon, his own many critics were equally unfair to him—giving him the nickname, "Dugout Doug" after his escape from the Philippines.

Of his overall performance as allied commander in the Philippines, MacArthur provided his own self-assessment as follows:

> Our tenacious defense against tremendous odds completely upset the Japanese military timetable, and enabled the Allies to gain precious months for the organization of the defense of Australia. [55]

As a matter of fact, Wainwright's forces held out until June of 1942, before finally surrendering and being forced to endure the savage "Bataan Death March".

For his valiant defense of Philippines, MacArthur was later awarded the Congressional Medal of Honor.

MacArthur declared from his headquarters in Australia to the people of the Philippines and the world, "I shall return". The Roosevelt Administration was not pleased with the egocentric wording of the pledge and the top Pentagon brass asked him to change it to "We shall return". MacArthur stuck to his guns and refused to make the pledge plural.

---

[54]   Ibid, p. 146.
[55]   Ibid.

MacArthur's pledge to return became both the rallying cry and mission statement for the U.S. effort in the Pacific against Japan. Although Admirals King and Nimitz considered the war in the Pacific to be primarily the province of the U.S. Navy, with all other forces playing a subsidiary role, MacArthur stole their thunder. His strategy for implementing his pledge to recapture the Philippines was brilliant in both concept and execution.

MacArthur described it as "a new type of campaign—three dimensional warfare—the triphibious concept."[56] In layman's terms the central premise of his strategy was island-hopping. Where Japanese forces were particularly formidable, he would simply bypass that island and go on to the next, and in the process cut off the channels of supply to the bypassed island, which would eventually be starved into submission. He thereby avoided frontal attack wherever possible with a huge savings of American lives and resources. He simply by-passed Japanese strongpoints, isolating them and neutralizing them. MacArthur employed this direct-target approach, popularly called "leap-frogging," all the way from Australia to Manila. Rather than constituting a new theory of warfare, it was an "adaptation of modern war instrumentalities to the concept of envelopment."[57]

The strategy demonstrated MacArthur's ability to learn quickly from his mistakes and adapt to present conditions. His ground forces were limited and the Japanese were adept at "fighting ferociously in defense of atolls where it would be hard to apply some of America's technological superiority."[58] Where the Japanese had more than one hundred thousand troops at Rabaul in the Solomons, "aching for a showdown," MacArthur by-passed them, cut off their supply lines and starved them out. David Halberstam described it in *The Coldest Winter* as a "military tour de force."[59] John Gunther, a highly-regarded journalist of the World War II era, wrote that "MacArthur took more territory, with less loss of life than any military commander since Darius the Great."

In 1945, MacArthur completed the liberation of the Philippines; and in August of that year accepted the unconditional surrender of Emperor Hirohito of Japan to the allies, aboard the U.S.S. *Missouri*.

---

[56] Ibid, p. 166.
[57] *The Coldest Winter*, op.cit., p. 122.
[58] Ibid.
[59] Ibid.

Upon the surrender, President Truman appointed MacArthur as military governor of Japan with a mission to enforce the surrender and reform the defeated Japanese nation. MacArthur went directly to Tokyo where he wielded the absolute power of a potentate over Japan with wisdom and compassion—restoring civil liberties and clearing the path for Japan to become a great and free modern nation.

One fact of MacArthur's professional life may say more about his devotion to duty than a thousand words could. Over a span of approximately fifteen years, he served without interruption as commanding general of the Philippines, allied commander of the Southern Pacific region, commander-in-chief of all U.S. Army Pacific Forces, military governor of Japan and commanding general of United Nations Forces in Korea, without once seeking the respite he might have received from a trip home to his native land.

Admiral Arthur W. Radford, USN, Commander in Chief, Pacific and Pacific Fleet (left) and General of the Army Douglas MacArthur, Commander in Chief, Far East, confer while awaiting the arrival of the Joint Chiefs of Staff, at Tokyo, Japan, 21 August 1950.

Major General Edward M. Almond, U.S. Army, Commanding General, Tenth Corps (left) and Lieutenant General Lemuel C. Shepherd, Jr., USMC, Commanding General, Fleet Marine Force, Pacific, confer at Tokyo, Japan, while awaiting the arrival of the Joint Chiefs of Staff, 21 August 1950.

General of the Army Douglas MacArthur, Commander in Chief, Far East, (center), greets Army Chief of Staff General J. Lawton Collins (left) and Chief of Naval Operations Admiral Forrest P. Sherman, as members of the Joint Chiefs of Staff arrive at a Tokyo airfield for conferences concerning future operations in Korea, 21 August 1950.

Admiral Forrest P. Sherman, Chief of Naval Operations, addresses the crew of USS Philippine Sea (CV-47) during his visit to ships and Navy installations in Japan and Korea, 23 August 1950.

Chapter 3

The President

Character is destiny.

—Heraclitus

ARRY S. Truman's time on earth covered a span of 88 years. Yet it was during a mere twelve year time period—from 1941 to 1953—that his brilliant star ascended on the upward path of its arc until reaching its apogee.

Before 1941 his life was as unremarkable as MacArthur's was luminous. But Truman's twelve year climb, beginning at age 56, from the lowlands of obscurity to the summit of international power and prestige, encompassed an impressive term as United States Senator, a short stint as Vice President and finally almost two turbulent terms as President of the United States.

A panel of well-known historians spanning the entire ideological spectrum, gathered by CSPAN in 2009, adjudged Harry S. Truman to be the fifth greatest American President—behind only Lincoln, Washington, and the two Roosevelts.

Born on May 8, 1884—only four years after MacArthur—and one of three children of John Anderson Truman and Martha Ellen Truman (formerly Martha Ellen Young), Harry Truman, by his own account, had a happy childhood, growing up in and near Independence, Missouri. From his earliest memories he recalled the twin joys of boyhood adventure on the farm outside of Independence owned by his maternal grandfather, and the more cultivated pursuits of music, art and reading which Independence had to offer. For the first six years of his life the Trumans lived on the Young farm where John Truman played a major role in its management. But in 1890, the Trumans left the farm and moved to Independence so that Harry could receive proper schooling. Young Harry was a natural student—a bright and eager learner—far more popular with his teachers than with his schoolmates.

On his tenth birthday his mother, with whom he had an especially close relationship, gave Harry a present which he would describe later as a turning point in his life. The gift was a four volume set of anthologies entitled *Great Men and Famous Women*. Hundreds of accomplished men and women were featured in the collection, ranging from Moses to Grover Cleveland. Among Harry's favorites were the profiles of Hannibal, Andrew Jackson and Robert E. Lee. At the age of ten, Harry Truman was already selecting role models from history who would, by their example, inform and inspire the rest of his life. Of Hannibal, Truman wrote, "There is not in all history so wonderful an example of what a single man of genius may achieve against tremendous odds." [60]

In Independence, John Truman emerged as an industrious businessman and an individual to be trusted. Correspondingly, the family's fortunes were on the up-swing. John Truman began enjoying success dabbling in real estate, trading in futures and as a minor inventor. He patented a staple puller for barb wire fences, from which he realized some impressive profits.

When the Missouri Railroad offered him an annual royalty of $2000.00 and the Chicago Alton Railroad offered him $2500.00, serious money in the 1890's, for the rights to an automated railroad switch he had invented, the elder Truman asked for double the amount. Both companies rejected his demand, pirated his idea and left John Truman with nothing. More than a small part of the stubbornness of Harry S. Truman as a world leader could be traced back to his enterprising but obstinate father.

Both John and Martha Truman placed heavy stock in serious reading and would sacrifice other things to purchase quality books for their home. As their financial situation improved they acquired a full set of Shakespeare, followed by *Plutarch's Lives*. Harry became a voracious reader, devouring everything in sight. History was his favorite, a predilection which lasted his entire life. Whatever major decision Truman made as President was first placed by him in an historical perspective. He would employ his deep knowledge of history as one of the acid tests, among others, for the correctness of his contemplated decision. The Roman general and consul, Cincinnatus, was one of his greatest heroes—a military man who knew the horrors of war and the dangers of absolute power, and accepted the position of "dictator" only until Rome's enemy could be defeated on the battlefield; and then immediately gave up the position and returned to his farm. He served as dictator for a total of only 16 days.

Harry's two siblings were a brother, Vivian, and sister, Mary Jane. Unlike the short, bookish and bespectacled Harry, who showed little physical prowess and who described himself decades later, as a bit of a

---

[60] *Truman*, op.cit., p. 43.

"sissy", Vivian was a strong, athletic and rugged physical specimen. Vivian and their boyhood chums, however, didn't remember Harry as either soft or a "sissy". True, he was short, fastidious in dress and grooming, bespectacled and played the piano, but many of the other boys still respected him because of his mastery of the mental requirements of each game they played and his "quiet" leadership.

Harry was in awe of his mother and sought her approval in almost all his endeavors. On the surface she was his favorite and he was hers. The other conventional family notion was that Mary Jane was her father's favorite. These assumptions were never tested in any rigorous way and even historians have fallen into the facile stereotype of a president whose greatest influence during his formative years was a mother to whose apron strings he was tied.

In fact, there were deeper similarities and shared characteristics between father and son, none more on display than during the Truman Presidency. John Truman was also short and compact, a wiry bantam weight. Though generally good natured, he possessed a no-nonsense aura of seriousness of purpose, toughness and brains. No one messed with John Anderson Truman—partly because of his fiery temper but mostly because of the respect which naturally flowed to him from other men, a function of his unshakeable integrity and courage. Anyone who ever accused him of lying did so at the great risk of going home with a black eye or bloody nose.

Harry undoubtedly inherited his fastidiousness from his father. John liked everything—his home, children, lawn, hedges, horses to be turned out just so—clean, neat, tidy and well-trimmed. [61]

Like Harry Truman, John was feisty and brave. "He had no use for a coward." [62] John Truman regularly professed a great faith in God but "raised his children to have faith in themselves and their potentialities as well." [63] He had unshakeable confidence in his own abilities—in his self-reliance and resourcefulness.

John Truman's driving passion was politics. As Harry gradually came to share that passion, the two of them attended the National Democratic Convention in 1900.

Inequality for Negroes was deeply embedded in late Nineteenth Century Missouri, as it was in every southern and border state. And despite their high principles and unshakeable integrity, the Trumans

---

[61] *Truman*, op.cit., pp. 46-47.
[62] Ibid.
[63] Ibid.

accepted it as part of the natural order of things. Independence was in terms of culture, tradition and philosophy a very southern town. There is little to suggest at this stage of Harry Truman's young life that seeking greater equality or an improved lot in life for Independence's black residents was even a minor part of his value system. Nevertheless, he was otherwise uncompromising and steadfast concerning his set of core principles. His credo included homespun aphorisms such as "Make yourself useful;" "Honesty is the best policy;" "Anything worthwhile requires effort;" "If at first you don't succeed, try again; Never, never give up;" "Honor thy Father and Mother;". "A good name is rather to be chosen than great riches;" and "say what you mean and mean what you say."[64] Most of these simple guideposts for living were handed down to Harry from his parents. The rest came from the Bible.

The pre-teen and teen-aged Harry Truman, however, was the farthest thing from being an unprepossessing clone of his parents, simply mimicking corny bits of folk wisdom falling from his parents' mouths. If he adopted as his own one of his parents' sayings or a bible passage, it was because it penetrated to the core of Harry's belief system, after first passing the rigorous inspection of his keen mind. True, he was no intellectual but by the time he graduated from high school, Harry was probably one of the best-read citizens of Independence—a prize garnered from untold hours spent in the Independence Public Library after school. The librarians were awe-struck by the sheer volume of books Harry Truman managed to devour and absorb—mostly histories of the ancient Greeks and Romans, particularly Plutarch's lives, sprinkled with a generous dose of Shakespeare. But as much as Harry Truman learned, he never considered himself superior to his less educated friends, relatives and fellow citizens of Independence. There was simply no pretense or superciliousness in the man's nature and no intellectual phoniness.

His wide and deep reading did not transport Harry Truman beyond the simple lessons of parental nurturing. He did not seek to transcend to a higher intellectual plane. What he believed were the fundamental truths. He took what he learned from books as confirmation of the universality of lessons first learned at home—the eternal virtues—honesty, courage, industriousness, charity, kindness, generosity and humility. It was not the ruthlessness and cunning of a Richard III or a Iago which he admired. It was the brave and wise citizen sol-

---

[64]   Ibid, pp. 54-55.

diers and statesmen, such as Cincinnatus, Cyrus the Great, Pericles, Cicero, Hannibal, George Washington and Robert E. Lee, whose attributes of courage and nobility he aspired to. Harry Truman was filled to the brim with the breathtaking accomplishments and qualities of heart and mind of the great men he read about in books. It wasn't just youthful exuberance and lofty idealism. The example of the great men of history forged his hard center as much as any experience he would have in his extraordinary life.

Truman had few friends in his early school years. Teased and tormented by other boys because of his size, his thick glasses and for being a "book worm," Harry somehow never let it get to him. His toughness and self-confidence were his armor. He persisted in studying the piano when playing baseball would have made him more popular. He loved music and was very serious about it, eschewing rag time for Bach, Mozart and Liszt, and attending classical concerts whenever he got the opportunity.

Everything changed for Harry Truman socially once he began high school. His cheerfulness, confidence and positive demeanor began to win him new friends. By his later teenage years, he had become an accomplished pianist. That plus his storehouse of jokes made him the life of the party. But, well before that happened he still had two special friends. One was the somewhat shy and gangly Charlie Ross, his best friend. Charlie was the smartest student in their class and rivaled Harry as a prodigious reader of books. They would remain life-long friends and Charlie Ross would figure prominently in the Truman-MacArthur drama of 1950-51.

The second special friend was the pretty, athletically-gifted and opinionated Elizabeth Virginia Wallace who everyone called Bess. Bess and Harry were classmates as far back as Kindergarten. She was the only girl Harry was ever interested in and though their paths diverged from time to time as they grew to adulthood, Harry always returned to his single-minded pursuit of Bess's affections. Most of those who knew Harry from early childhood had no doubt that he had always been in love with Bess. Yet, Bess turned down Harry's first proposal of marriage and they didn't marry until 1919 when he was 34 and she was 33.

The bottom fell out for John Anderson Truman in 1901 at about the time Harry, the eldest of the three Truman children, was making plans to attend college the following fall. John Truman always wanted to get rich. That driving ambition led him to gamble more than he could afford in grain futures. When the market tanked, John Truman lost everything. The Trumans were forced to sell their house and move to more modest quarters in Kansas City, approximately ten miles from Independence.[65] Harry, whose role models were mostly great generals, yearned for a military career and hoped to attend one of the service academies—West Point or Annapolis. Sadly, he was turned down by both because of his poor eyesight. Without funds to attend a private college, it looked as though Harry's promise for a brilliant academic career had come to a sudden and unexpected end. After graduation he was forced to go to work and took a job as a time keeper with the Santa Fe Railroad.

Despite their shocking reversal of fortune, the Trumans were far from destitute. Martha Truman had inherited 600 acres of prime Missouri farm land from her father, Solomon Young. Unable to get back on his feet financially, John Truman returned to farming and in 1906 persuaded Harry, who was then showing promise as a bank clerk, to join him in working the family farm. It was back-breaking work but Harry approached it just as he did every other task in life—with total commitment. He literally got behind the plow—tilling the fields with a gangplow pulled by a team of horses many hours a day, an exercise which made him hard and lean with a rugged physique. Plowing a straight furrow became a frequent leadership metaphor employed by him in his later public life. To Harry Truman being straight with the American people was like "plowing a straight furrow."

Later on in life Truman complained about how he had hated farming. But, throughout his 20s he gave everything he had to it with a determination that knew no respite. Farming was arduous labor from the break of dawn until well after darkness descended upon rural Missouri. But it demanded more than just physical exertion. It required patience and equanimity as well. Its disappointments and frustrations were potentially unlimited—everything from drought, flood, freeze, blight, animal disease, crop failure, a poor harvest and a bad economy, could and did happen. But the Trumans had what it took to deal with all of it. They were patient, methodical and deliberate in whatever they did. They took disappointments in stride and never gave up. Farming was a major factor in the development of Harry Truman's character. It gave him the grit to later become a better soldier, administrator, legislator, and chief executive than he otherwise might have been had he not had that experience.

---

[65] Unlike Independence; the fast-growing Kansas City was considered a "Yankee" town.

After John Truman died in 1914, Harry Truman ran the family farm for a few years but increasingly shifted his main attention to the Missouri National Guard which he had joined in 1905. Prior to America's entry into World War I he helped organize the 2nd Regiment of the Missouri Field Artillery. He was placed in charge of its battery in Kansas City, a unit infamous for its lack of discipline and rowdiness. Applying the same patient and deliberate approach he had brought to farming, Truman managed to shape and mold the outfit into an effective unit prior to its insertion into combat in Europe as part of the American Expeditionary Force. He turned out to be a natural leader and a skillful organizer.

When the United States entered World War I, Truman was promoted to Captain and named the Commanding Officer of the regiment's Battery D. The regiment was re-designated the 129th Field Artillery. Battery D under Truman's command saw action in France in the Vosges, Saint Mihiel and Meuse-Argonne campaigns.

Harry Truman and his outfit left Missouri to go to war in 1918 but before entering combat in France, Truman trained his men relentlessly. He worked them hard, insisting on strict standards of behavior.[66] He drove himself equally hard and as Battery D was slowly chiseled into a cohesive unit, it went from being one of the worst in the regiment to one of the best. Truman took great pride and satisfaction in what he had accomplished and for the first time in his life came to experience the heady and intoxicating effect of power.[67]

The inevitable time lag in getting General Pershing's expeditionary force fully trained, equipped, mobilized and inserted into combat clearly worked to the advantage of the Germans in late 1917 and the first half of 1918. Part of the reason for the delay was Pershing's insistence that the U.S. forces operate as an autonomous army under his command only. Eventually, the impracticality of this position became apparent and for reasons of allied strategy, U.S. military forces were placed under the overall command of the allied commander, Marshal Foch of France.

On July 15, 1918, an empowered German Army unleashed its full strength in an offensive which became known as the Second Battle of the Marne. Thirty-four Allied divisions, which included nine American, were pitted against fifty-two German Divisions. The German objective was to take Paris. Battery D was deployed to a remote location

---

[66] *Truman*, op.cit., p. 118.
[67] Ibid.

in the Vosges Mountains along the French-Swiss border on the east-ernmost front. Far removed from the main thrusts and counter-thrusts of the competing armies, the Vosges was an ideal location in which to initiate green troops into battle. After first undergoing the enormous physical exertion of hauling its horse-drawn artillery pieces up a mountain road, the battery, upon Truman's command, fired a barrage of poison gas artillery shells at the German position. In the German counter-bombardment of poison gas, the green and confused troops of Battery D scrambled to get gas masks on themselves and the horses. Men, horses, wagons and guns seemed to be headed in every direction at once. Truman commanded his charges from horseback but soon in the clamor and chaos of the German bombardment, the horse fell, landed on top of Truman and trapped him beneath its weight. His air supply was cut off and he gasped for breath as he was slowly extricated from under the horse by his men. In the meantime, most of Battery D was retreating down the mountain. Truman, however, stayed put in the center of the action gasping for breath, shouting commands and unleashing a barrage of profanity at his fleeing troops. His tirade, how-ever, did the trick. His troops, totally shocked by hearing the prim and proper Truman cursing at them, and calling them every name in the book, regrouped, ended the rout and made an orderly withdrawal of men, guns and horses down the mountain road. From that day for-ward, Truman had the full respect and affection of his men. Over the years his spectacular array of curse words aimed at his charges at the Vosges became legendary and was a source of great hilarity at Battery D commemorative dinners and reunions, whenever their former commander, Captain Truman, was in attendance, and when the men boisterously reminisced about their wartime experiences.

The 129th Field Artillery's next engagement made it part of histo-ry. Battery D and the rest of the Regiment "were part of the first big American push."[68] A half a million men marched first to San Mihiel, south of Verdun, where they scored a smashing victory over the Ger-mans in less than forty-eight hours.

Then on the night of September 16, 1918, the huge American ex-peditionary Army began a forced march of epic proportions—almost one hundred miles to the Argonne Forest. "The Supreme command had decided on a colossal, all-out offensive to end the war."[69] In his diary Truman wrote: "It was march all night and part of the day, grab

---

[68] Ibid, p. 124.
[69] Ibid, p. 125.

a few hours sleep and march some more."[70] By far the largest campaign of the war, the attack was to extend along the entire Western Front—from Verdun to the Sea. It came to be known as the Meuse-Argonne offensive and constituted the single largest action in American military history up to that point. The numbers were staggering—600,000 men; 3000 artillery pieces, countless supply wagons, trucks, tanks, ambulances and other vehicles; and more than 90,000 horses. The logistics alone seemed beyond the reckoning of mere mortals. They were, however, worked out well by a brilliant officer on General Pershing's staff, George C. Marshall. Harry Truman witnessed the results of Marshall's meticulous and ingenious planning for the first time. It would clearly not be the last.

The 100 mile march to the Argonne Forest was exhausting. To avoid adding weight for the tired horses to pull, the men were ordered not to hold on to the rolling artillery pieces. Colonel Klemm, a regimental higher-up, would ride up and down the column to enforce the edict. Under cover of darkness, some of the men could not resist the temptation to occasionally grab hold of the nearest gun for support. For many it was either do that or fall down from exhaustion. Truman noticed that some of his men were actually falling asleep standing up and finally on his own authority took them off the road to rest. This led to a fierce chewing-out from Colonel Klemm in front of the men. Truman stayed cool and unapologetic during the dressing-down which further endeared him to his men. In addition to Klemm's verbal barrage for letting the men rest, he severely chastised Truman for letting a man with a twisted ankle, Sergeant Jim Doherty, ride his horse instead of march. Truman remained unflappable on the surface but underneath he was seething. That night he wrote in his diary: "The Colonel insults me shamefully. No gentleman would say what he said. Damn him."[71] The seeds of Harry Truman's later powerful resentment of the abuse of power by some members of the officer corps had been planted. By 1945 it was in full bloom.

The American force finally arrived at the front at about 4:30 a.m. on September 26, 1918. Battery D shot off an artillery barrage soon after arriving but the real bombardment by the entire regiment commenced at about 5:30 a.m. with a deafening and prolonged cascade of staggered and synchronized firing. Later in the morning Captain Truman, accompanied by a Battery D lieutenant and a sergeant, moved

---

[70] Truman Papers, Harry S. Truman Library and Museum.
[71] Ibid.

considerably forward of the battery's position at a peach orchard in order to find a better vantage point from which to observe the German positions. Suddenly and quite by surprise an enemy artillery contingent appeared in an opening about a quarter of a mile away from Truman's forward observation post with its big guns aimed in the direction of the American 28th Division. There were standing orders to the 29th Division that they were not to fire on any German artillery not pointed at the 35th Division. Truman sent orders to Battery D to open fire on the German artillery anyway. His action saved the lives of men in the 28th Division but again ignited the wrath of Colonel Klemm who later phoned Truman and threatened him with a court martial. But nothing ever came of it. Klemm shot himself in his Chicago business office in 1925.

The Meuse-Argonne campaign was not the decisive victory that the allies expected. But it did force the Germans to engage in serious peace talks and on November 11, 1918 at 11:00 o'clock—the 11th hour of the 11th day of the 11th month—an armistice was finally signed and World War I was over. The Vosges, Saint Mihiel and Meuse-Argonne campaigns had taken their toll on Harry Truman. He wrote to Bess of the great sense of tragedy he felt over the useless loss of life. The elation of victory was heavily tempered by the sadness and human suffering all around him—as if, in his words, "he had marched on the graves of 500,000 fighting Frenchmen." Physically he was exhausted and depleted—he lost twenty pounds in just a few months. But, overriding all of this was the deep pride and newly found confidence which embraced him. He had led Battery D into action in three campaigns and lost not a single man. In many ways, Truman's service in France had been the most exhilarating experience of his life.

By the time he became President of the United States in 1945, Truman had developed into "a keen student of warfare."[72] He was the first former soldier since Theodore Roosevelt to ascend to the presidency.

Harry S. Truman's first taste of real power—as a commanding officer of an army artillery unit, may have whetted his appetite for more, but if it did, it was tempered by the example of his heroes, Cincinnatus, George Washington and Robert E. Lee, who gladly relinquished power when its retention was no longer beneficial to the people they served. Truman, like George C. Marshall, Dwight D. Eisenhower and Theodore Roosevelt of his own century, was a citizen-soldier, in that

---

[72] *Harry and Ike*, by Steve Neal (Scribner: 2001), p. 1.

TRUMAN AND MACARTHUR

order. He was always a citizen first and a soldier second. His firm convictions about the proper balance to be struck by a wise leader between the sometimes competing interests of military power and civilian authority; between individual command and collective decision—making, would later collide dramatically with the singularly authoritarian views of Douglas MacArthur. Given the fact that the two men were polar opposites in their orientations as to military versus civilian and individual versus collective authority, the constitutional crises of 1950-51, in which they found themselves, was probably inevitable.

Upon his return to Kansas City after the war, Truman went into partnership with his National Guard buddy, Eddie Jacobsen, in the ownership of a men's furnishings store (shirts, ties, underwear, socks, hats, etc.). Truman hoped to parlay his immense popularity with the returning men of the 129th Field Artillery Regiment into commercial success for his retail venture. Like his father before him, he dreamed of a quick strike of opportune ingenuity which would lead to dramatic financial success. His foray into the world of commerce, however, ended in failure.

The name selected for the store was "Truman and Jacobsen." During its first year the store did well, partly because the agrarian economy in Missouri was prospering, but mainly because Harry's Battery D boys came into the store in droves, purchased its wares and talked it up among their friends. Their enthusiasm was a residue of the strong feelings of loyalty and allegiance the men felt for "Captain Harry," less than a year after he had brought them home safely from what was simultaneously the greatest danger and greatest adventure of their lives. But in 1920, the price of wheat plunged dramatically and the Kansas City Grain Exchange began to register heavy losses. This adversely affected the entire local economy. The Battery D boys still came in but now it was more likely just to chew the fat with Captain Harry and their other battery-mates. From the time of its opening the store had served as an informal meeting hall for the veterans of Battery D. By mid-1920 the former artillerymen were more likely to put the arm on "Captain Harry" for a loan than they were to make a purchase. On his part, Truman considered them to be family and almost never said no when one of his boys needed a five dollar bill to carry him over to pay day. There was, however, a clear line which was never crossed. Truman never invited his army buddies to his home. For that matter, it wasn't really his home anyway. It belonged to his mother-in-law, Madge Wallace, and by every indication, both Madge and Bess considered the Battery D boys to be roughnecks and riff-raff. Eddie Jacobsen and his wife were never invited over either. Madge Wallace was like aristocracy in Independence and the anti-Semitism of the era which permeated the upper-crust precluded such an invitation from being extended to a Jewish couple.

One of the veterans who often came into the store was Jim Pendergast, nephew of the legendary Kansas City wholesale liquor entrepreneur and Democratic political boss of the same name. Though the elder Jim Pendergast died in 1911, his even more politically-talented brother, Tom Pendergast, succeeded him as an alderman and as boss of the powerful and deeply entrenched Democratic political machine. Intelligent and charismatic, Tom Pendergast's acumen was augmented by that of his brother, Mike Pendergast, who was young Jim's father.

The Pendergasts were generous to the down-trodden; civic-minded and loyal to a fault. They protected the legions of blue-collar workers who inhabited the wards of the inner-city and they got results for their large and dedicated following. But, any sense of propriety in the use of naked political power to achieve commercial success for themselves was simply not part of their gospel.

The elder Jim Pendergast had had a strong interest in politics and civic affairs for their own sake but his younger brother, Tom, saw politics mainly as a hammer to be used to pound out profits from the family's various interlocking businesses. Perhaps the most egregious example of the craven application of political power for personal gain was brother Mike Pendergast's use of his position as Tom's hand-picked county liquor commissioner. As commissioner, Mike Pendergast had the final say as to which of the many hundreds of taverns under his jurisdiction would be granted liquor licenses, or have existing licenses renewed; and which would not. Purchasing their supplies from the Pendergast wholesale liquor business in sufficient quantities almost guaranteed a tavern owner the granting of a license; whereas a failure to do so usually doomed his application to rejection.

As his friendship with the politically—connected Jim Pendergast ripened into a life-long relationship, Truman's business continued its decline. "Truman and Jacobsen" was a classy, top-of-the-line establishment with only quality brands. Harry Truman had always liked good clothes and the store was a reflection of his tastes. But, in tight economic times, it was far beyond the pocket-book of the average veteran of Battery D and his circle of friends.

As *Truman and Jacobsen* listed towards insolvency, Harry appeared at the store less and less frequently. Eddie Jacobsen pretty much took over its day-to-day operations while Harry stepped up his involvement in local politics and civic affairs. John Truman was a Pendergast man and his son, Harry, did not escape the notice of the politically attuned Pendergast family. His strong involvement in local rotary-like service organizations, his meticulous planning of city commemorative events and his impressive war record were all on the Pendergast radar screen. But the thing that particularly engaged their attention was his squeaky-clean image. The corrupt Pendergast machine was badly in need of a public-perception face lift and they needed an infusion of men like Truman into public office—men they could point to when accused of running a strictly patronage system.

So it was that Jim Pendergast prevailed upon his wealthy and powerful father to invite the Trumans to their home for dinner. At about the same time, Truman and Jacobsen had decided to close the store but not to file for bankruptcy. They were heavily in debt but each agreed to pay off half the store debts. Jacobsen was a natural-born salesman and had no trouble finding work as a drummer. But, in his occasional lean years, he was unable to keep up his end of the bargain and Harry Truman wound up paying off the majority of the debts. This had no effect on their friendship which was enduring and close throughout their lives.

The Trumans were proud and excited to be invited to the house of a person of such influence as Mike Pendergast. Jim was also along to make the introductions and help the Trumans feel more at ease. The elder Pendergast, a political powerhouse, was both garrulous and congenial; and by all accounts the Trumans had a wonderful time.

The reality was that at that stage of their lives, in 1922, the Trumans were down on their luck and very worried about money. Whatever income Harry and Bess earned from the farm was woefully insufficient to provide a living for them, much less pay off their debts. Surely the Trumans had heard many of the stories about the abuses of power and corrupt activities of the Pendergasts. Their primary concern, however, in 1922 was to make some money. Over his long career, Harry Truman was never known to have personally engaged in illegal or corrupt activities, but there can be no denying that Harry Truman considered the Pendergasts to be his friends and felt a permanent debt of gratitude to them for launching and promoting his political career.

In 1922 Tom Pendergast arranged for Harry Truman to be appointed as a Judge of the County Court of the Eastern District of Jackson County, Missouri. Of course, Truman had no legal training but this type of judgeship in Missouri was not a legal or judicial position. It was strictly an administrative job, akin to that of a county executive. Truman did such a good job in managing the financial and other governmental functions in his district that after one four year term, he was named presiding judge in 1926, a position he held until 1934. As presiding judge he adroitly steered Jackson County through the worst part of the Depression and managed its affairs successfully during the most difficult of circumstances. It was during this period of his life that Truman first showed signs of the grit and mettle of a crusading public servant, when he took on the Ku Klux Klan, an organization at the pinnacle of its power in rural Missouri during the 1920s and early 1930s. In condemning their activities, he also took the risky step of challenging their manhood by suggesting that only cowards would hide under a white hood; and attacking their patriotism by referring to them as "cheap un-American fakers." [73]

The press and public appeared to look past Truman's association with the Pendergasts as he developed a wide reputation for unimpeachable integrity.

In 1934, with the help of the Pendergast machine, Truman was elected to the United States Senate. During his first six year term in the Senate, Truman worked hard and applied himself assiduously to the job of learning to be an effective legislator. He did not, however, either enjoy much success in getting legislation enacted or make much of a name for himself. Those things would have to await his second term.

Washington, however, was not Missouri. There was no reservoir of local pride in a favorite son, as there was in Independence and Kansas City, to buffet Truman against the barbed criticism and contempt for him in the U.S. Senate, because of his association with the Pendergasts. It was just assumed that because Harry Truman was the hand-picked candidate of the Pendergasts, he was simply there to do their bidding—in other words, their hand-controlled puppet. The assumption was not unreasonable. There was no way that his detractors could know that Harry Truman was no one's stooge—that he was and always would be his own man.

The first test of Truman's independence came with the Utility Holding Company Act. An unregulated national utilities industry was breeding inefficiency, corruption and waste. Tom Pendergast lobbied Harry Truman hard to get him to oppose the legislation with its stringent regulatory provisions designed to reform the industry. Truman,

---

[73] *Harry S. Truman*, op.cit., p. 68.

however, showed that on matters of principle he was a maverick. He voted for and actively promoted the bill, much to Tom Pendergast's disappointment. The exquisite irony of the episode was that in voting his principles, Truman was branded by the press as a mere pawn of President Franklin D. Roosevelt. This was almost laughable because Truman had rarely exchanged even a single word with Roosevelt during his first year in office. As a freshman senator he had the usual pro forma photo opportunity with the President about a month after he arrived in Washington, in February of 1935, but in his own words was "tongue-tied" and unable to speak with any cogency.[74] Truman later attributed his diffidence to being in awe of the office of the Presidency rather than of Roosevelt personally.[75]

Isolated and largely friendless during his first months in the Senate, Truman by dint of his hard work, intelligence and resolute approach to legislation, eventually came to be noticed by the Senate insiders—also known as "the Club". The Club was the hand-full of movers and shakers who dominated the committees and shaped and molded the leadership's legislative agenda. They were an elite group but Harry Truman attracted their attention mainly because of his indefatigable work regimen away from the Senate floor in whatever committee on which he served. Truman could always be counted on to do the research, make the phone calls, lobby other Senators and their staffs, write memos in support of proposed legislation, brain-storm with the experts or meet with the press, whenever that's what was needed to advance a particular cause. Another requirement of membership was sociability. Truman was at his core a friendly man. He loved to talk, laugh, tell stories and play poker. His ability to play the piano at parties was no drawback and his flinty manner when engaged in conversation with his peers marked him as a man possessed of great self-confidence. Thus, after his first two years in office he was welcomed into and became an active member of "the Club".

It was during Harry Truman's second term as Senator from Missouri that he gained a nation-wide reputation—one which would eventually propel him into the Vice Presidency.

In 1941 when Truman began his second full term in office, World War II had already been raging for more than a year and a half. France had been defeated and had acquiesced by setting up its pro-Nazi, Vichy government. England was under siege and being kept alive by a com-

---

[74]   Ibid, p. 91.
[75]   Ibid.

bination of its own indomitable spirit and United States Lend-Lease. The United States was also moving towards a war-footing with tremendous growth underway in building and improving military camps across the nation. Having heard rumors of massive waste and graft going on in the rapid build-ups of Army installations, Truman's first act as a second-term Senator was to embark on a one-man inspection tour of military facilities from Florida to New England and from the Atlantic to the heart of the mid-west. Upon his return to Washington he gave a major speech on the floor of the senate, one that shook the foundations of the U.S. defense establishment and earned for Harry Truman the reputation as a man to be reckoned with. He reported bluntly that the Department of Defense build-up program at the nation's military installations was rife with waste, inefficiency and fraud, and was costing the taxpayers millions of dollars in unnecessary and wasteful spending.

In the wake of Truman's tour de force, a groundswell of public and Congressional clamor for an investigation of the military— industrial partnership was loudly heard in the halls of Congress and in public forums throughout the country.

The Roosevelt Administration immediately jumped out in front of the movement in order to prevent the investigation from falling into hostile Republican hands.

The political calculation was that the investigation should be conducted by a Southern Democrat to pre-empt an investigation by Northern Republicans in pro-Roosevelt southern regions of the country where most of the Army forts and camps were located. Georgia Republican Senator Eugene Cox quickly maneuvered to head-up an investigation. He was, however, an avowed Roosevelt-hater and Democratic Senator James (Jimmy) Byrnes of Georgia, a powerful Roosevelt ally, used his considerable influence to steer the investigation to Harry Truman as a safe compromise. Hence, the Truman Committee to oversee Department of Defense spending was born. Truman received an initial budget of $15,000.00 per year, a paltry sum. But Truman wisely used the lion's share of this budget to hire first-rate committee counsel at what was in 1941 a lavish salary of $9,000.00 per year. The Truman Committee's investigation and public hearings were a model of professionalism, mainly due to his initial decision to spend heavily on skilled and experienced counsel. When the Truman Committee exposed a hundred million dollars in wasteful spending by the Defense Department, mostly at military installations, Congress increased Truman's annual budget to $85,000.00 per year. In addition,

Truman was given the mandate to continue his investigation throughout America's involvement in the Second World War. As a keen student of history, Truman knew how Congressional interference in the war effort had made things so difficult for President Abraham Lincoln in the early years of the Civil War, and, therefore, vowed not to oversee Roosevelt's conduct of the war itself, but rather to confine his investigation to defense spending and efficiency in the war effort. Politically, this was a wise decision as well. There is little likelihood Roosevelt would have agreed to have Truman as his Vice-Presidential running mate in 1944 had Truman been looking over the President's shoulder for the previous four years.

The Harry Truman who attended the Democratic National Convention in August of 1944 bore no resemblance in terms of national prestige to the obscure Midwestern politician who first arrived in Washington ten years earlier. By July of 1944 he was a respected national figure whose star was on the ascendancy; and though he was not the top pick of many of the convention's power brokers to be the number two man on the ticket, he was on the short list of most.

The selection process which ultimately landed Truman the Vice Presidential nomination at the Democratic National Convention in Chicago in July of 1944, left a crowd of embittered politicians in its wake. The bitterness was not openly directed at Truman who neither sought nor wanted the nomination. It was the Democratic Party's powerful bosses and even more significantly FDR himself in whose direction the vitriol ultimately flowed. Roosevelt was at his game-playing best. Unwilling or unable to express a strong preference for any one of the leading candidates, all of whom he encouraged into thinking they were the President's number one choice, Roosevelt threw the process into the hands of the Democratic Party Chairman, the CIO[76] leadership and the Democratic machine bosses from big cities such as New York and Chicago. The result was that Roosevelt War Operations director, James Byrnes, and Vice President, Henry Wallace, each thought that he had gotten the nod from the President. Others believed to be in contention were Senator Albin Barkley, Speaker of the House, Sam Rayburn, and Supreme Court Justice, William O. Douglas. In fact, the only candidates Roosevelt ever expressed his written approval for were Truman and Douglas. Jimmy Byrnes and Vice President Henry Wallace, each clearly led by Roosevelt into thinking he was the anointed one, waged exhausting and divisive floor fights at

---

[76]   Congress of Industrial Organizations.

the national nominating convention. But it was the unenthused Truman, who spent most of the convention sequestered in his hotel room, that got the nod. Roosevelt ultimately agreed with the bosses that the pro-segregation southerner, Jimmy Byrnes, would cost the ticket hundreds of thousands of Negro votes and that the ultra-liberal Henry Wallace could cost Roosevelt much of his support in the South. The reluctant warrior, Harry S. Truman, a Midwesterner with a moderate voting record, was a safe compromise.

As for Truman himself, who secured the nomination after several ballots, when the momentum swung key delegations to change their votes and throw their support to him, the entire process was extremely unsavory and demeaning. That he should have so little control over his own destiny, which seemingly, was solely in the hands of the political pros, was appalling to him. John Truman had to be looking down from somewhere with a look of disgust on his face. It wasn't that Truman had anything against being Vice-President or even President for that matter. He just didn't want to succeed this particular President to the White House. As the saying goes, Roosevelt was a tough act to follow.

Byrnes and Wallace left the convention furious at Roosevelt and embittered at the dishonest way in which they were treated. Truman left with the belief that neither Byrnes nor Wallace were likely to seek political revenge against a man as popular and powerful as Roosevelt; but might just transfer their anger to him as a target by proxy for political vengeance. Justice William O'Douglas never left the convention at all because he never attended in the first place. Off mountain climbing in the western United States, he was unaware that he was even under consideration for the high post.

After the Roosevelt-Truman ticket won the 1944 Presidential election handily, Truman had just one meeting with Roosevelt before the latter died suddenly from a brain hemorrhage on April 12, 1945 at Warm Springs, Georgia. It was a luncheon meeting at which only the two of them were present. The meeting went well and gave Truman some reassurance that he would play an important role in the Administration. But, Roosevelt failed to bring Truman into his confidence on any of the major policy initiatives which were in process. When Truman suddenly succeeded Roosevelt to the Presidency on April 12, 1945 he did not even know that America had developed the atomic bomb and was considering using it against Japan.

When First Lady Eleanor Roosevelt informed Truman of Franklin Roosevelt's death, Truman asked if there was anything he could do for her. "No Harry" she replied, "Is there anything I can do for you? For you are the one in trouble now."[77]

President Truman, after the initial shock, overcame his sense of being overwhelmed by his awesome new responsibilities as President. Despite not being prepared to take over by Roosevelt, he worked tirelessly to learn the job. Truman went on to handle the remainder of Roosevelt's term admirably after some expected initial bumbling and false starts. He acquitted himself well at the Potsdam summit conference with Stalin and Churchill; he forthrightly made the decision to drop the atomic bomb on Japan to end the war; and made George C. Marshall his Secretary of State. This led to the Marshall Plan, the Berlin Airlift and NATO. Truman and Marshall then implemented the Truman Doctrine for Greece and Turkey and shepherded the United Nations through its infancy. Truman also courageously overcame his initial reluctance to recognize the State of Israel after some intensive lobbying from old friend Eddie Jacobsen; he ended racial segregation in the Armed Forces and steered the national economy wisely and competently into a period of growth.

Former United States President and Nobel Laureate, Jimmy Carter, provided a fitting tribute to Harry S. Truman when he spoke the following words:

> Among those who have served during my lifetime, Harry Truman is the President whom I've admired most. He was honest, modest, plainspoken, courageous and bold in the face of crisis.[78]

Truman himself best summarized his view of government and his political philosophy in an address which he gave at the home of Thomas Jefferson, Mt. Vernon, Virginia, on July 4, 1947:

> The first requisite of peace among nations is common adherence to the principle that governments derive their just powers from the consent of the governed. ... A second requisite of peace among nations is common respect for basic human rights. ... So long as the basic rights of men are denied in any

---

[77] *My Fellow Americans*, Sourcebooks, Inc., 2003, p. 136.
[78] Ibid, p. 138.

substantial portion of the Earth, men everywhere must live in fear of their own rights and their own security.[79]

This core philosophy of government formed the underlying principle of the Truman Doctrine.

As Truman and MacArthur continued on their collision course in 1950 towards America's greatest crisis of command, there was little disagreement between them over the proposition that Korea was a "substantial portion of the Earth" where the "basic rights of men" were in great jeopardy and needed to be secured.

They shared a similar view as to the palpable threat by the communists to the entire Far East. Their ultimately irreconcilable differences were not rooted in a deep chasm of ideology. They stemmed more from differences in approach to the formulation of policies geared to implement their jointly held beliefs. Their differences in approach in turn emanated from each man's entire set of attitudes on life, which expressed themselves in vastly different disciplines and personalities. Each man's make-up was the product of his genetic, educational, class and experiential history. Both of them had been tested by intense life challenges and choices. The decisions they made and lessons they learned created in each of them certain rock-solid and intractable traits of character. Each man's resolve, convictions and self-confidence in times of crisis was unshakeable.

When these two powerful personalities reached diametrically opposed conclusions over matters of war and peace—of life and death for peoples and nations—the result would be shattering for both of them and deeply unsettling for America.

---

[79]   Ibid, p. 137.

Six months before Truman's dramatic recall of General MacArthur after the two disagreed about the future course of the Korean War, political cartoonist John Chase ridiculed the president's capacities as a military leader with this caricature of the Commander-in-Chief dwarfed by his General's outsized hat.

President Harry S. Truman (right), with Admiral Arthur W. Radford, USN, Commander in Chief Pacific, Commander in Chief Pacific Fleet, at Hickam Air Force Base, Honolulu, Hawaii, after the President's arrival in mid-October 1950. Truman was en route to Wake Island for the conference with MacArthur that began on 15 October.

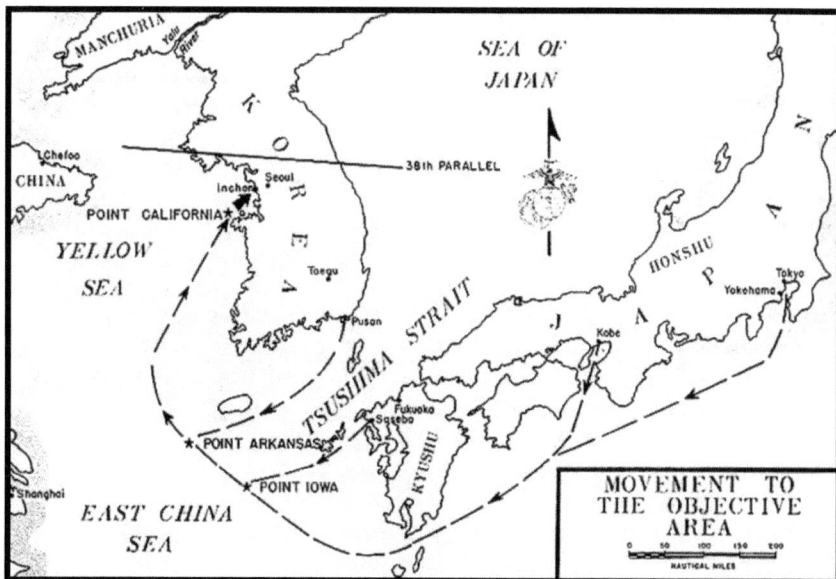

Route taken by the invasion forces to reach Inchon.

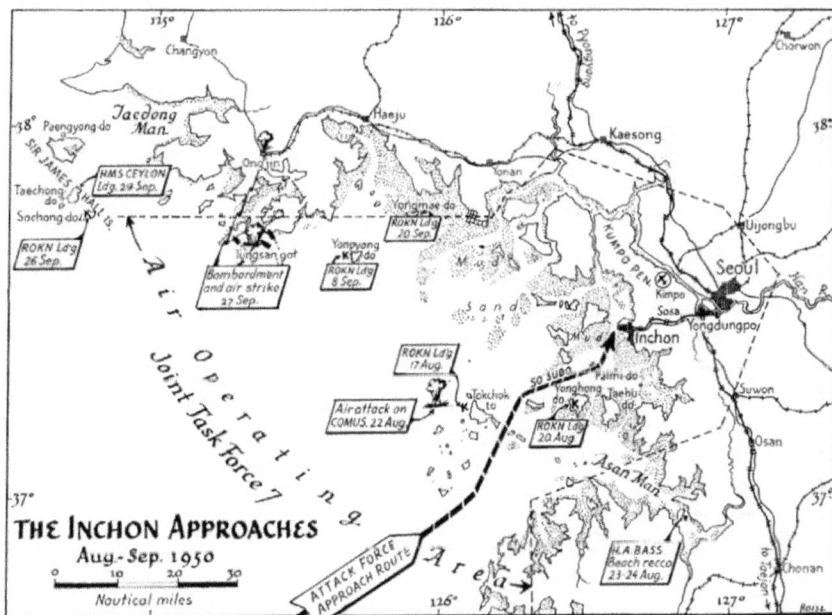

The Inchon Assault, 15 September 1950

Chapter 4

The Inchon Landing

The tragedy of life is not that man loses but that he almost wins.
—Heywood Broun

THE first two months of the Korean War were a period of crushing defeat for the South Korean Army and United Nations forces. By June 28, 1950, a mere three days after the North Korean offensive began, Seoul, the South Korean capital, was in Communist hands and the South Korean Army in a state of near-collapse.

Despite the fact that UN troops poured into the Port of Pusan from Japan and elsewhere, the initial UN tactical mission was strictly a defensive one—to defend the 50 mile by 50 mile Pusan Peninsula and to keep its perimeter intact. South Korean President Syngman Rhee lobbied MacArthur for a bold strike against the North—one that would be so stunning and breathtaking as to purge Rhee's humiliation at the hands of his implacable Communist foe, Kim Il-Sung. MacArthur needed no encouragement.

The early honeymoon between MacArthur and Truman came to an abrupt end when on August 17, 1950, MacArthur in a message to the Veterans of Foreign Wars (VFW) encroached upon Truman's territory by presenting a plea for American support for nationalist Chinese leader-in-exile, Chiang Kai-shek. MacArthur stressed in his message the strategic importance of Formosa to the defense of the Pacific.

Truman had appointed MacArthur to win the Korean War, not to meddle in foreign policy, and was justifiably irked. He saw MacArthur's action as a direct challenge to his authority. He ordered MacArthur to publicly retract his statement and after some initial resistance, MacArthur complied. Nevertheless, Truman had barely been able to contain his wrath and considered relieving MacArthur of command. But Truman decided against firing MacArthur in the interests of the long-term security of the United States and the more immediate exigencies of the War.

MacArthur's views themselves came as no surprise to Truman, Acheson and Marshall. He had voiced them many times before. But to go public with them at such a critical time for the Administration and the Nation was a blatant provocation by a subordinate. For five years Truman had been trying to get MacArthur to come home from Japan for a series of meetings. Truman's "invitations" to MacArthur were in essence orders from the commander-in-chief. MacArthur refused each invitation with a transparent excuse. Only MacArthur could have gotten away with such insubordination. Again in August of 1950, instead of strongly rebuking MacArthur's usurpation of Presidential authority, the only penalty Truman imposed upon him was an order to retract his statement to the VFW, and even that was not immediately forthcoming from the General. MacArthur had given Roosevelt pretty much the same treatment during the war years, with impunity.

For a full decade two presidents as well as the Joint Chiefs had appeased MacArthur and in so doing became his enablers. It was the price they chose to pay to keep his genius at work for them and to avoid political embarrassment. It was beginning to appear that the price had been far too high—but then came Inchon.

The United Nations forces in Korea, with American troops comprising the overwhelming majority but also including British, Australian, Turkish, Italian, Greek, Canadian, French, Dutch and a smattering of others as well—were pinned down on the Pusan Peninsula with the Naktong River as the last natural northern barrier. A breakout seemed impossible and at best, a long shot, unless MacArthur could open a second front.

The Communist forces were attempting to cross the Naktong River but the massive number of UN troops, arms and matériel flowing steadily into the Port of Pusan was holding them at bay and preventing Pusan from becoming an American "Dunkirk". The American leadership could not help but draw parallels between the type of bloody stalemate extant in South Korea in July and August of 1950 and the brutally destructive and wasteful stalemate of World War I, which had paralyzed the French and British in their trenches on one side of the Western Front and the Germans on the other, on the battle fields of France from 1915 through 1917. MacArthur knew that the forces under his command desperately needed to break the stalemate.

As early as July 2, 1950 MacArthur had formulated a plan to destroy the North Korean Army with an amphibious envelopment.[80] The place chosen was Inchon, a city on the West Coast of the Korean

---

[80] *MacArthur: A Biography* by Richard B. Frank (Palgrave MacMillan 2009), p. 153.

Peninsula just slightly southwest of Seoul and about 150 miles Northwest of the Pusan perimeter.

Most thought the natural barriers, comprised of a tidal cycle which made a landing feasible only at high tides, the approach through a narrow twisting channel protected by shore batteries and a high seawall extending along the entire Inchon waterfront, made a landing there all but impossible. And aside from the navigational difficulties and natural barriers, an invasion at Inchon presented a major strategic gamble. MacArthur would have to withdraw badly needed troops from the Pusan Perimeter for the strike force, including the Marine Brigade, and divert to the Inchon operation reinforcements headed for the Port of Pusan from America and Europe.

The plan called for the UN strike force to drive inland once Inchon was secured, seize South Korea's capital, Seoul, and sever the supply lines of the North Korean armies. By choking-off their supplies and reinforcements, the North Korean Army, then-laying siege to the Pusan Peninsula, would be trapped between MacArthur's forces to their North and Walton Walker's Eighth Army to their south.

The plan was a natural for MacArthur for he had enjoyed many successes with just such amphibious envelopments in the Pacific during World War II.[81] An example was his victory at Hollandia on New Guinea in April of 1944.

The code-name for the planned operation was "Chromite". But the only person with any enthusiasm for a landing at Inchon was MacArthur himself. Army and Navy planners both at the Pentagon and at MacArthur's headquarters in Tokyo found only reasons why Inchon was a totally unacceptable place at which to stage an attack. General J. Lawton Collins, the U.S. Army Chief of Staff, usually referred to as Joe Collins, and Admiral Forest Sherman, the Chief of Naval Operations, flew from Washington to Tokyo with the mission of talking MacArthur out of it.[82]

A briefing session was held in Tokyo at Headquarters in the Dai Ichi Building on August 23, 1950. It turned out to be a fateful meeting of great historical significance.

The session opened on a clearly negative note. Nine Navy briefers "presented the decidedly problematic details of Chromite."[83] As the

---

[81]   Ibid.

[82]   *The Secrets of Inchon*, by Eugene Franklin Clark (GP Putnam's Sons, 2002) p. 9.

[83]   `*MacArthur: A Biography*, op.cit..

speakers droned on, General Collins, in particular, became even more opposed to the operation than he was upon entering the room. Nothing but pessimism seemed to pervade the atmosphere as MacArthur sat with apparent imperturbability, puffing on his corn-cob pipe. Some of the previously-designated commanders for the planned operation had urged MacArthur, with no success, to target Posung-Myon, a city about twenty miles south of Inchon, for the landing. A Navy staff officer involved in the planning quipped: "We drew up a list of every conceivable and natural handicap and Inchon had 'em all." [84]

After the last briefer finished his presentation, MacArthur stood and addressed Collins, Sherman and the contingent of other staff officers present. He spoke without notes for a full forty five minutes. It was a virtuoso performance—an eloquent peroration exceeding all others in his long career. His full array of oratorical skills was on display and most of those present were mesmerized—perhaps with the exception of the skeptical J. Lawton Collins. MacArthur brilliantly flipped the arguments concerning the incredible, if not impossible, challenges of an Inchon landing, to his own advantage. "No enemy general would believe any sane commander would attack" [85] [at Inchon] argued MacArthur, and that fact would guarantee to him the element of surprise. The prestige of the Western world was hanging in the balance in Korea, said MacArthur. Communism had chosen Asia for its march to global domination. Perhaps in Europe we were able to fight Communism with words but that would not be enough here in Asia. Here, argued the General, we had no choice but to do it with deeds, and Inchon was a deed that would resound throughout the civilized world— and save 100,000 lives. After goading the Navy briefers and Navy brass present by declaring, "I seem to have more confidence in the Navy than the Navy has in itself," MacArthur concluded with the daring prediction, "We shall land at Inchon and I shall crush them." [86]

As the meeting drew to a close, no one in the room had yet voiced any support for MacArthur's plan. A tense silence enveloped the participants until finally Rear Admiral James G. Doyle, the commander of the amphibious branch of the operation, broke the ice by proclaiming, "General, I have not been asked nor have I volunteered my opinion about this landing. If I were asked, however, the best I can say is

---

[84]   Ibid, p. 154.
[85]   Ibid.
[86]   Ibid.

Inchon is not impossible."[87] General Collins departed without offering his endorsement, unmoved by MacArthur's dazzling eloquence. Admiral Sherman on the other hand had been converted into a believer.

Back in Washington, D.C., Collins and Sherman gave a detailed report of the arguments—pro and con—which had reverberated throughout the Dai Ichi building. With great reservations, the Joint Chiefs of Staff conditionally approved the landing at Inchon.

MacArthur had courageously decided to go ahead with virtually no allies backing him up. The Chiefs however, could not be accused of having that kind of backbone. They knew that the fate of the non-communist world might well be riding on the success of the operation. To cover their posteriors, however, they sought Truman's explicit permission to go forward with the landing. They passed the buck to Harry Truman as if to validate the hard truth of the sign on the President's desk—"The buck stops here."

Truman did not even hesitate in making the momentous decision. The ex-artillery captain said it sounded like a worthy plan and gave it "the green-light".[88]

The two tough and decisive warriors did not like each other but at this pivotal moment in American history, Truman and MacArthur by their courage and decisiveness, proved why they stood so much taller than most of the men around them.

To keep Inchon and future operations completely under his control, MacArthur split Eighth Army into two contingents, in effect, spinning off his own force totally independent from Eighth Army, called "X Corps," and put his hand-picked general, Edward (Ned) Almond, in charge. Almond, a highly ambitious officer, went back to the Bataan days of 1941-42 with MacArthur and owed his career to him. He was a one hundred percent loyal MacArthur man. X Corps was comprised mainly of the 1st Marine Division and the 7th Infantry Division. It was completely free of Eighth Army, then under the Command of General Walton W. Walker.

When Army Chief of Staff, Joe Collins, heard that MacArthur had selected Ned Almond as his Inchon Commander, he was furious. Collins did not like Almond and considered him unqualified for such a command. And MacArthur had kept the operation shrouded in secrecy and failed to provide the Joint Chiefs with the plan of battle until the very morning of the invasion itself, September 15, 1950, when a

---

[87] *The Secrets of Inchon*, op.cit., p. 10.
[88] Ibid.

young staff officer, Lieutenant Colonel Lynn Smith, delivered the exact plans for Inchon to General Collins. By the time Collins was handed the multiple volumes containing the final plans for the landing, the operation was already underway.[89] The evidence seems clear that MacArthur withheld from the Joint Chiefs, technically his superiors, the details of what he was doing until it was too late to stop him.[90] To then compound the grievance, MacArthur named his own man, the unpopular Edward Almond, to command the historic operation without first clearing it with the Joint Chiefs. Within the culture of the military, MacArthur had committed an unpardonable sin. He had treated the four-star generals and admirals—technically his bosses—with a total lack of respect. It wasn't just that he had completely shredded any semblance of protocol—it was the dismissive, bordering on contemptuous, manner in which he did it. Eight months later the chiefs would have their opportunity for revenge against MacArthur for blind-siding them on Inchon.

MacArthur's first stroke of good fortune concerning Inchon was North Korean leader Kim Il-Sung's rejection of the possibility of the UN forces conducting an amphibious landing behind his lines. Inchon, like Seoul, was south of the 38th Parallel but fell into North Korean hands after June 25th. Kim Il-Sung simply did not comprehend the brilliance and audacity of MacArthur. This gave MacArthur the benefit of surprise, which combined with the meticulous and intelligent planning of Rear Admiral James H. Doyle, enabled MacArthur's strike forces to approach Inchon Harbor without mishap. His initial landing force consisted of the Fifth and Seventh Marine Regiments—thirteen thousand men in all—followed by the First Marine Regiment. The overall mission was to take Inchon, then Kimpo and finally Seoul, about thirty miles from Inchon.

Preliminary to the approach and landing at Inchon Harbor, were massive naval and air bombardments of the harbors and the Flying Fish Channel, which narrowed and emptied into the Inchon Channel. Despite the early positive signs, the actual landing still posed immense challenges. A high tide measuring thirty one feet in height was a natural obstacle no amount of planning could neutralize. MacArthur had a narrow window of opportunity to get the Marines ashore at high tide. Otherwise, landing vehicles, equipment and the troops themselves would become mired in the mudflats of coastal Inchon, once the tides

---

[89]   *The Coldest Winter*, op.cit., p. 301.
[90]   Ibid.

receded, where they would be sitting ducks for North Korean artillery, mortars and small arms fire. If that happened, the Marines would lose the advantages of surprise, speed and superior fire power, in all likelihood dooming the entire operation.

Another logistical problem for MacArthur was that Inchon had very few beaches on which to land. The Marines landing crafts would be able to navigate the Inchon channel, provided it had not been mined, right up to the city's waterfront, but once there would have no place to land thousands of marines. They would have to scale a high seawall in order to penetrate the perimeter of the city. Fortunately, there was another way. Deep into the Inchon Channel and just west of Inchon were two islands with beaches suitable for an amphibious landing. Their names were Wolmi-do and a smaller companion island, Sowolmi-do. Admiral Doyle and his staff had planned the timing of the landings with great precision and the 1st Marine Division executed the plan with perfection. At sunrise on September 15, 1950, 230 ships from seven navies, swarms of LST and smaller craft—the entire UN invasion fleet—assembled in the waters of Inchon Harbor. In perfect sync with high tide, a battalion of the Fifth Marine Regiment stormed both Wolmi-do and Sowolmi-do at 6:33 a.m. on September 15. They expected ferocious resistance from North Korean infantry and shore batteries and were pleasantly surprised when it failed to materialize. The Navy's advance reconnaissance mission had revealed machine-gun nests lining the shore and big gun emplacements well back from the beaches. The machine gun nests had been reduced to rubble by the massive U.S. combined sea and air bombardments; and the big guns to scrap metal.

Both Wolmi-do and Sowolmi-do were captured after Marine landings at high tide with unusually light casualties—one Marine fatality and only seventeen wounded. The first landing took place at the area designated as "Green Beach" on Wolmi-do and upon alighting from their LSTs, the Marines had to scale twelve foot high seawalls under enemy fire. After negotiating the steep seawalls handily, they swept over Wolmi-do in just two hours with only token resistance by the NKPA. The Navy and Marine command expected to have to defend against a strong North Korean counter-attack over the next twelve hours, but it never came.

"Red Beach" further up the channel fell with little resistance to the Fifth Marines Regiment. "Blue Beach," about three miles south of Inchon, was a little more difficult for the Marines to capture, but not because of an effective defense by the North Koreans. Strong currents, another natural impediment to the landing, threw the LSTs off course. This, however, did not affect the overall landings.

Roughly twelve hours after the initial landings at Wolmi-do, and with the returning high tides, Marines from Wolmi-do and in landing craft in the Inchon Channel, stormed into Inchon Harbor. Two battalions from the Fifth Regiment scaled the seawall in downtown Inchon while simultaneously the First Regiment hit the seawall in a suburban area a few miles southeast of central Inchon.

A reporter in one of the landing crafts later wrote that the seawall looked as high "as the RCA building."[91] But the Marine assault reflected careful and ingenious advance planning. They were well-prepared for every obstacle in their way. The landing crafts were equipped with ladders protruding upwards from their bows. As the landing crafts slammed into the concrete walls with engines running to keep them from drifting, the Marines scrambled up the ladders. At the same time Marine contingents at Wolmi-do directed a blizzard of suppressing fire into the area of downtown Inchon beyond the seawall, to provide cover for the exposed Marines climbing over the walls, and to destroy remaining pockets of resistance.

Again anticipating that the next cycle of low tides would delay the Marines' further progress once they were over the walls, the high command directed ten LSTs loaded with supplies and ammunition to remain in place in the mud on the channel-side of the seawall once high tide again receded. The Marine strike force thereby had the food, medical supplies and ammunition it needed to sustain the beachhead.

It took less than two days to subdue and secure Inchon. The total UN invasion force consisted of more than seventy thousand men, but casualties were relatively light. The Inchon landing was a towering feat. MacArthur had taken complete ownership of the risky venture from the start and deservedly took ownership of the prodigious victory it produced, the greatest of his long and singularly transcendent career.

In response to skeptics who dismissed the victory as pure luck, General O. P. Smith observed, "We had a break at Inchon all right—we had the know-how." In a more expansive explanation, Admiral Doyle wrote in his after-action report,

The successful accomplishment of the assault on Inchon demanded that an incredible number of individual and coordi-

---

[91]   *The Secrets of Inchon*, op.cit., p. 322.

nated tasks be performed precisely in the face of almost insu-
perable difficulties...because of their many years of specialized
training in amphibious warfare, in conjunction with the Navy,
the Marines had the requisite know-how to formulate these
plans flawlessly without additional training or rehearsal.

A less modest man might have found a way to mention his own
essential contribution, which was the tireless and skillful anticipation
of everything that could go wrong, and, putting exhaustive plans in
place to meet those contingencies.

At the August 23 meeting at the Dai Ichi building, Admiral Doyle
had disregarded General Almond's admonition to him to speak only in
generalities to MacArthur and the assembled top brass about the extreme difficulties and risks attendant upon a landing at Inchon. Doyle
steadfastly believed that an operation of such critical importance made
it imperative that the overall commander be made aware of all the important details.[92] When Doyle's turn to speak came, he ignored Almond's warning that MacArthur wasn't interested in the details by
presenting a totally unvarnished appraisal of the natural obstacles to
success at Inchon—the tides, the narrow channel, the currents, the sea
walls and so on. He forcefully stated his preference for a landing at
Posung-Myong.

Because of his strong convictions against Inchon as the landing site,
rather than in spite of them, Rear Admiral James H. Doyle became the
ideal commander of naval operations for the landing.

General Omar Bradley was quoted as calling Inchon "the luckiest
military operation in history," and without question luck played a major part in its success. But luck was only a part of the vast interwoven
tapestry which produced victory, and at Inchon luck was the residue of
design.

Things did not go quite as smoothly in General Almond's drive to
capture Seoul. While the battle for Inchon raged, Kim Il-Sung rushed
one full division and three separate regiments to Seoul to bolster its
defense—about twenty thousand troops in all. When added to the
North Korean defenders already at Seoul, there was now a sizable force
in place of 35,000 to 40,000 troops to protect Seoul from once again
falling under the control of South Korea and its allies.

---

[92] *Warrior or Wordsmith* by Bernard K. Duffy and Ronald H. Carpenter
(Greenwood Press, 1997).

General O.P. Smith, Commander of the First Marine Division, now part of X Corps under Ned Almond's immediate command, was tasked with the mission of moving across the Han River and taking Seoul with about two Marine Regiments. Outnumbered by the North Korean forces and under constant pressure from Almond to keep moving forward regardless of the cost in Marine lives, Smith grew deeply resentful of Almond's intrusions into ground operations and was not afraid of telling him so—although this did not end the interference. Smith finally drew the line when Almond started giving commands directly to officers serving under Smith. The respected and combat-seasoned Smith simply told his officers that they were to obey no orders unless they came directly from him. Had Smith been an Army officer, Almond would probably have stripped him of command immediately. But, inter-service politics and protocol prevented Almond from tampering with the command of a senior Marine officer- especially one in such a high profile position, who had just led one of the most spectacular assaults in American military history—the taking of Inchon. Smith even went so far as to reject Almond's battle plan to split his forces and enter Seoul from opposite sides of the City, concerned that in the general confusion and chaos engendered by the fog of war, the advancing forces might wind-up shooting each other. Smith's refusal to carry out the order bordered on insubordination but Almond and MacArthur took no action against him. MacArthur was instead focusing his ire upon Eighth Army commander, General Walton Walker. The plan for recapturing Seoul entailed a two-pronged pincer movement with Walker's Eighth Army breaking out of the Pusan Peninsula, crossing the Naktong River and moving north to link up with Almond's forces, while smashing the North Korean Army caught in between. But with only two bridges over the Naktong and much of Walker's engineering equipment siphoned off by X Corps for the Inchon campaign, Walker was finding the breakout to be difficult and was moving at a pace, which MacArthur back in Tokyo, found unacceptably slow. MacArthur was, by his vocal criticism, laying the groundwork for Walker's eventual replacement.

The pressure on Smith to take Seoul, coming directly from Almond and indirectly from MacArthur back in Tokyo, was intense and unwelcome. The Marines' resentment against Almond and MacArthur was a simmering cauldron that would soon boil over.

By December when the First Marine Division was surrounded by tens of thousands of Chinese troops at Chosin Reservoir and barely escaped total destruction by fighting their way out of the Chinese envelopment, the resentment had hardened into an intense dislike. The commonplace term applied to Almond and MacArthur by Marines on the ground was "Pogues," a derisive acronym for non-combat personnel. The reference was particularly biting in the context of the harrowing conditions at Chosin Reservoir, Fox Hill and Turkey Hill because of the belief by the Marines that the two aforementioned "Pogue generals"—driven by ego and a lust for publicity—had recklessly placed the 1st Marines in peril.

O.P. Smith's Marines reached the outskirts of Seoul on September 25 leading Almond to make the misleading claim that X Corps had retaken the beleaguered South Korean Capital. In fact, it took three more days of fierce fighting before it was safely back under UN control; and then only after superior United States firepower had demolished large parts of the city.

The Eighth Army under Walker, and X Corps under Almond, finally linked up on September 27. By September 28 they had effectively suppressed all pockets of major resistance. In the next two weeks, MacArthur's forces would consolidate their gains and re-take virtually all territory south of the 38th Parallel. The Inchon plan had been an astounding success and had seemingly transformed a humiliating defeat in Korea for the United States into an incredible victory, within a period of less than three weeks.

The North Korean army had "sustained huge losses and would never again be able to field more than a corps-sized fighting force."[93] After Walker had executed his breakout from Pusan, the North Korean Army, finding itself surrounded, collapsed and was pushed back into North Korea. During the Inchon-Seoul campaign, UN troops discovered many North Korean atrocities—including 8300 Korean and 485 Americans massacred by North Korean forces. Richard B. Franks in *MacArthur: A Biography*, summed up the psychological climate in Seoul and Tokyo following the discovery of the brutal acts of the North Koreans, in the following passage:

> This [the discoveries] exacerbated the incendiary issue of whether MacArthur should cross the 38th parallel, and if so, for what purpose. MacArthur and Rhee enjoyed the enormous advantage of a clear, shared purpose: unify Korea by force under Rhee.[94]

---

[93] *MacArthur: A Biography*, op.cit., p. 154.
[94] Ibid.

The shared purpose of Rhee and MacArthur notwithstanding, it was now time for a long-delayed meeting in which Rhee would have no role and play no part.

USS Rowan (DD-782) silhouetted against the sun on 14 September 1950, as she escorts USS Mount McKinley (AGC-7) off the Korean coast en route to Inchon.

Five U.S. Navy destroyers steam up the Inchon channel to bombard Wolmi-Do Island on 13 September 1950, two days prior to the Inchon landings. Wolmi-Do is in the right center background, with smoke rising from air strikes. The ships are USS Mansfield (DD-728); USS DeHaven (DD-727); USS Lyman K. Swenson (DD-729); USS Collett (DD-730) and USS Gurke (DD-783).

TRUMAN AND MACARTHUR

Wolmi-Do Island under bombardment on 13 September 1950, two days before the landings at Inchon. Photographed from USS Lyman K. Swenson (DD-729), one of whose 40mm gun mounts is in the foreground. Sowolmi-Do Island, connected to Wolmi-Do by a causeway, is at the right, with Inchon beyond.

A Chaplain reads the Last Rites service as Lieutenant (Junior Grade) David H. Swenson is buried at sea from USS Toledo (CA-133), off Inchon, Korea. He had been killed by North Korean artillery while his ship, USS Lyman K. Swenson (DD-729) was bombarding enemy positions on Wolmi-do Island, Inchon, on 13 September 1950. Lyman K. Swenson is in the background, with her crew at quarters on deck.

Major General Oliver P. Smith, USMC, Commanding General, First Marine Division (left) and Rear Admiral James H. Doyle, USN, Commander, Task Force 90, confer on board USS Mount McKinley (AGC-7), in mid-September 1950, immediately prior to the Inchon invasion.

Rear Admiral James H. Doyle, USN, Commander, Task Force 90, on the bridge of his flagship, USS Mount McKinley (AGC-7), in mid-September 1950, immediately prior to the Inchon invasion.

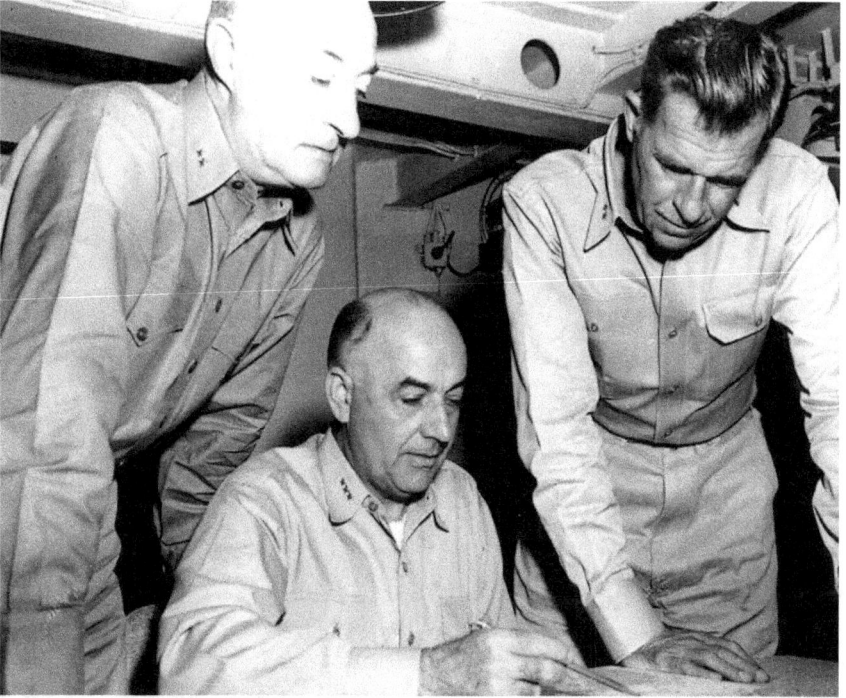

Flag conference on board USS Rochester (CA-124), flagship of Joint Task Force Seven, during the Inchon operation. Those present are (from left to right): Rear Admiral James H. Doyle, USN, Commander, Task Force 90, Vice Admiral Arthur D. Struble, USN, Commander, Joint Task Force Seven, and Rear Admiral John M. Higgins, USN, Commander, Task Group 90.6.

Crew of one of the USS Toldeo's (CA-133) 40mm quad gun mounts stands ready during the Inchon invasion, circa 15 September 1950.

Three Hospital Corpsmen relax on board USS Toledo (CA-133) during a lull in the Inchon invasion action, circa 15 September 1950. These men are (from left to right): Bob Hays, Jack R. Allen and Stephen J. Lazorchak. Note: Life vests, white helmet with red cross, and red cross armbands.

An LST slips into Inchon harbor in the early hours of 15 September 1950, just prior to the landings there.

Truman and MacArthur

LCVPs from USS Union (AKA-106) circle in the transport area off Inchon, prior to going to the line of departure on the first day of landings, 15 September 1950. An LST, wearing the side number QO-12, is in the center background.

First wave of U.S. Marines head for the landing beach in LCVPs, 15 September 1950. Lighting in sky indicates that these Marines may be bound for the "Green" Beach landings on Wolmi-Do Island.

First wave of U.S. Marines head for the landing beach in LVTs, 15 September 1950. Island in the background is Wolmi-Do. This may show the landings on Wolmi-Do's "Green" Beach in the morning of 15 September. Control ship in the right center background is a PCE.

LCVPs from USS Noble (APA-218) wait their turn to go up to the Inchon pontoon docks to unload troops and supplies, on the first day of the landings, 15 September 1950.

LCVPs prepare to land troops and equipment on Green Beach, Wolmi-Do Island, during the first day of landings at Inchon, 15 September 1950.

A LSMR (Landing Ship, Medium, Rocket) fires rockets as LVTs (Landing Vehicle, Tank) cross the line of departure to take Marines to Blue Beach on the first day of landings, 15 September 1950. Wolmi-Do island is in the left center background. The Inchon waterfront is in the right center distance, with heavy smoke rising from pre-invasion bombardment.

TRUMAN AND MACARTHUR

First Lieutenant Baldomero Lopez, USMC, leads the 3rd Platoon, Company A, 1st Battalion, 5th Marines, over the seawall on the northern side of Red Beach, as the second assault wave lands, 15 September 1950. Wooden scaling ladders are in use to facilitate disembarkation from the LCVP that brought these men to the shore. Lt. Lopez was killed in action within a few minutes, while assaulting a North Korean bunker. Note M1 Carbine carried by Lt. Lopez, M1 Rifles of other Marines and details of the Marines' field gear.

Colonel Lewis B. Puller, USMC, studies the terrain before advancing to another enemy objective, during operations beyond Inchon, Korea, circa September 1950. He was in command of the Marine Regimental Combat Team One of the First Marine Division.

Left to right, Brig. Gen. Courtney Whitney, Gen. Douglas MacArthur, Command-in-Chief of UN Forces, and Maj. Gen. Edward M. Almond observe the shelling of Inchon from the USS Mt. McKinley, 15 September 1950.

General of the Army Douglas MacArthur (center) confers with other senior officers on board USS Mount McKinley (AGC-7) during the landings at Inchon, 15 September 1950. Officer directly behind MacArthur is Major General Edward M. Almond, U.S. Army, Commander Tenth Corps. Brigadier General Edwin K. Wright, MacArthur's Operations Officer, is also present, wearing a ball cap.

General of the Army Douglas MacArthur (seated, center), Commander-in-Chief, Far East Command, on board USS Mount McKinley (AGC-7) during the Inchon landings, 15 September 1950. The others present are (from left to right): Rear Admiral James H. Doyle, U.S. Navy, Commander, Task Force 90; Brigadier General Edwin K. Wright, U.S. Army, MacArthur's Operations Officer, and Major General Edward M. Almond, U.S. Army, Commander, Tenth Corps.

Senior U.S. commanders inspect the Inchon port area, 16 September 1950. This appears to be in the Red Beach area, with the northern end of Wolmi-Do island in the background. Those present in the front row are (from left to right): Vice Admiral Arthur D. Struble, USN, Commander, Joint Task Force Seven; General of the Army Douglas MacArthur, Commander in Chief, Far East Command, and Major General Oliver P. Smith, USMC, Commanding General, First Marine Division.

General of the Army Douglas MacArthur, Commander in Chief, Far East Command, makes a jeep tour of Inchon port facilities on 16 September 1950, soon after the city was captured by U.S. forces. Seated immediately behind him are Major General Oliver P. Smith, USMC, Commanding General, First Marine Division (left center) and Vice Admiral Arthur D. Struble, USN, Commander, Joint Task Force Seven (at right).

Four LSTs unload men and equipment while "high and dry" at low tide on Inchon's Red Beach, 16 September 1950, the day after the initial landings there. USS LST-715 is on the right end of this group, which also includes LST-611, LST-845 and one other. Another LST is beached on the tidal mud flats at the extreme right. Note bombardment damage to the building in center foreground, many trucks at work, Wolmi-Do island in the left background and the causeway connecting the island to Inchon. Ship in the far distance, just beyond the right end of Wolmi-Do, is USS Lyman K. Swenson (DD-729).

LSTs on "Yellow" Beach, on the Inchon waterfront, 16 September 1950. Second ship from the front is probably USS LST-914. Next beyond her is USS LSM-419. The other two LSTs present are Japanese-manned, and therefore unarmed.

LSU-1160 moves onto Inchon's "Yellow" Beach to land supplies, 17 September 1950. Taken by a photographer from USS Mount McKinley (AGC-7).

LCM stranded on the side of a sunken ship off Inchon, 17 September 1950. Its position, some twenty feet above the water level, shows the great tidal range that is typical of Inchon.

Troops unload landing craft at Inchon's "Red" Beach on 18 September 1950, three days after the initial landings there. The LCVP in the center is from USS Alshain (AKA-55). Wolmi-Do Island is in the background.

TRUMAN AND MACARTHUR

A LST and a LCM are stranded by low tide near the Tidal Basin on In-chon's waterfront, during the post-assault logistics buildup, 20 September 1950. The LST (bearing the side number QO-18) is suspended on the end of a pier, with other landing craft beached nearby. Sowolmi-Do Island is in the far right background, with invasion shipping visible in the distance.

Unloading operations on "Green" Beach, Inchon, 20 September 1950. The beached ship is a Japanese-manned LST. USS Eldorado (AGC-11) is in the center distance.

General of the Army Douglas MacArthur, Commander in Chief, Far East (left), greets Admiral Arthur W. Radford, USN, Commander in Chief Pacific and Pacific Fleet, at a Tokyo airfield. Photo is dated 20 September 1950. This is a wirephoto, with vertical transmission lines and some electronic "noise".

General of the Army Douglas MacArthur boards USS Missouri (BB-63) off Inchon, Korea, 21 September 1950.

Truman and MacArthur

Rear Admiral James H. Doyle, USN, Commander, Task Force 90, congratulates four sailors who have just received the Silver Star Medal for service as coxswains of LCVP landing craft during the Inchon invasion. Taken during ceremonies on board USS Rochester (CA-124). The original photograph is dated 22 September 1950. The men are (left to right): Seaman Chancey H. Vogt, Seaman William H. Ragan, Engineman-Fireman Richard P. Vinson, and Seaman Apprentice Paul J. Gregory.

U.S. Marines engaged in street fighting during the liberation of Seoul, circa late September 1950. Note M1 rifles and Browning Automatic Rifles carried by the Marines, dead Koreans in the street, and M4 "Sherman" tanks in the distance.

View of the transport area, looking southwestward from over Inchon, with Sowolmi Do in the foreground. The original photograph is dated 29 September 1950, two weeks after the Inchon assault and the day that liberation ceremonies took place in Seoul. USS Rochester (CA-124), flagship of Joint Task Force Seven, is in the center. USS Mount McKinley (AGC-7), flagship of Task Force 90, is the nearest of the three ships at left, seen straight out from the Sowolmi Do seawall.

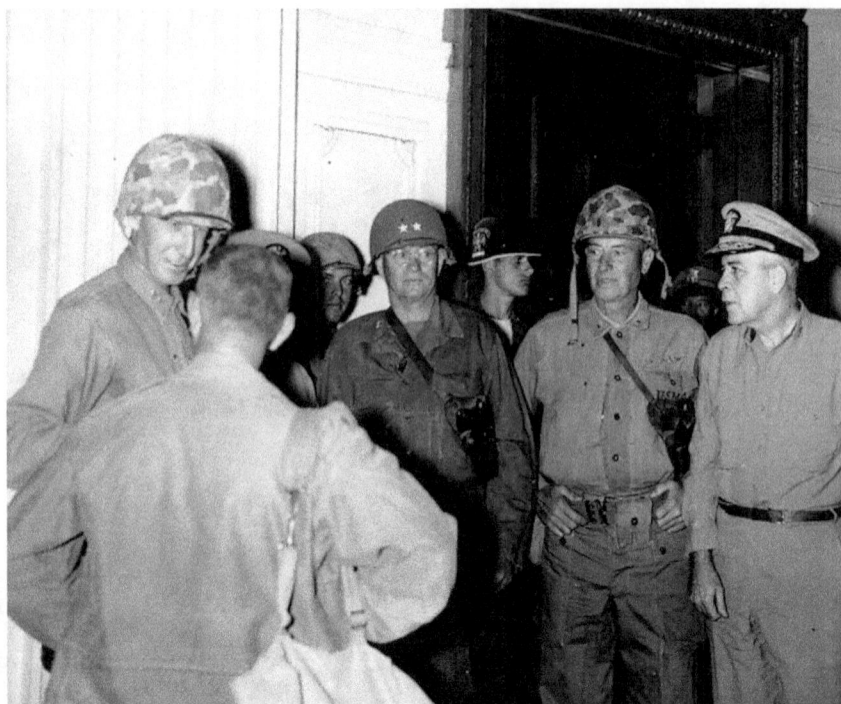

Liberation of Seoul, Korea, September 1950. Senior U.S. commanders assembled for the formal ceremonies in which General of the Army Douglas MacArthur returned the capital city to the Republic of Korea government, 29 September 1950. Those present are (from left to right, facing camera): Major General Oliver P. Smith, USMC, Commanding General, First Marine Division; Major General David G. Barr, U.S. Army, Commanding General, Seventh Infantry Division; Brigadier General Thomas J. Cushman, USMC, commanding forward echelon, First Marine Air Wing, and Vice Admiral C. Turner Joy, USN, Commander, U.S. Naval Forces, Far East. Photographed by Sgt. Ed Barnum, USMC.

Navy Corpsmen Herald B. Williams, James E. Carr and William N. Shipworth help carry a wounded man from a U.S. Marine Corps HO3S-1 evacuation helicopter to a hospital in Korea. Helicopter is from squadron VMO-6. Original photo is dated 3 October 1950, in which case it was probably taken during Marine Corps operations in the vicinity of Seoul, Korea. Note extensive "Quonset" hut facilities in the distance.

Chapter 5

The Wake Island Summit

Boast not thyself of to-morrow; for thou knowest not what a day may bring forth.

—Bible, Proverbs 27:1

IN a display of gross overconfidence, MacArthur blithely entered into what was probably the worst period of generalship of his career. He severely handicapped the advance of Walker's Eighth Army by evacuating X Corps by sea from the West Coast of Korea and transporting it on a southerly route, around the horn of the Korean peninsula and then north again to a landing on the east coast at Wonsan, north of the 38th parallel. The objective was to have X Corps attack the North Korean capital of Pyong Yang across the narrow neck of the Korean peninsula while Eighth Army attacked from the South. But the amphibious landing, after a long and cumbersome sea voyage, had created a nightmare of wasted time, logistical snafus and loss of the momentum and morale gained from MacArthur's Inchon triumph. The demands the Wonsan operation imposed, overloaded the UN transportation system. It required so many naval vessels of all types that thereafter it became difficult to supply Eighth Army.

Did MacArthur make this odd move, which split his forces in two and placed X Corps on the opposite side of the Korean peninsula from 8th Army—with a mountainous spine between them—to enhance Almond's prestige while undermining Walker's? This was the opinion of many MacArthur observers, but it does not seem credible. As much as MacArthur favored Almond, it would have been totally out of character for him to ever make a strategic decision in order to promote a subordinate. What is clear, however, is that MacArthur consistently sought to keep X Corps and 8th Army separate and thereby bereft of a unified command. But, overconfidence is a more likely reason for his curious military moves after Inchon than anything more sinister.

The objective of the Wonsan landing was outstripped by events when the NKPA virtually collapsed while X Corps was still at sea. By the time the 1st Marine Division waded ashore at Wonsan on October 25, the ROK Army had already secured Wonsan; and Pyongyang had fallen to the U.S. 1st Cavalry Division and the ROK 1st Division, on October 19.

Truman thought the time was right for a face to face meeting with MacArthur; and this time he would not be put off.

His main reason was to look MacArthur in the eye and engage in some straight talk about Korea as he took the measure of the man and assessed his future plans. Sensing that MacArthur's stunning victory at Inchon would make him more difficult to deal with than ever, Truman felt the need to meet with him man-to-man and hopefully reaffirm his own authority as Commander-in-Chief.

Truman's secondary and ulterior purpose was to derive some political benefit from MacArthur's success and resurgent popularity. The midterm Congressional elections were less than a month off and the Democratic Party wanted to cash in on MacArthur's high-flying stock—to have it pay some handsome dividends at the voting booths. Truman himself had no qualms about basking in MacArthur's reflected glory for political gain. After all, he was a politician before he became a statesman. And, Truman felt totally justified in his ambitions. Yes, MacArthur was deserving of all the kudos he could muster for pulling off a stupendous feat at Inchon. But, without Truman's approval, there would have been no Inchon landing. Both men had risked everything on the operation. They let it all ride on the tides, the currents, the brilliant planning of the Navy and the skillful daring of the Marines. In Truman's view MacArthur could afford to share some of the abundant residue of victory.

As Eighth Army and X Corps, twin mastodons of different masters, prepared to rumble north towards a common fate at the Yalu, Truman ordered MacArthur to meet with him.

Original plans called for a meeting at Honolulu but MacArthur demurred on the grounds that he could not afford to be that far away from his armies. MacArthur counter-proposed Wake Island and requested October 15th as the date. Truman accepted the compromise. It meant he would have to travel 4900 miles to MacArthur's 1900 but Truman seemed not to be phased by this fact.

Most of Truman's White House staff had pushed hard for the conference and managed to wear down the President's initial resistance. One or two dissident voices, however, were appalled by the idea of the Chief of State having to bend to the wishes of an impertinent subordinate with a maddeningly imperious manner. Of all the key personages at the Washington seat of power, only Chairman of the Joint Chiefs, General Omar Bradley, and Secretary of the Army, Frank Pace, agreed to accompany the President to Wake Island. Army Chief of Staff Joe Collins declined and Secretary of Defense George C. Marshall wanted no part of it. Marshall and MacArthur had locked horns far too many times and their relationship was toxic. Secretary of State Dean Acheson also demurred. He wrote later that he had "a vast distaste for the whole idea."[95] "While General MacArthur," wrote Acheson, "had all the attributes of a foreign sovereign,...it did not seem wise to recognize him as one."[96]

Even having to leave Tokyo and fly to Wake Island displeased MacArthur. MacArthur had been mostly autonomous and free from any real control by his civilian and military superiors for fifteen years. Those same higher-ups had fed his Napoleonic tendencies by their permissiveness the entire time, leading to his deluded view of himself as something akin to a head of state—a viceroy of Japan. MacArthur believed people should come to him, not the other way around.

Putting politics, ego and ambition aside, the situation in Korea was far more tenuous and fraught with grave overtones than any of the principal players perceived in early October of 1950. Whatever political jockeying may have been going on in the early fall of 1950 by MacArthur, Truman, Almond, Acheson, Trygve Lie and others, there were enough weighty military issues to amply justify the planned Truman—MacArthur conference.

MacArthur was not the only one who seemed carried away by the euphoria born of the Inchon triumph. There were indeed great reasons to be concerned about the intentions of both Communist China and Soviet Russia. Yet, the State Department, the Joint Chiefs and the UN leadership seemed oblivious to the ominous signals being received in both Washington and Tokyo. Nations with strong diplomatic ties with Peking, especially India, reported that Mao Tse-tung had declared that he would send troops into Korea if UN forces crossed the 38th parallel. The Indian Ambassador to Peking, Krishna Menon, seemed to have been designated by mainland China's President Chou En Lai, as a go-between to communicate this threat to Washington, since the U.S. did not have diplomatic relations with Communist China. China was said to have the full backing of the Soviet Union for its intentions. The Chinese even reinforced the dire warning by announcing it over their official government radio station. Truman promptly relayed the warning to MacArthur. But, Major General Charles A. Willoughby, Mac-

---

[95] *The Coldest Winter*, op.cit., p. 365.
[96] Ibid.

Arthur's G-2—his Chief of Intelligence—was dismissive concerning the threat, referring to it as mere "political blackmail,"[97] designed solely to frighten the United Nations away from seeking to impose a unified Korea. Willoughby's intelligence estimates had not served MacArthur well from the very beginning—consistently misreading the strength and capabilities, of first the North Korean Army and later the Communist Chinese forces. He also incorrectly interpreted the intelligence data gathered by his operatives—concluding erroneously that Red China would not enter the War. He then failed to detect the presence and strength of numbers of Red China's vast army once it crossed the Yalu River in late October and throughout November, 1950, and penetrated deep into North Korea.

Willoughby, however, was not the only highly placed officer to underestimate the enemy in Korea. Many of the staff officers serving MacArthur at headquarters in the Dai Ichi building held a dim view of the fighting capabilities of the Chinese. General Ned Almond held them in special contempt—referring to the Chinese soldiers as a bunch of "laundrymen" who would never be able to stand toe-to-toe with American GIs and could not possibly prevail in battle. As later events would prove, he could not have been more deluded by his prejudice. It was true that the Chinese infantryman occupied a lowly status in society and was callously mistreated by both China's military and civilian leaders. But he was generally a skilled and devoted soldier. The Chinese Army was composed of battle-hardened veterans of years of Civil War against the nationalist forces of Chiang Kai-Shek. They were indoctrinated in Chinese revolutionary teaching and were highly motivated. Before he could be inducted into the Army, each man had to sign a pledge to destroy Imperialism.

The resolve, skill and might of the Chinese Army plus the determination of China's leaders to keep Western forces away from their border seemed no real part of the equation in the minds of the U.S. leadership in early October of 1950—a fatal mistake.

Inchon had made all the difference in both UN and United States thinking. Before the Inchon landing they had been submerged in gloom and pessimism. After Inchon the UN did a complete about-face by voting overwhelmingly for a resolution calling for a "unified, independent and democratic government" of Korea. After Inchon no one was willing to stand up to MacArthur and tell him he was wrong about anything. All of the higher-ups in Washington, with the excep-

---

[97] *Harry S. Truman*, op.cit., p. 482.

tion of Truman, had been highly skeptical about MacArthur's chances for success at Inchon. Now that he had proved them all wrong and that he had been right all along, no one was willing to speak out in opposition to him a second time. MacArthur, on the strength of Willoughby's intelligence estimates minimizing the possibility of Communist Chinese intervention, wanted to go after the crippled North Korean Army in hot pursuit and, in particular, capture Pyongyang, the North's capital city. The Joint Chiefs of Staff enthusiastically endorsed the concept upon the condition that "there has been no entry into North Korea by major Soviet or Chinese Communist forces, no announcement of intended entry, nor a threat to counter our operations militarily in Korea." This proviso seemed blatantly transparent and another example of Pentagon posturing. Communist China had made its intentions clear—to intervene in Korea if the UN widened the war, both through diplomatic back-channels and on its official state ratio. To condition MacArthur's permission on the absence of an overt threat or action by China in advance of the American initiative made no sense. China could move against UN forces at any time—either with or without a prior threat and with or without announcing its action in advance.

The reservations of many notwithstanding, Truman enthusiastically flew off across the Pacific in the *Independence* to meet MacArthur for the first time, and as events would prove, the last time, on October 14, 1950. "I thought that he ought to know his commander-in-chief and that I ought to know the senior field commander in the Far East," Truman said later.[98] The Presidential party, including special presidential advisor, Averell Harriman; Omar Bradley, Chairman of the Joint Chiefs; Frank Pace, Secretary of the Army; plus, Philip Jessup and Dean Rusk from the State Department, came bearing gifts—several boxes of Mrs. MacArthur's favorite treat, Blum's candy.

Truman's high spirits were in stark juxtaposition to MacArthur's foul mood as the latter embarked by plane from Tokyo. During the flight he grumbled constantly to John Muccio, the American Ambassador to Korea, about "being forced to make the trip"—of having "to fly so far to meet the president."[99] MacArthur felt put-upon and burdened by such an inconvenience. It also "violated his unofficial sense of hierarchy."[100] He saw himself more as a head of state than a military

---

[98]   *Harry and Ike* by Steve Neal (Scribner, 2001), p. 209.
[99]   *The Coldest Winter*, op.cit., p. 365.
[100] Ibid.

commander and viewed Truman as not so much his boss as simply another visiting head of state, who should be coming to him.

What undoubtedly irked MacArthur even more was that his and Truman's planes arrived at Wake Island at roughly the same time on October 15, 1950 and protocol required that MacArthur's plane land first so that he would be on hand to greet his commander-in-chief as the President alighted from the Independence. As it turned out MacArthur kept Truman waiting in his plane for a brief time before he finally appeared on the tarmac to greet Truman as the President reached the bottom step of the plane's ladder.

Then MacArthur committed a serious breach of protocol by failing to salute his commander-in-chief. Whether the snub was the product of pique, imperiousness, hubris or just plain forgetfulness by the seventy year-old MacArthur, Truman simply chose to ignore it. This in itself was an exercise of presidential prerogative. The two men cordially shook hands as Truman said "I am glad you are here. I have been a long time in meeting you." "I hope it won't be so long next time, Mr. President," [101] replied MacArthur.

MacArthur was dressed in fatigues, a loose fitting jacket and a battered old Army cap dating back to pre-World War II days. He was tieless and smoked a corn-cob pipe. He didn't even deign to greet Secretary of the Army, Frank Pace, though Pace was above him in the chain of command.

No American president could have felt warmed by the greeting MacArthur gave Truman. The general's appearance, manner and breach of protocol bespoke an attitude that no one in the United States hierarchy was above him.

Truman himself succinctly chronicled the highlights of the Wake Island conference in a memo dictated to his secretary, Rose Conway, the key portions of which appear below:

> We arrived at dawn, General MacArthur was at the Airport with his shirt unbuttoned, wearing a greasy ham and eggs cap that evidently had been in use for twenty years.
>
> He greeted the President cordially and after the photographers had finished their usual picture orgy the President and the General boarded an old two door sedan and drove to the quarters of the Airline Manager on the island.

---

[101] *Harry and Ike*, op.cit., p. 210.

For more than an hour they discussed the Japanese and Korean situation.

The General assured the President that the victory was won in Korea, that Japan was ready for a peace treaty and that the Chinese Communists would not attack. [102]

MacArthur was a big enough man to bring up the Veterans of the Foreign Wars incident and told the President that "he was sorry for any embarrassment he'd caused;" [103] and Truman was likewise big enough not to mention MacArthur's failure to salute him—then and even in his later private memo.

Two meetings took place between the President and the General— one private between the two men only and one with their respective advisers present. By fortunate happenstance an accurate historical record was made of the meetings. Philip Jessup's secretary, Vernice Anderson, was waiting in the next room for a post-conference communiqué to be dictated to her, which the President would issue concerning the meeting. The door was partially open and she could hear everything that was being said. On her own initiative she decided to take notes in shorthand of everything of substance said during the conference—simply believing that it was important that there be an accurate record of what transpired. Probably not appreciating the full significance of what she was doing, Ms. Anderson created a valuable historical document.

The transcript of the notes taken by Ms. Anderson reveals that the President asked MacArthur: "What are the chances for Chinese or Soviet interference?" "Very little," replied MacArthur, and added, "Had they interfered in the first or second months it would have been decisive. We are no longer fearful of their intervention ... The Chinese have 300,000 men in Manchuria. Of these probably not more than 100-125,000 are distributed along the Yalu. Only 50-60,000 could be gotten across the Yalu River. They have no air force. Now that we have bases for our Air Force in Korea, if the Chinese try to get down to Pyongyang there would be the greatest slaughter..." [104]

---

102 *The President's Private War*, Harry S. Truman Library and Museum, Truman Papers, Korean War File 1947-52; *Harry S. Truman*, op.cit., p. 484-485.

103 Ibid.

104 Ibid.

Chairman of the Joint Chiefs of Staff, Omar Bradley, betraying a concern about U.S. strength in Europe in the face of the Soviet threat there, asked General MacArthur: "Could the 2nd or 3rd Division be available to be sent to Europe by January?" "Yes," MacArthur answered, "...I hope to get the Eighth Army back by Christmas." [105]

As the meeting began to wind down, MacArthur urged Truman to proclaim a "Truman Doctrine" for the Far East. By seeking to contain Communist aggression in Korea, Truman, by his actions, already had. And in implementing that doctrine, MacArthur had received "a mandate from the UN to move across the 38th Parallel for the purpose of uniting all Korea." [106]

The historic Wake Island conference ended like many summit meetings—with effusions of good will masking deeper underlying differences and problems. MacArthur later expressed relief that the warnings he had received about Truman's impatience and abruptness turned out not to be valid, and that the President couldn't have been more pleasant. Publicly, he even told reporters, "No commander in the history of war has had more complete and admirable support from the agencies in Washington than I have during the Korean operation." [107]

In a similar vein, the President pinned a Distinguished Service Cross on MacArthur's chest, presented him with the boxes of Blum's candy for Mrs. MacArthur, boarded the *Independence* and flew off. The following day upon landing in San Francisco, he described the conference to reporters as "very satisfactory." In a later address at the San Francisco Opera House, he described the crux of the meeting with MacArthur as having made it,

> Perfectly clear...that there is complete unity in the aims and conduct of our foreign policy....I want Wake Island to be a symbol of our unity of purpose for world peace. I want to see world peace from Wake Island west all the way around and back again. The only victory we seek is the victory of peace.

Truman further beseeched those countries within the Communist orbit to contribute to world peace by adhering to the principles of the United Nations Charter.

---

[105] Ibid.
[106] *Harry and Ike*, op.cit., p. 210.
[107] *The President's Private War*, Truman Papers, op.cit..

Once you got past the rhetoric and political posturing of both President Truman and General MacArthur, the actual events of the Wake Island conference were deeply troubling—although admittedly such a reaction stems partially from the wisdom of hindsight. For one thing, Wake Island was disturbingly political. It would seem that both men felt somewhat liberated by their recently-acquired sublime confidence that eventual victory in Korea was a fait accompli. This shared attitude left them free to succumb to the temptation to use the event for personal political gain. At this point in time both men had their eyes on the 1952 U.S. Presidential election. They could not have known then that subsequent events related to Korea would destroy the further presidential aspirations of both of them.

The transcript of the Wake Island conference reflected in the words of one MacArthur biographer "a wide but extremely shallow skating over an array of issues..." [108] In response to the President's one and only question to him on the subject of the Red Chinese threat, MacArthur assessed the risk of Soviet or Communist Chinese intervention in Korea if the UN forces took their offensive north of the 38th Parallel, as "very little," and predicted the enemy would be slaughtered by U.S. airpower. In the face of such an extraordinarily glib pronouncement, one would expect at least some probing by the members of the presidential party to test the factual basis of MacArthur's assumptions. Amazingly, neither the President, General Bradley, Secretary of the Army Pace, Ambassador Harriman, Ambassador Jessup or Under-Secretary of State Rusk asked a single follow-up question. The MacArthur mystique notwithstanding, the situation screamed for a thorough and probing examination of this vital issue of war and peace. Yet, one question by Truman and one brief answer by MacArthur constituted the full extent of the discussion as to the possible vast implications of taking the UN offensive right up to the border of Communist China.

At Wake Island, MacArthur told the conferees that "The Chinese have 300,000 men in Manchuria. Of these probably not more than 100-125,000 are distributed along the Yalu. Only 50-60,000 could be gotten across the Yalu River." [109] But, roughly six weeks later on November 25, 1950, the Chinese Fourth Field Army, the thirteenth Army Group and the Ninth Army Group, totaling twelve divisions and 300,000 men, poured across the Yalu River from Manchuria and from other

---

[108]   *MacArthur, A Biography*, op.cit., p. 156.
[109]   *The President's Private War*, Truman Papers, op.cit..

positions inside North Korea, sending UN forces under Generals Almond and Walker down to a devastating and bloody defeat. MacArthur radioed to the Joint Chiefs of Staff in Washington: "We face an entirely new war." [110]

In later years, after Truman and MacArthur were well-ensconced in retirement, statements made by both of them revealed just how fragile and fleeting was the positive feeling of Wake Island. By then both had suffered deep personal political losses but still, in general, enjoyed the overall acclaim of their fellow Americans. Citizen Harry S. Truman often complained about MacArthur's failure to salute him at Wake Island and MacArthur wrote the following in his memoirs:

> The conference at Wake Island made me realize that a curious and sinister change was taking place in Washington. The defiant rallying figure that had been FDR was gone ... The original courageous decision of Harry Truman to boldly meet and defeat Communism in Asia was apparently being chipped away by the constant pounding whispers of timidity and cynicism. The President seemed to be swayed by the blandishments of some of the more selfish politicians of the U.N ... of openly expressing fears of over-calculated risks that he had fearlessly taken only a few months ago. [111]

This passage penned by an eighty-something General MacArthur is astonishing. The transcript of the Wake Island conference reveals nothing which could have remotely caused MacArthur to draw such conclusions. To the contrary, MacArthur's plans to extend the war northward went unchallenged. Everything he said was readily accepted and indorsed by the President. The disaster soon to follow lays at the feet of both men.

---

[110] *Taking Command* by H. Paul Jeffers (Pilgrim Group [USA] Inc.—ValCaliber, 2009), p. 260.

[111] *Reminiscences*, op.cit., p. 363.

Truman is greeted by MacArthur upon his arrival on Wake Island, 15 October 1950.

Truman shakes MacArthur's hand after decorating him with the fourth oak leaf cluster of the Distinguished Service Medal, during their meeting on Wake Island, 15 October 1950.

President Harry S. Truman (left), with Admiral Arthur W. Radford, USN, Commander in Chief Pacific, Commander in Chief Pacific Fleet, returning to their automobile, at the time of the Wake Island conference, 16 October 1950. This is a "wirephoto", with vertical streaking from transmission "noise".

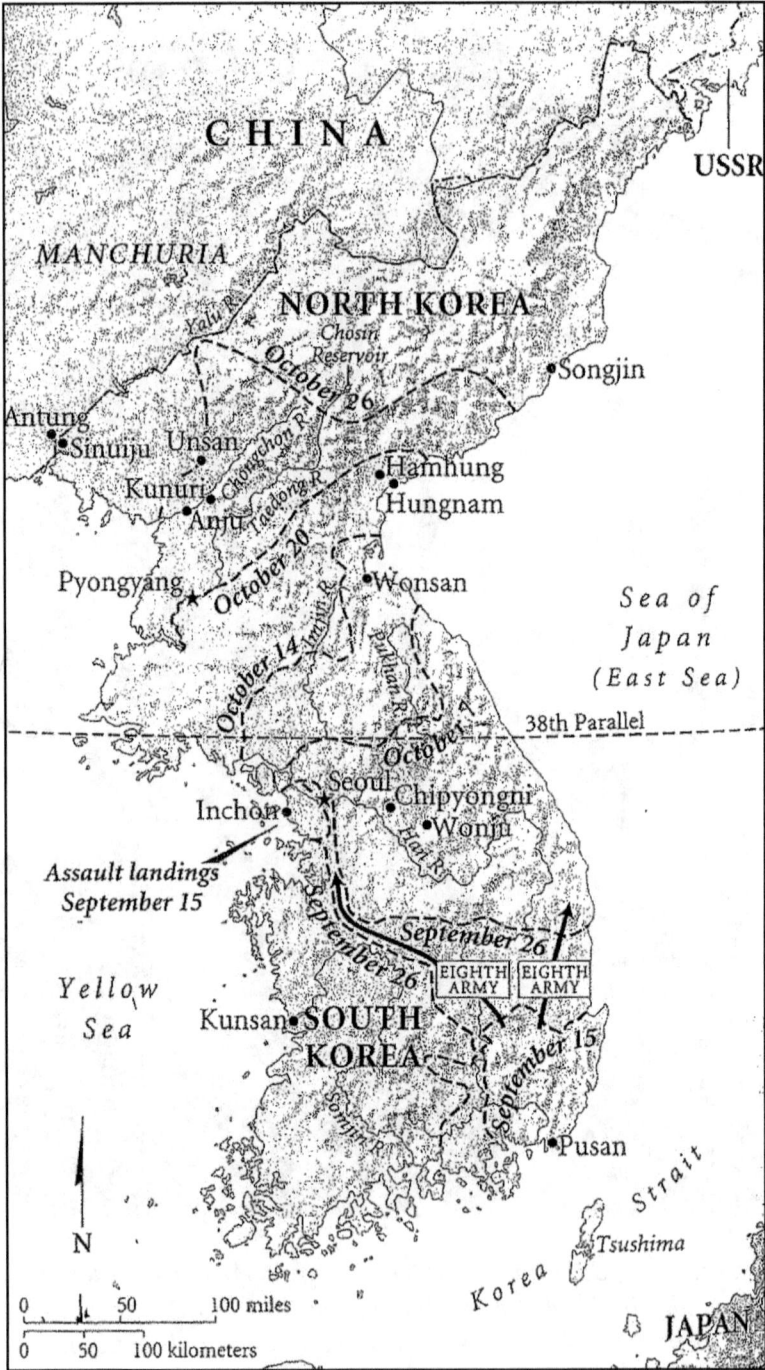

The U.N. Fall Offensive, 1950

Chapter 6

The Advance to the Yalu

But time strips our illusions of their hue, and one by one in turn,
some grand mistake casts off its bright skin...

—Lord Byron

IN mid-October, 1950, an exhilarated MacArthur told a group of his assembled officers:

> The war is over. The Chinese are not coming ... The Third Division will be back in Fort Benning for Christmas Dinner. [112]

On September 26th, the Joint Chiefs of Staff had authorized MacArthur to operate throughout North Korea provided there was no "major" Soviet or Chinese incursion across the border. The absence, however, of any clear directions to MacArthur as to what he was to do in the event of a major intervention by Communist forces once his army was firmly embedded in the North, rendered the authorization hollow. Given the timing of the directive, it would seem to have been influenced by the post-Inchon euphoria. In fairness, however, to the JCS, MacArthur was cautioned that his operations north of the 38th Parallel were not an "occupation" of North Korea. Only South Korean units, therefore, were to be deployed in the Soviet and Chinese border areas. But, this caveat by the JCS was then clearly undermined by a personal message from the new Secretary of Defense, George C. Marshall, to MacArthur sent on September 28, 1950:

> We want you to feel unhampered strategically and tactically to proceed North of the 38th Parallel ... Rhee's (i.e. Syngman Rhee's) authority should remain confined to the South. [113]

---

[112]   *The Coldest Winter*, op.cit., p. 388.
[113]   *MacArthur, A Biography*, op.cit., p. 155.

It was unanimous. The United Nations, the JCS and the civilian leadership in Washington were, with certain restrictions, encouraging MacArthur to take aggressive action in North Korea—in fulfillment of the clear, shared purpose of MacArthur and South Korean President Rhee—"to unify Korea by force under Rhee." [114]

With his forces bifurcated—X Corps to the east of Korea's mountainous spine and Eighth Army to the West, MacArthur directed both elements to move north towards the Yalu River and the Manchurian border in October of 1950. X Corps under General Almond was to reach the border north of Chosin Reservoir and then pivot west, eventually joining up with Walker's Eighth Army which would similarly pivot to the East at the Yalu River. The concept was to form an unbroken northern defensive perimeter and an envelopment of all North Korean forces, which would secure the entire northern border of Korea and solidify control of the peninsula.

By splitting his forces in two, however, MacArthur had greatly weakened their overall strength and effectively prevented one from reinforcing the other on the trek north, should conditions on the ground require it.

Intense tri-partite discussions among Red China, the Soviet Union and North Korea were underway no later than the recapture of Seoul by UN forces on or about September 26 and probably earlier. The subject was China's probable military intervention into Korea.

The three Communist nations were engaged in an intricate diplomatic dance. Before the June 25, 1950 invasion, Mao Tse-tung had offered major military assistance to North Korea's Kim Il-Sung. The latter, however, turned him down—fearful that China would thereby gain too much influence over North Korea and weaken his own power and control. But now on September 30th, as the Republic of Korea (ROK) Army pushed north across the 38th Parallel, with the U.S. First Cavalry Division only a week behind them, North Korea was desperate for China's military intervention. Mao had every intention of intervening but didn't want to show his cards too early. He knew that Soviet Russia had invested a huge amount of resources, prestige and credibility in its satellite, North Korea. Mao wished to exploit that fact to his own advantage. Although China is now believed by most historians to have firmly decided weeks before to cross the Yalu in a full scale attack upon its formidable American foe, it first wanted to leverage its position to the maximum with the Soviet Union. It is believed

---

[114] Ibid, p. 154.

that sometime in late September, Red China finally won the concession it was looking for—an apparent agreement by the Soviets to supply air cover for the advancing Chinese Armies. [115]

As the U.S. First Cavalry Division was capturing Pyongyang around October 14th and South Korean forces marched steadily northward towards the Manchurian border, elements of the army of the Chinese People's Republic were stealthily crossing the border at various points, into North Korea.

By late October, personnel of the same Naval intelligence unit which performed valuable covert reconnaissance at Inchon well in advance of the invasion, were using their Korean agents to seize islands in the mouth of the Yalu River, where they made an alarming discovery. "Large numbers of Chinese Communist troops were crossing the Yalu into Korea." [116]

This dramatic development was immediately transmitted to MacArthur's headquarters in Tokyo. It did not, however, go immediately to MacArthur's desk. First it had to pass through the filter of Willoughby's G-2 apparatus, which meant the news was analyzed, synthesized, diluted, discounted and minimized before it even reached MacArthur's desk. Instead of giving MacArthur bad news immediately and accurately, Willoughby's practice was to first spin it to conform to his own preconceived notion that the threat from the Red Chinese and Soviets was being over-stated and over-dramatized. He thought he knew what MacArthur wanted to hear and did not want to disappoint him. MacArthur at this critical point in history needed hard-headed, courageous and independent advice, based on reliable data, from his senior staff. He desperately needed an Eisenhower, Bradley or Ridgway instead of the mediocre band of sycophants whom he had allowed to surround him in positions of great responsibility, for which they were abysmally unqualified. And, to make things worse, the American High Commands in both Tokyo and Washington were still mesmerized by the success of Inchon and as a consequence, resisted any negative reports. The vital intelligence from the Navy's forward reconnaissance elements was simply ignored—with disastrous consequences.

MacArthur, his senior staff and the Pentagon could hardly argue afterwards that the Naval Intelligence sightings of heavy Yalu River crossings were isolated reports with little corroboration. As early as October 3, 1950, Chinese diplomats had sent a message via their inter-

---

[115] *The Coldest Winter*, op.cit., p. 345.
[116] *The Secrets of Inchon*, op.cit., p. 324.

mediary, the Indian government, that "China would confront a U.S. entry into North Korea, but not an advance by the South Koreans." [117] Combined intelligence from Army, Navy and CIA indicated 300,000 to 400,000 Chinese troops in Manchuria. "Washington and MacArthur both discounted the warning as a bluff and the troop movements as defensive." [118] Even when the first 260,000 Chinese troops entered North Korea between October 19 and 22, MacArthur failed to detect them. [119]

The first Chinese POWs were captured on October 26, 1950. This event was met by official silence from MacArthur's Headquarters. It was only five days later that MacArthur finally conceded that Red Chinese units had crossed the border into North Korea. The following week on November 6, MacArthur issued a demand to the JCS to bomb the Yalu River bridges. Reporting that Chinese men and matériel were pouring across them, he exclaimed that "this movement not only jeopardizes but threatens the ultimate destruction of forces under my command." [120] This statement was in stark contrast with his pronouncement of mid-October that "The War is over...The Chinese are not coming." MacArthur's demand to bomb the bridges was rejected by the JCS.

To the overwhelming majority of Americans—totally dependent on a national news media, which knew nothing of the worrisome signs of Chinese encroachments—the war couldn't have been going better. By October 14, ROK forces had secured Wonsan on the east coast of the Peninsula. By October 26, Pyongyang was comfortably under the control of Walker's Eighth Army and the eastern coastal cities of Hamhung and Hungnam had fallen to Almond's X Corps and the ROK Army. By October 28, forward elements of Eighth Army had reached the Yalu River. On the other side of the peninsula, Almond's combined Marine and Army forces continued their relentless northward march to the Chosin Reservoir, which was to be followed thereafter by a push to the Manchurian border.

The seemingly unstoppable advance to the Yalu and total envelopment of the Korean peninsula by UN forces was, however, a mirage. At the Pentagon, in Tokyo and among those having access to the most

---

[117] *MacArthur: A Biography*, op.cit., p. 158.
[118] Ibid.
[119] *The Years of MacArthur*, Vol. 3, by D. Clayton James (Houghton Miffin, 1985).
[120] *Harry S. Truman*, op.cit., p. 490.

up-to-date intelligence in the war zones, only a hidden agenda or a case of deep denial could have prevented them from acknowledging the deeply troubling sign-posts which were everywhere.

Sixteen Chinese soldiers were captured on October 30 near Hamhung. Under interrogation they revealed that they had crossed the Yalu River by train over one of its railroad bridges on October 16, the day after the Wake Island conference.

On November 1, the U.S. 8th Cavalry Regiment of the First Cavalry Division was attacked by heavy Chinese Communist forces at Unsan, after first being softened up by mortars and Russian Katyusha rockets.

The battle raged through the night. On the following day, the Regiment attempted an organized retreat but were emphatically repulsed by a heavily fortified Chinese road block. The 8th Regiment, finding itself surrounded and greatly outnumbered, was routed and quickly disassembled into multiple small units, many of which escaped into the hills and found their way south to safety. They were the lucky ones. One battalion was trapped and almost completely wiped out.

General Walton Walker's telegram to Tokyo described the debacle in the following blunt language: "An ambush and surprise attack by fresh, well-organized and well-trained units, some of which were Chinese Communist forces." In response he was ordered by headquarters to resume his northward advance, with no mention by Tokyo of the Chinese forces whose presence he had reported.

MacArthur took unwarranted liberties with both the letter and the spirit of the directives from the JCS. His excuse for pre-empting South Korean units in the vicinity of the northern border was that he was merely softening up the areas in order to prepare them for a South Korean take-over. This was clearly disingenuous. Almond pushed his forces steadily northward regardless of what resistance or signs of Chinese intervention he encountered, ignoring all troubling intelligence reports and seemingly oblivious to the JCS order that only ROK forces were to occupy the border regions. Admittedly, George C. Marshall's message to MacArthur was ill-advised and needlessly encouraged an aggressive Tokyo Command, which needed no encouragement, to contravene its orders. But, MacArthur had received clear directives on the issue of military operations in the border regions through his direct chain of command and was intentionally disobeying them. He did little, if anything, to check Almond's X Corps' rapid advance and may have explicitly authorized it. MacArthur was incrementally destroying his relationship with the Joint Chiefs—a political and strategic blunder which would have serious consequences for him. As to the Chinese presence in North Korea, it wasn't only MacArthur who discounted the threat. General Pack Sun Yap, a highly competent ROK Commander, asked Chinese POWs during interrogation, "Are there many of you here?" They replied "many, many." [121] MacArthur, the President's Washington military advisers and the JCS were in full accord, however, that Mao had sent only a small number of troops into North Korea—merely as a face-saving measure. Such a serious miscalculation on their part made it easy for them to dismiss the growing number of reports of heavy Chinese troop movements in Korea, as a mere fantasy.

While MacArthur needed better military intelligence and should have paid more heed to the intelligence already at his disposal, Truman clearly was in need of better political intelligence. Washington misapprehended the underlying political winds of change. Its assumption of a monolithic Communist movement in Eastern Asia was beginning to reveal its fault lines. The State Department was convinced that Soviet Russia would not permit its ally, Red China, to intervene in the Korean War because of the risk of a wider—possibly even nuclear—war with the United States. What was missed was the gradual emergence of Communist China from the shadows of Soviet stewardship to a new status of partial autonomy. Mao was inexorably taking the colossus of mainland China from revolutionary state to major international player, and no longer felt shackled by the global power-politics of the Kremlin. In Korea, he sought Soviet approval and support but was prepared to take on the United States in North Korea without it, if it came to that. His confidence was chiefly a function of China's huge population—an unlimited source of manpower; and his highly-trained and battle-seasoned army, which would compensate for its lack of heavy weaponry by its overwhelming numerical superiority. Mao bristled at the notion of China's being a puppet state of Stalin and the Kremlin. He needed to keep the United States away from China's international borders and the Korean conflict provided him with the perfect opportunity to both check the U.S.'s military might and cast off the yoke of Russia's political domination at the same time.

Soviet Russia, on the other hand, while fully aware of its loosening control over Red China as a satellite state, was even more anxious to maintain the viability of North Korea, its true puppet in the Asian-Pacific area.

---

[121] *The Last Stand of Fox Company*, op.cit., p. 51.

Such subtleties of shifting power alliances and hardening national imperatives seemed to be lost on both Truman and MacArthur as Walker's Eighth Army and Almond's X Corps marched north towards a common destiny in November of 1950, one of the most disastrous months in American military history.

Republic of Korea minesweeper YMS-516 is blown up by a magnetic mine, during sweeping operations west of Kalma Pando, Wonsan harbor, on 18 October 1950. This ship was originally the U.S. Navy's YMS-148, which had served in the British Navy in 1943-46.

Vought F4U-4B "Corsair" fighters, of Fighter Squadrons 113 and 114 (VF-113 and VF-114) prepare for launching aboard USS Philippine Sea (CV-47), during strikes on North Korean targets, circa 19 October 1950. Note small bombs, with fuse extensions, on the planes' wings.

Douglas AD "Skyraider" attack planes from USS Valley Forge (CV-45), fire 5-inch rockets at a North Korean field position. Photo is dated 24 October 1950.

TRUMAN AND MACARTHUR

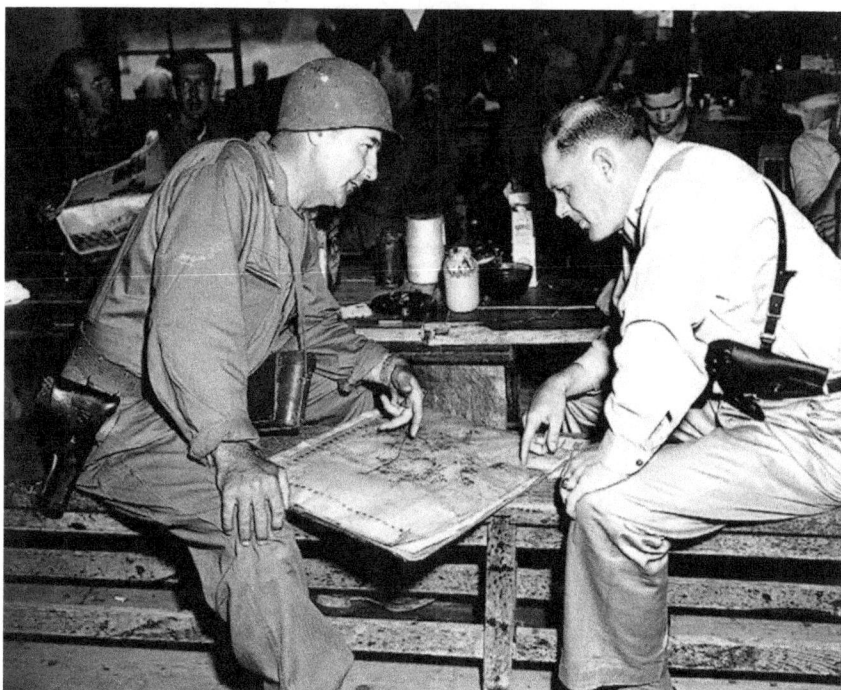

Commander L.E. Hubbell, USN, Operations Officer of USS Helena (CA-75) (right), confers with Lieutenant Colonel Rollins S. Emmerich, U.S. Army, at Korean Military Advisory Group Headquarters, 19 October 1950. Helena was then providing gunfire support for the United Nations' forces offensive in Korea. Note Cdr. Hubbell's shoulder holster.

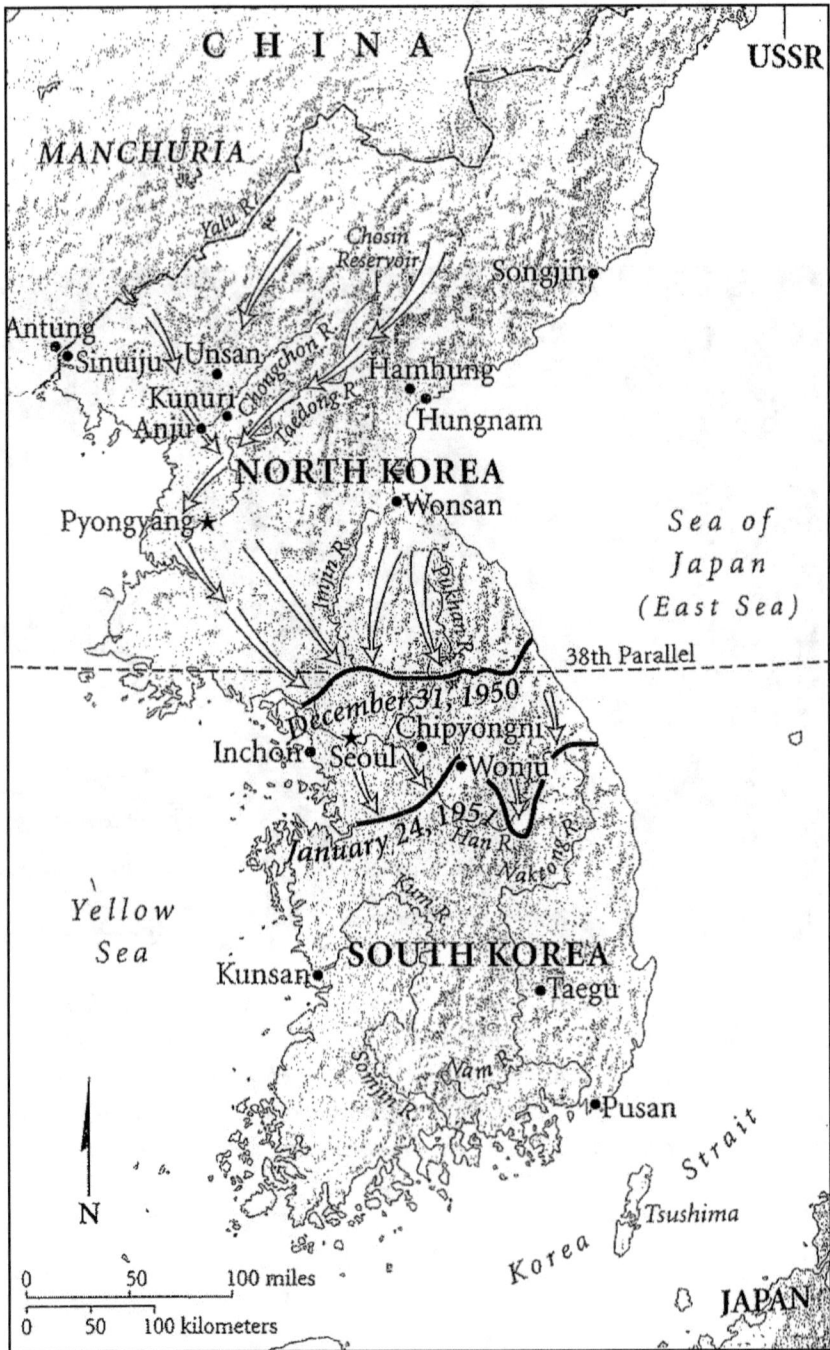

The Chinese Intervention, 1950-51

TRUMAN AND MACARTHUR

Chapter 7

The Chinese Intervention

It is difficulties that show what men are.

—Epictetus

THE massive onslaught of Communist Chinese troops numbering more than 400,000, against the UN forces in late November
and early December, 1950 came as a great shock to MacArthur
and the UN Command. Clearly, however, it shouldn't have. There
were many portents of disaster in the preceding five or six weeks
which only a myopic leadership could have missed. It was not a case of
lack of skill or experience—rather one of vastly skewed perceptions
caused by over-confidence and grandiose thinking. And the full
month's delay in deploying UN forces on both sides of the peninsula
for their northern advance, caused by the Wonsan landing, had allowed the CCF to establish strategic attack points along the Manchurian border.

The South Korean (ROK) Army was technically the vanguard of
the UN push to the North. Its Sixth Division reached Choson on the
Yalu River only nine days after the October 15th Wake Island Conference. Once there it engaged North Korean troops in a firefight and
quickly overwhelmed them. The North Koreans sought refuge by fleeing under fire across a pontoon bridge into Chinese territory. The following morning the Chinese retaliated—crossing the Yalu undetected
in great strength and routing the ROK Second Corps. Two full Chinese divisions participated in the attack. The after-action report of the
encounter worked its way up the chain of command through General
Walker to MacArthur headquarters in Tokyo and finally to the desk of
Army Chief of Staff, General J. Lawton Collins in Washington.

Collins read the reports with consternation. He was particularly
disturbed that the right flank of Eighth Army's forward offensive was
exposed by the total collapse of the ROK First Division. [122]

Eighth Army Commander, Walton Walker, a highly regarded tank
commander under General George S. Patton in World War II, tapped

---

[122] *Taking Command*, op.cit., pp. 260-261.

fellow Patton alumnus, Major General Hobart R. Gay, Patton's Chief of Staff in Europe, to take the First Cavalry Division on a mission to plug the gaps in the UN front line. But, after an impressive earlier victory with its capture of Pyongyang, the American First Cavalry met much the same fate as the ROK 1st Division when one of its battalions was decimated at Unsan. The Chinese infantry then quietly withdrew into the snow-covered hills north of the front line of the UN forces, where they would lay in wait to stage their next powerful attack.

To the east of the central mountain ranges, General Edward Almond ordered the Seventh Army Division under Major General David Barr to advance toward the Yalu on the east side of the Chosin Reservoir. It took Barr's troops until November 21 to reach the Yalu, a temporary occupancy from which they would be rudely and violently evicted several days later.

A week earlier, the 1st Marine Division on the opposite side of the Chosin Reservoir under the command of the widely-admired Marine General, O.P. Smith, had advanced up a mountain path, only to encounter and drive off a full Chinese Regiment.

MacArthur, 400 miles away from the combat zones in Tokyo, was still denying any serious Chinese intervention, even in the face of overwhelming evidence to the contrary.

Shortly after his victory at Inchon, MacArthur began seriously beating the drum for a far wider war. In early November he confided to his headquarters staff that he wanted "to strangle the Chinese Communist government in its infancy, before it could accumulate more power and territory." [123] These were not mere musings on his part. Beginning in November, with the encouragement of Air Force General and World War II legend, Curtis LeMay, MacArthur engaged in a massive bombing and Napalm campaign against North Korean cities—some of which were mostly vaporized. His primary political goal was to restore Chiang Kai-Shek to power in mainland China. His message was not lost on Mao Tse-tung whose forces in Korea had simply disappeared after the defeat of the U.S. 1st Cavalry at Unsan in late October. MacArthur's next step towards escalation was his report to Washington that enemy planes were engaging in hit-and-run raids across the Yalu, coupled with his demand that he be authorized to pursue them into their sanctuary in Manchuria. The JCS emphatically denied his request. They considered his plan far too risky. U.S. planes were flying into Korea from privileged sanctuaries in Japan, and the

---

[123] *The Last Stand of Fox Company*, op.cit., p. 43.

last thing both the civilian leadership and military command in Washington wanted was for the U.S. to hand Russia and China a pretext for attacking our aircraft in Japan. But, MacArthur was left free in November of 1950 to continue his relentless drive north to the Yalu.

MacArthur has received great criticism from historians for his heedless disregard of all the obvious signs of danger as he pushed his army north—and deservedly so. But, the curious passivity of the Joint Chiefs of Staff in the face of his recklessness does them no credit either. Surely, General Collins fully briefed Joint Chiefs Commander, General Omar Bradley, and the other chiefs as to the implications of the devastating defeats suffered by the South Korean First Division at Choson and by the U.S. 1st Cavalry at Unsan, at the hands of the Chinese during the last week in October. They also knew that the Chinese Army (CCF) had then virtually disappeared into the hills and mountains—in all likelihood to consolidate their forces and then spring a trap on the advancing UN forces, near the Yalu. Yet for the greater part of a month they allowed MacArthur and Almond to throw all caution to the wind, when the JCS could have ordered a halt to the advance and sought to join with MacArthur in devising a more prudent strategy. In a time of great crisis, the top military command of the nation failed to discharge its obligations to the American people.

MacArthur continued to disobey orders with impunity. In direct disobedience of the JCS's order to use only Republic of Korea forces in the northern-most regions of Korea, he told the Joint Chiefs that he was using Americans for the advance but would substitute ROK troops for the Americans once an area was cleared. This rank insubordination went unchallenged by the JCS.

On November 24, 1950, MacArthur launched what he predicted in his own words would be the "home by Christmas" final offensive to fully occupy North Korea. The 1st Marine Division which was well-up the mountain road along the Chosin Reservoir was having none of it. Entrenched on frozen hills guarding snowy passes between the mountains, with temperatures as low as forty below zero, fighting frost bite and diarrhea—some of it caused by the frozen turkey they consumed for their Thanksgiving dinner, the Marines could actually feel the presence of the enemy forces gathering around them. Many of the Marines had not seen an enemy soldier in four weeks but they knew they were there—distant grey shadows moving into position and getting ready to pounce—in great numbers under cover of darkness and in the middle of the night. It was eerily quiet—too quiet, and the seasoned veterans knew in their gut that a major attack was imminent. General O.P.

Smith was particularly contemptuous of MacArthur's "home for Christmas" talk. To his command staff he openly scoffed at what he referred to as "the home by Xmas baloney." [124] He expected major Chinese resistance to the 1st Marines' advance towards the Yalu west of the Chosin Reservoir.

On the night of November 25, 1950, the Communist Chinese Army struck along the entire 300 mile UN front from the west coast to the east. By the sheer force of numbers and their total disregard for their own casualties, they swarmed over fixed UN positions, routed them and forced them into retreat. Wave after wave of Chinese soldiers in white quilted uniforms and soft winter caps—carrying Russian made weapons—with little air or artillery support, just kept coming. They attacked relentlessly even where the Americans held the high ground; and even where American forward artillery observers with excellent vantage points were able to precisely pinpoint the locations of the attacking Chinese and enable U.S. artillery and mortars to rain devastation down upon them. There were so many dead Chinese on the frozen hillsides and fields that the Americans piled up their frozen bodies and used them as barricades in front of their fox holes. Yet, still the Chinese kept attacking—almost exclusively at night. They often eschewed a direct frontal attack in favor of slipping along the flanks of the U.S. defensive perimeters, probing for soft spots and gaps, while moving to the rear of the U.S. positions in order to cut off any retreat. Surrounded American companies and battalions were reduced to chaos by the multiple breaches of their perimeters and deaths of their officers and non-coms. The Chinese were everywhere. Dazed and bedraggled American soldiers were forced to escape into the trees and hills in groups of threes and fours, tens and twenties, often dragging or carrying their wounded with them; and for days faced the multi-perils of freezing to death in the sub-zero temperatures, dying in skirmishes with the Chinese, becoming crippled by frost-bite, being captured by the enemy, or collapsing from sheer hunger and exhaustion. Scores of such fractured units with no senior leadership and short on ammunition and food staggered in a southbound retreat—usually with the pursuing Chinese not far behind them.

The Chinese were especially adept at causing terror. A sudden massive attack in the cold and dark hours of the night against nervous and fatigued UN troops was accompanied by the blowing of bugles

---

[124] *The Last Stand of Fox Company*, op.cit., p. 16.

TRUMAN AND MACARTHUR

and the shrillness of whistles, producing a frightening and shocking effect.

Americans in southerly retreat on the narrow North Korean roads suffered many of the same agonies as those in the countryside. The Chinese were behind them, on both sides of them and in front of them. The attackers fired and lobbed grenades into the retreating forces from revetments above the roads and erected road blocks to halt their forward progress. The Chinese Army's clear objective was to annihilate the fleeing American forces. But although the U.S. battalions, regiments and divisions sustained terrible casualties—in some units more than fifty percent dead or wounded—they fought bravely and resourcefully. Superior U.S. firepower compensated somewhat for ratios of Chinese to Americans of seven to one or greater. U.S. tanks fired into and smashed the roadblocks and American Corsairs rained their bombs and other ordnance down upon the swarming Chinese infantrymen. For U.S. forces, the late November Red Chinese offensive left them with only one viable option—escape, regroup and resupply. If they could just make it to the next secure U.S. garrison they would be okay, or so they thought. Once there, however, they frequently found it too, to be under attack or siege and preparing to retreat south. Great acts of U.S. heroism were combined with some instances of cowardice—the abandonment of wounded on the arduous trek towards what they hoped would be safe havens; and the retreat, or surrender by some units to the enemy without a fight. But these were for the most part isolated incidents. Hundreds of Americans fought hard, only to be captured when surrounded and facing immediate extinction. American POWs—even when wounded—were often marched non-stop for days without food or medical attention to Chinese Army encampments.

The size and scope of the Chinese attack on November 25 was mind-boggling—about 180,000 Chinese soldiers struck Walker's Eighth Army. Two days later approximately 120,000 Chinese attacked Almond's X Corps. Wearing canvas shoes, the Chinese infantrymen had moved silently and quickly through the snows to their points of attack. Their massive intervention caught MacArthur's headquarters in Tokyo completely by surprise.

In most instances, it was impossible for American troops to form a perimeter on the retreat. There were simply too many Chinese and they were too close to the fleeing UN troops.

One of the largest Chinese assaults was the attack on the Army's Second Infantry Division on November 25 and 26 by the Chinese 40th

Army near the Chongchon River. This was the beginning of the long and harrowing retreat south by the Second Division towards Kunuri and then to Sunchon.

No retreat by UN forces in late November was orderly. They were essentially fighting retreats despite the comments by General O.P. Smith that the First Marines were not retreating at Chosin Reservoir but "just attacking in another direction." Given the need to buck-up the morale of the imperiled First Marines, Smith can be forgiven his rhetorical flourish.

On the tortuous trek south by the Second Infantry Division, its units were constantly harassed by pursuing Chinese troops from both sides of the road and from the rear. On the road from Kunuri south to Sunchon the Second Infantry was surrounded and attacked continuously by the CCF from point of origin to destination. The infamous stretch of road came to be known in military history as "the Gauntlet." But still the Second Division kept moving—punching through everything the CCF placed in their way—but at the cost of many Americans killed or severely wounded. The Second Engineers Battalion was hit the hardest. The battalion originally had 900 men before the November 25 attack. When their retreat ended, there were only 266 effectives remaining. They had become a ghost battalion.

November 30, 1950 was clearly one of the worst days in the history of the United States Army. In particular, it marked the end of the worst week in the history of the Second Infantry Division. An infantry regiment is at full strength at about 3800 men. At the end of their retreat, the Ninth Regiment had only 1409 men still fit for duty—the 38th Regiment, 1700 and the 23rd Regiment, 2200.

To General Walker's credit, he had learned the lessons of the June invasion when so many ROK and American units were cut-off by the North Koreans and left with no means of escape. On the Eighth Army's long slog to the Yalu, he made sure to secure the roads which would serve as his forces' exit routes if such an unhappy event became necessary. By doing so, he probably saved Eighth Army from annihilation. But, on both coasts of the peninsula, the sheer size and scope of the Chinese offensive was beyond anything that even Walker could have envisioned. As a result, he was somewhat slow to react to the initial attacks, misapprehended the full gravity of the situation and erroneously believed he could establish a line of defense at the narrow neck of the Korean peninsula near Pyongyang, which was essentially the position at which he believed Eighth Army should have stopped on its northern advance. As it turned out he was probably right about where

American forces should have stopped but wrong about what still could be defended after the massive Chinese attacks had occurred. The Chinese Army not only overran Pyongyang, it pushed Eighth Army all the way back to well below the 38th Parallel—a staggering retreat and defeat.

By contrast, Walker's counterpart on the eastern coast of the peninsula, General Edward (Ned) Almond, continued to function in a self-created fantasy world. Seemingly oblivious to the full dimensions of the catastrophe and to just how imperiled his X Corps really was, he continued to mindlessly advocate launching a full attack north against the Chinese. As late as November 28, he still refused to acknowledge the magnitude of the Chinese intervention. When informed that elements of the 5th and 7th Marine Regiments, which had reached Yudam-ni near the northern part of the Chosin Reservoir—numbering about 3000 infantry and artillery soldiers in all—had sustained 35 percent casualties when attacked by at least two Chinese divisions, Almond in a disconnect from any semblance of reality, incredibly proclaimed, "That's impossible, there aren't two Chinese divisions in the whole of North Korea." In fact, by November 28 when Almond made his statement, there were likely more than 20 Red Chinese Divisions in North Korea. The First Marine Division, stretching from Koto-Ri, northwest of the coastal city of Hungnam to Hagaru-ri near the southern tip of the reservoir and all the way north to Yudam-ni—were quickly becoming surrounded by about 40,000 Chinese.

Almond had fragmented his command—sending the Marines under General Smith north on the MSR, the Korean Road (N.K. 72) which ran almost due north from Koto-ri to Hagaru-ri, but then forked sharply west at Hagaru-ri until it reached Toktong Pass, where it again sharply changed direction to lead due north, roughly following the western shore of the Chosin Reservoir, to Yudam-ni, one of the last stops before reaching the Manchurian border at the Yalu River. The right fork from Hagaru-ri also ran due north, but snaked along the contours of the eastern shore of the Chosin Reservoir.

Almond further fragmented the Seventh Division to the east of the Chosin into two separate task forces—Task Force MacLean and Task Force Faith. When Almond helicoptered into the 31st Regiment Command post for a visit on November 28, Colonel Allan MacLean and his task force were being pummeled by a numerically superior Chinese force. At that point in time, prudence dictated that Almond order a retreat in an attempt to link up with the western wing of his corps—the 1st Marine Division, which was also being hammered. Almond, however, chose to push on and gave no such order.

The next day, Colonel Allan MacLean was killed trying to lead the 31st Regiment out of a Chinese encirclement. Three days later, Lt. Col. Don Carlos Faith, the Commander of the 32nd Regiment (Task Force Faith) was also killed along the Chosin Reservoir. Greatly outnumbered and victimized by "friendly fire" from Marine Corsairs, Task Force Faith was decimated. A mere 500 survivors managed to struggle into Hagaru-ri.

Almond's forces had been soundly beaten on both sides of the Chosin. The Seventh Infantry Division was in tatters. The only course of action left for the First Marine Division was a southbound retreat and break-out in order to prevent their total destruction.

The First Marine Division's break-out from Yudam-ni and other points along the Chosin has been recorded as one of the greatest feats in the annals of American military history.

With the Fifth and Seventh Marine Regiments under heavy attack at Yudam-ni, and in danger of having the one good road out interdicted by the Chinese, General O.P. Smith ordered an immediate withdrawal of all units from the Chosin Reservoir. ("just attacking in another direction"). This was clearly the only choice Smith had. The First Division was virtually surrounded and outnumbered by about seven to one. Either attacking to the north or remaining in place would have resulted in the destruction of his division and probably the entire X Corps as well.

It was critical, however, to keep the road open and passable—particularly the mountain passes which were vulnerable to being seized by the Chinese. Under-strength Marine rifle companies were dispatched from Koto-ri, Hagaru-ri and Yudam-ni to strategic hill tops above the passes, such as Fox Hill and Turkey Hill, to prevent the Chinese from gaining a foothold in the pass or on either side. The most critical of these passes was Toktong Pass at the junction where the MSR (N.K. 72) sharply changed its direction from west to north. Fox Company, Second Battalion, Seventh Regiment with only 192 men fit for combat dug in on the top of Fox Hill with an open view of Toktong Pass and a clear field of fire, on November 26, 1950. The Chinese had just made a devastating attack on the Marines on Turkey Hill to the north and the men of "Fox Company" expected more of the same.

The battle of Chosin Reservoir was about to begin in earnest with X Corps—approximately 30,000 troops pitted against approximately 150,000 Chinese.

The remaining elements of Fifth and Seventh Marine Regiments, including foot soldiers, vehicles, tanks and artillery began their southward trek from Yudam-ni down the MSR. The wounded who were too seriously injured to march were loaded onto trucks. The conditions for the retreat were horrendous—sub-zero temperatures, 30 to 40 below at night; battle-weary troops; snow banks and icy patches on the road; a narrow, winding mountain road cutting through rugged terrain with cliffs, ridges and abutments on both sides at various points along the way, giving the Chinese perfect cover and location for firing their weapons, lobbing hand grenades and propelling mortar shells down onto the road and into the midst of the retreating Marines.

On December 1, 1950, Fifth Regiment led the way out of Yudam-ni, marching southeast on the MSR. Their orders were to attack and seize the high ground on both sides of the road to provide cover for the Seventh Regiment led by Marine Colonel Homer Litzenberg, which would follow them out of the village. Several Chinese Regiments surrounded Yudam-ni and they weren't expected to sit idly by while the Fifth and Seventh Marines simply walked away. A Marine rear guard was, therefore, established composed of part of the Fifth Regiment plus some big guns from the Eleventh. Its job was to ward off any attacks from the rear.

At Turkey Hill, a battalion of Marines peeled off from the main force into the countryside east of the road, under cover of darkness. Their mission was to stealthily move through the deep snow, across frozen streams, through heavily wooded areas and over mountains for a distance of seven miles; neutralize any Chinese troops they encountered along the way and ultimately relieve Fox Company's beleaguered band of exhausted, mostly wounded and frost-bitten Marines on Fox Hill.

Entrenched in their fox holes, the gallant guardians of Toktong Pass had fought snipers during the day and turned back wave upon wave of attacking Chinese during the last four nights. Fox Company had sustained casualties of more than sixty percent dead or seriously wounded but they had killed many hundreds of attacking Chinese troops and had miraculously kept Toktong Pass open and unobstructed. Had they failed in their mission, the First Marine Division would have been trapped, surrounded and probably destroyed at Chosin Reservoir.

The cross-country warriors arrived at Fox Hill on the fifth day of the battle at Toktong Pass and relieved the weary, frozen and starving men of Fox Company, who enjoyed their first hot meal in five days and then immediately began their march south to Hagaru-ri and hopefully some sleep, hot chow and medical attention.

In the meantime, the main force retreating from Yudam-ni picked up surviving elements of other embattled units along the way. As they moved south towards Toktong Pass they were assaulted by the Chinese at all points, from their elevated redoubts above the road—by mortars, hand grenades and small arms fire. But capturing some high ground out of Yudam-ni gave the Marines an initial base from which they launched patrols each night of the long forced march to Hagaru-ri, with a mission to locate Chinese troops on the ledges and hill-tops on both sides of the road and kill them or drive them off. These patrols moved out in the dead of night into the unknown against overwhelming numerical odds. But they were Marines and their superior fighting skills enabled them to engage the Chinese successfully enough to enable the long column on the road below to keep moving.

But the southbound column was beset with every type of hindrance imaginable along the way—fire fights with the enemy, sniper fire, many additional wounded and killed, mortar explosions in their midst, vehicle engines freezing up due to the Arctic temperatures and blocking the road, severe frost-bite and road blocks set up by the Chinese—usually at passes, junctions and other road narrowings—which had to be blasted and cleared by U.S. tanks, artillery and planes before forward progress could resume.

The non-wounded and walking-wounded grunts had it the worst. Most of them fought a losing battle to keep their socks dry and as a result suffered severely frost-bitten feet. The worst frost-bite cases could no longer walk and were forced to climb onto trucks, tanks and jeeps or be left behind.

The danger of freezing to death at night in their sleeping bags when temperatures plummeted to 30 or 40 below zero was a real one. The grunts also had to worry that each time they lowered their pants to defecate, they would become frost-bite victims and as a result many simply defecated in their trousers. Then there was the constant harassment from the Chinese soldiers who tried to kill as many of the retreating Marines as they could. But the Marines fought back hard, pursuing their attackers, calling in air and artillery strikes against them and sending out patrols at night to sneak in behind the Chinese positions and trap them between the Marine patrols and the road.

All told, the First Marine Division's break-out and long march from Yudam-ni to Hungnam, where they were evacuated by U.S. Navy ships, covered a distance of approximately seventy miles and took eleven days. Whatever rest they were able to gather along the way at stop-overs at Hagaru-ri and Koto-ri were of brief duration, because those villages were also under heavy attack from the Chinese and, in any event, the main Chinese Force was in hot-pursuit and arrived at Hungnam less than half an hour after the last remnants of the Marine First Division and Army Seventh Regiment were safely on board the evacuation ships.

The retreat had been one long battle and the haggard, frost-bitten and sleep-deprived Marines defended and counter-attacked—mostly in squads and platoons—along the entire route. The spirit of the First Division was embodied in the officer in immediate charge of the operation, Marine Colonel "Chesty" Puller who was attributed with expressing the sentiment that at least when the Marines are completely surrounded, things are simplified because then they know exactly where the enemy is, so they can go out and get him. Led by Puller, a task force of U.S. marines and British Royal Marines actually broke in to the surrounded Hagaru-ri.

The Marine First Division gave as good as they got—inflicting huge casualties on the attacking Chinese. But at the end of the day, the devastating losses suffered by the Marines, which they blamed on the high command, left them embittered. Upon getting orders that on the next morning they would break-out of Hagaru-ri by marching on the same open and exposed road to Koto-ri; and then all the way to Hungnam on the coast, a common sentiment expressed by the Marines of the Fifth and Seventh Regiments was that "the pogue Army generals, MacArthur and Almond, had failed to get them all killed...and now they were determined to get it right." [125]

The fighting withdrawal from "Frozen Chosin" was a brilliant operation, one of the proudest in the illustrious history of the Marine Corps.

On the morning of November 28, General Omar Bradley, Chairman of the Joint Chiefs of Staff, had delivered the devastating news of the rout at the Yalu to President Truman. The Chinese had struck UN Forces north of the 38th Parallel in huge numbers and everywhere MacArthur's armies were reeling and in disarray. Thus began one of the grimmest days of the Truman Presidency. Non-stop conferences in

---

[125] *The Last Stand of Fox Company*, op.cit., p. 287.

the War Room that day and the days to follow were characterized mostly by expressions of alarm. The frequently expressed fear was that MacArthur had been steadily plunging toward disaster. But no one seemed to have the courage or decisiveness to set forth a clear plan of action. Finally General Matthew B. Ridgway, who the top brass were relying upon to closely monitor and assess the Korean situation, asked for permission to be heard. It took guts on his part to speak out because he was not a member of the Joint Chiefs of Staff and had no vote. He then forcefully declared that they all "owed it to the men in the field and to the God to whom we must answer for these men's lives, to stop talking and to act." [126] Ridgway's eloquent plea was met with stony silence. [127]

Later at a White House staff meeting, Truman gave the following grim report:

> We've got a terrific situation on our hands. General Bradley told me that a terrible message had come from General MacArthur. MacArthur said there were 260,000 Chinese troops against him out there. He says he's stymied. He says he has to go over to the defense. It is no longer a question of a few so-called volunteers. The Chinese have come in with both feet. [128]

MacArthur had told Collins and Bradley on November 28 that "we face an entirely new war." The plan he proposed to counteract the massive Chinese intervention was a departure from anything he had overtly advocated before, and "reflected his shock." [129]

> Eighth Army would withdraw to a Pusan bridgehead. X Corps would undertake a fighting withdrawal to Hungnam. Nationalist Chinese troops would enter the war to shore up battered UN forces.

Washington vetoed the use of Nationalist Chinese troops. This only heightened MacArthur's anxiety when General Collins arrived in Tokyo on December 6 to meet with MacArthur and assess the battle-

---

[126]   *Harry S. Truman*, op.cit., p. 491.

[127]   Ibid.

[128]   *Harry S. Truman*, op.cit., p. 492.

[129]   *MacArthur, a Biography*, op.cit., p. 159.

field situation. A shaken but resolute MacArthur had honed his argument to achieve the greatest shock value.

Unless he was sent major reinforcements, or freed of restrictions on where he could attack [130] and with what weapons, said MacArthur, "Korea should be evacuated." [131]

Collins viewed MacArthur's argument as an overreaction. Where MacArthur's request for nationalist Chinese troops was a departure from his previous position, his suggestion for a withdrawal from Korea was a radical change in his thinking. Only seven (7) weeks before MacArthur had declared that the "war is won." While MacArthur was undoubtedly engaging in rhetorical dramatics to achieve a particular effect, Collins was taken aback. He did not see the situation as nearly so dire.

It was true that UN Forces had been dealt a catastrophic blow, but the war was far from over. Thanks to the foresight of Marine General O.P. Smith who had set up supply centers all the way from Koto-ri to Hagaru-ri; and General Walton Walker who kept his escape routes open and secured, X Corps and Eighth Army, though badly battered, had escaped to fight another day.

As he had done throughout his career, MacArthur took no responsibility for the late-November debacle in North Korea and looked to blame the Administration. Eisenhower recalled years later that MacArthur "had an obsession that a high commander must protect his public image and never admit his wrongs." [132] Eisenhower's personal opinion was that MacArthur had left his forces far too vulnerable to attack—over a 300 mile front—and shouldn't have been pointing fingers. [133]

To deflect attention from his own mistakes, MacArthur began a press campaign, granting no less than seven interviews between November 28 and December 3, 1950. His excuse for being overrun in Korea was that Washington had tied his hands. In a statement dripping with hyperbole, he maintained that his inability to bomb Manchuria was "an enormous handicap without precedent in military history." [134] No attempt was made to explain the gaping 80 mile hole he had left in

---

[130] In particular MacArthur wanted to attack Chinese bases inside Manchuria.
[131] *MacArthur, a Biography*, op.cit..
[132] *Harry and Ike*, op.cit., p. 211.
[133] Ibid.
[134] *Harry S. Truman*, op.cit., p. 494.

his lines between Eighth Army and X Corps into which the Chinese had poured in droves.

Truman had no public comment on MacArthur's attempt to cast the blame on the Administration, but in an expression of his inner thoughts and feelings, he penned the following passage on a calendar page for November 30, 1950:

> This has been a hectic month. General Mac, as usual has been shooting off his mouth. He made a pre-election statement that cost us votes and he made a post-election statement that has him in hot water in Europe and at home. I must defend him and save his face even if he has tried on various and numerous occasions to cut mine off. But I must stand by my subordinates.

The shared purpose and empathy between the two men which had been prevalent, at least on the surface, at the Wake Island conference, was quickly dissipating. In his numerous interviews, MacArthur was suggesting widening the war by bombing the Chinese mainland—even using nuclear weapons, if necessary. This was contrary to U.S. policy and left the Joint Chiefs stunned. MacArthur was repeatedly dissenting from his government's foreign and military policies. Two days after he gave a highly controversial interview to *U.S. News and World Report*, Truman issued the following order on December 7, 1950:

> No speech, press release, or other public statement concerning military policy should be released until it has received clearance from the Department of Defense. [135]

MacArthur paid no heed to this directive. Eisenhower, on the other hand, was Commander in Chief of all NATO forces in Europe at the time and took the directive seriously because it applied to him as well. In his diary he wrote that "because people believe that MacArthur is trespassing on purely civilian functions, it becomes difficult for anyone in uniform to discuss public issues." [136]

Nevertheless, Truman knew that the credibility of his commanding general in Korea was critical to the war effort at this time of great crisis. He strenuously defended MacArthur at a presidential press con-

---

[135] *Harry and Ike*, op.cit., p. 213.
[136] *Harry and Ike*, op.cit..

TRUMAN AND MACARTHUR

ference on November 30 in the following exchange with Washington Post reporter, Edward T. Folliard:

> *Question*: The particular criticism is that he [MacArthur] exceeded his authority and went beyond the point he was suppose to go.
> *The President*: He did nothing of the kind. He has done a good job, and is continuing to do a good job.

Then another reporter, Tony Leviero, asked Truman if attacks in Manchuria would depend on action in the United Nations. "Yes, entirely" replied Truman. Leviero pressed on: "In other words, if the United Nations resolution should authorize General MacArthur to go further than he has, he will..."; cutting him off, Truman announced, "We will take whatever steps are necessary to meet the military situation just as we always have." Given an opening, Jack Dougherty of the N.Y. Daily News pounced, "Will that include the atomic bomb?"

"That includes every weapon that we have" said Truman, adding that the "A Bomb was always under consideration."

Ever the wily politician, Harry Truman had to know how politically controversial his remarks about possible use of the atomic bomb would be. But as the X Corps and Eighth Army fought for their very survival, by extension America's Korean War effort also hung in the balance. Truman and MacArthur, despite their vast differences and criticism of each other, were standing shoulder to shoulder in presenting a common front to enemies and allies alike.

Truman had either wittingly or unwittingly set off a media firestorm. White House Press Secretary, Charlie Ross, was appalled and rushed to put out a clarifying statement, but the damage had already been done. The afternoon dailies contained banner headlines suggesting that the President had given MacArthur carte blanche to start a nuclear war.

In the days to follow, the White House did enough damage control to quell the media frenzy over Truman's remarks, and the issue was pushed off the front pages by news of the dramatic break-out by the First Marine Division from Chosin Reservoir. The issue, however, was now out there. Was the world on the brink of nuclear war over Korea? History cannot provide a definitive answer to that question because Truman's comments were made at a time of dramatic U.S. military reverses. Within the weeks and months to follow, conditions on the ground would change greatly and the "A"-bomb issue would temporarily be put on the shelf.

MacArthur displayed none of the support and unity for Truman that Truman extended to him. In the wake of the late November–early December disaster, MacArthur added his own postscript in the following letter dated December 26, 1950, to the Filipino Secretary of Foreign Affairs, Carlos P. Romulo:

26 December 1950

Dear Carlos:

I am most grateful for your fine note of the 14th and the heartening loyalty it reflects.

The commitment of the military resource of China to war against the United Nations Command was of course a risk inherent in our decision to give military support to the Republic of Korea. That risk from the start hung over our heads like the sword of Damocles, and I realized that our only hope of avoiding it lay in speedily bringing the campaign to a close. In retrospect, it is now clear that the decision of the Chinese authorities was taken even before launching of the North Korean aggression on June 25th, and that nothing we did or could have done could exert the slightest influence upon that decision.

The campaign of vituperation initiated against me as a result of Red China's entry into the war was not unexpected. I had warnings from various sources, all reliable, long before Inchon that such a campaign was being planned by the radical fringe. Success at Inchon caused the plan to fail to materialize, but the new situation created by the Chinese offensive was apparently seized upon as the most favorable opportunity for its revival and effectuation. Calm judgment on the issue in the long run will prevail and the understanding will govern that the cards were stacked against us from the start, and campaign strategy alone gave us timely warning of political decisions and military preparations, both aimed at the build-up of an offensive so powerful as to destroy the Command, if caught off guard, with one mighty blow. The Chinese failed to achieve this decisive result but their eleventh hour intervention did block our efforts to complete the prescribed mission.

The efforts through a shocking perversion of truth to shape public thinking along the line that the entry of Communist China into the war was responsive to incidents of the campaign has been scandalous. The dominant group spearheading the drive has of course been the Communists and their friends, but they have received powerful assistance from those who are so infatuated with the safeguard of Europe that they would sacrifice Asia rather than see any support diverted from Europe. My views, of course, are well known. I don't believe either Europe or Asia should be abandoned if American resources can effectively assist toward their security, but the problem is a global one and must be considered on a global basis if it is considered at all. This group of Europhiles just will not recognize that it is Asia which has been selected for the test of Communist power and that if all Asia falls, Europe would not have a chance—either with or without American assistance. In their blind and stupid effort to undermine public confidence in me as something of a symbol of the need for balanced thinking and action, they do Europe the gravest disservice and sow the seeds to its possible ultimate destruction. Asia no less than Europe must be free if global peace is to be secured.

I see by the press that you are soon to return to Manila. Yours is a continuing and vast opportunity for public service, and I know that the free world may continue to look to you during these troubled times for wise and fearless counsel.

With warm regards,
Most faithfully,
Douglas MacArthur [137]

---

[137] *War Letters*, edited by Andrew Carroll (Washington Square Press, division of Simon and Schuster), pp. 47-48.

Rear Admiral Albert K. Morehouse, USN, Chief of Staff to Commander Naval Forces, Far East, disembarks from a Douglas AD "Skyraider" after being flown to the USS Philippine Sea (CV-47) on 13 November 1950. Assisting him is Captain Joseph C. Clifton. Note the decoration on his flying helmet (the back view of a cat) and life jackets worn by RAdm. Morehouse and Capt. Clifton.

Crewman operates a winch on board USS Mockingbird (AMS-27) during mine clearance operations off Wonsan, North Korea. The ship's name is seen on a life ring mounted on the bulwark in the lower right. Original photo is dated 14 November 1950.

Navy carrier-based planes attack bridges over the Yalu River, at Sinuiju, North Korea. Note anti-aircraft emplacements along the river embankment in right center and at left, and bomb craters closer to the bridges. Photograph is dated 15 November 1950, but may have been taken a few days earlier.

Yalu River bridges at Sinuiju, North Korea, under attack by planes from USS Leyte (CV-32). Three spans have been dropped on the highway bridge, but the railway bridge (lower bridge) appears to be intact. The Manchurian city of Antung is across the river, in upper right. Photograph is dated 18 November 1950, but may have been taken on 11 November. Compare bomb damage on and around the river embankment, in the lower part of this photo, with that of previous photo, which was taken earlier.

Secretary of the Navy Francis P. Matthews (right), talks with Vice Admiral Arthur D. Struble, Commander Seventh Fleet (left), and Vice Admiral C. Turner Joy, Commander Naval Forces Far East, (center), upon his arrival at Wonsan airfield, North Korea, for Korean war conferences. The original photograph is dated 23 November 1950, but may have been taken on 20 November.

Secretary of the Navy Francis P. Matthews (center) disembarks from a Douglas AD-4N "Skyraider" aircraft, after being flown aboard USS Philippine Sea (CV-47) off Korea, 22 November 1950. He is being welcomed by the carrier's Commanding Officer, Captain Willard K. Goodney. Secretary Matthews was visiting Navy units involved in Korean War operations. Note his leather flight helmet and inflatable life vest.

"Weapons Company, in line with Headquarters and Service Company, 2nd Battalion, 7th Marines, trying to contact the temporarily cut off Fox Company in a glancing engagement to permit the 5th and 7th Marines to withdraw from the Yudam-ni area. November 27, 1950." Quoted from original picture caption, released by Headquarters, U.S. Marine Corps, on 22 December 1950. Yudam-ni, at the western extremity of the Chosin Reservoir, was the scene of early combat in the campaign, as Chinese forces attacked the two Marine regiments there. The Marines subsequently had to fight their way back to Hagaru along roads surrounded by the enemy.

"Leathernecks inch forward under fire on the central Korean front." Quoted from the original photo caption. This view was taken in late 1950 or early 1951, and was published in All Hands magazine's May 1951 issue. Note scarf worn around the neck of this Marine and billed cap under his helmet. Photographed by Cpl. W.T. Wolfe, USMC.

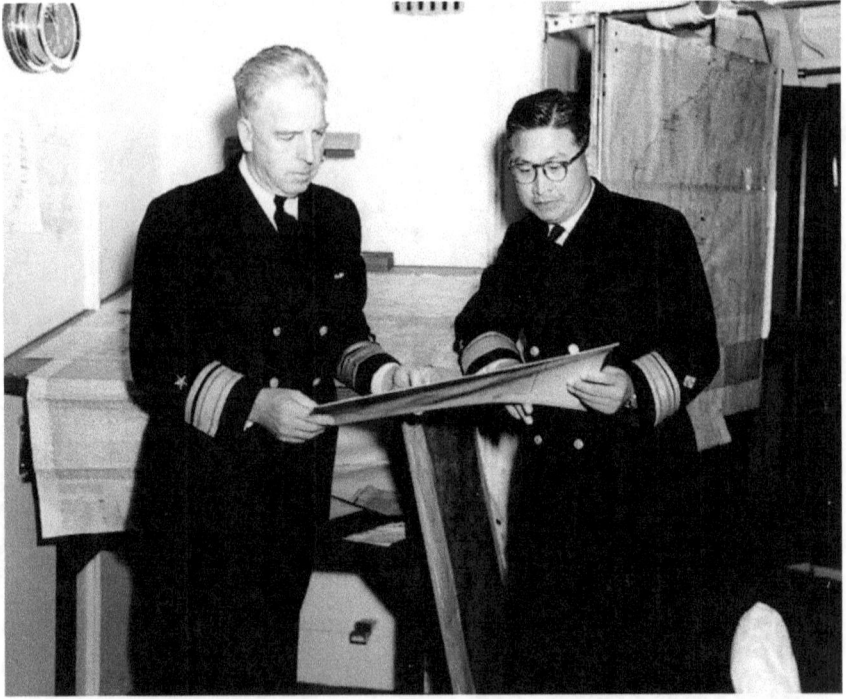

Rear Admiral Allan E. Smith, USN, Commander, Task Force 95 (left), discusses Korean War operations with Rear Admiral Won Il Sohn, Republic of Korea Chief of Naval Operations, on board USS Dixie (AD-14), 6 December 1950.

Rear Admiral James H. Doyle, USN, Commander Task Force 90, Major General Field Harris, USMC, Tactical Air Commander for Tenth Corps, and Lieutenant General Lemuel C. Shepherd, Jr., USMC, Commanding General Fleet Marine Force Pacific, confer at Yonpo airfield, near Hungnam, North Korea, on 8 December 1950, shortly before the Hungnam Evacuation was undertaken. Note planes in the background, including a F7F "Tigercat" (at left) and F4U "Corsairs".

Captain Fremont B. Eggers, USN, shows Major General David G. Barr the course to another port, on board the USS General J.C. Breckinridge (AP-176), during operations off Korea. Maj. Gen. Barr commanded the Seventh Infantry Division. The photo may have been taken during that unit's evacuation from Hungnam, North Korea, on about 21 December 1950.

Port facilities at Inchon, South Korea, are destroyed as U.N. forces evacuate the city in the face of the Chinese Communist advance. Photograph is dated 4 January 1951. The final evacuation of Inchon took place on 5 January.

Chapter 8

The Fallout From Defeat

As always, victory finds a hundred fathers but defeat is an orphan.

—Count Galeazzo Ciano

NO true democracy could suffer the type of humiliating defeat which the United States had just endured against the Communist Chinese Army without there being significant political fall-out.

Predictably, there was a great deal of panic. Prime Minister Clement Atlee of Great Britain urged the Truman Administration to initiate peace talks with the Chinese aimed at a negotiated settlement. This elicited a terse reply from Truman: "We did not get into this fight with the idea of getting licked. We will fight to the finish to stop this aggression...I want to make it perfectly plain that we cannot desert our friends when the going gets rough."

At a meeting with the British Prime Minister, Truman and Acheson pointed out to Atlee that it was their firm opinion that the fate of Western Europe was inextricably connected to the effort and outcome in Korea. How could the U.S. appease and surrender to the Communist aggressors in Asia and at the same time credibly maintain a policy of resistance and negotiation from strength in Europe? Atlee was unable to mount any strong challenge in the face of the firmness of the U.S. leadership.

The panic which was palpable in many quarters was mixed with politics in the United States Congress.

Most Congressional leaders called for the declaration of a national emergency. Having received first-hand reports from the battlefield, Truman knew by December 15 that so far Walker's defensive perimeter was holding, all UN forces were regrouping and for the time being the very worst of the crisis had passed. Much of Eighth Army and X Corps were still in retreat and Seoul was in danger of again falling to the Communists, but the long retreat was now more orderly and strategic. He did, however, go on television and radio on the evening of

December 15 in order to try to allay some of the public's worst fears and to rally the populace to the cause.

Truman spoke bluntly and honestly in reporting that "aggression has won a military advantage in Korea. We should not try to hide or explain away that fact." He issued a plea to his countrymen to make a national effort to meet the crisis.

In an exercise of demagoguery, the House of Representatives called for the dismissal of Dean Acheson as Secretary of State. By its resolution the House blamed the entire disaster on Acheson, claiming that he was soft on Communism. General MacArthur was totally exonerated—not a word of criticism was uttered concerning his splitting his Army in two with a mountain range between them and gaping holes along his 300 mile front, stretching across the peninsula. His gross underestimation of the massive Chinese intervention was neither second-guessed nor even mentioned in the House resolution.

If Truman didn't know what he was up against in terms of public perception at that time, he should have. Truman was not a charismatic figure but even if he were, he would never be given the same deference by the public as was accorded to MacArthur, a national hero and legend. But the calls for Dean Acheson's resignation were too much for Truman to take. At a December press conference he fought back against Acheson's critics, with the following compelling words:

> How our position in the world would be improved by the retirement of Dean Acheson from public life is beyond me. Mr. Acheson has helped shape and carry out our policy of resistance to Communist imperialism...If communism were to prevail in the world—and it shall not prevail—Dean Acheson would be one of the first, if not *the* first, to be shot by the enemies of liberty...

But, the recriminations continued. Former President Herbert Hoover also severely criticized Dean Acheson and his foreign policy. Acheson had clearly become the flashpoint for the U.S. reverses in Korea. In point of fact, he had made one big mistake when, in a foreign policy speech many months before, he failed to include South Korea within the global containment perimeter of the United States. But Acheson subsequently repudiated that statement and clearly extended the parameters of the Truman Doctrine to include South Korea. Nevertheless, the criticism of him for his original position was fair. To accuse him, however, of appeasement and being solely responsible for the catastrophe along the Yalu was not only unfair but intellectually dishonest. The acts and omissions which led to the debacle were primarily military and had little to do with the State Department and foreign policy.

Acheson could be arrogant and at times inflexible but he was no appeaser. On the contrary, he was a cold warrior who had skillfully negotiated the creation of an integrated European Army as part of the U.S. action to resist Stalin's aggression in Europe. With the onset of the Korean War, his focus had been greatly broadened to include the coordination of Asian and European defense policies to achieve a unified global strategy.

The clamor continued through the first few weeks in December 1950—and not all of it from Republicans. On December 12, Joseph P. Kennedy, Franklin D. Roosevelt's Ambassador to Great Britain, called for the immediate withdrawal of United States forces from Korea, Berlin and Europe. In reverting to his pre-World War II brand of isolationism—in which he felt comfortable in not opposing the march of Nazism—Kennedy labeled American foreign policy in 1950 as "suicidal, and politically and morally bankrupt." [138]

The sheer nonsense, born of panic, spewing forth from members of both major political parties, prompted Truman to meet with Congressional leaders on December 13, together with some of his top aides, to attempt to restore some sanity to the national discourse on Korea. He felt the need to present to them a macro view of U.S. international defense policy, which included maintaining the freedom and territorial integrity of South Korea as an integral part of a global policy to contain international communism.

Truman read to the Congressional leaders from top secret CIA reports forecasting probable moves by the Soviet Union around the world. The reports detailed Russian designs upon Iran, and told how it was fiercely attacking U.S. aid under the Truman Doctrine to Greece, Turkey and Yugoslavia. The Kremlin, said Truman, had also belligerently announced that it "would not tolerate the rearmament of Germany, which had become an essential part of our NATO strategy." [139] Forcing the U.S. to expend so much of its blood and treasure in Korea was designed in part to drain resources and manpower away from NATO's defense of Europe—but Korea had to be defended—it was key to America's maintenance of stability in the Pacific. Like World War

---

[138] *Harry S. Truman*, op.cit., p. 504.
[139] Ibid.

II, the Cold War was now being fought in two separate theaters—the European Atlantic and the Asian Pacific.

As Truman attempted to reverse the tide against him in Congress, he began to pick up vocal support from key allies. Marshall, Bradley, Acheson and Eisenhower all flocked to support the Administration's policies on Korea.

Secretary of Defense, George Marshall, had assured the Congressional leadership during the December 13 meetings that the situation in Korea was already improving—our army was regrouping and making a stand. Fortunately General Walker had left himself well-protected routes of escape and the First Marine Division had miraculously escaped at Hungnam. The bitter disappointment and alarm left in the wake of the Chinese intervention forced the Administration to do a sober reassessment of the Korean situation. A re-definition of American objectives was clearly necessary. Truman and his top advisers all agreed that the situation had brought America much closer to global war with the Soviet Union. They determined to drop the objective of liberation of North Korea in favor of a policy of containment.[140] The President, however, committed the error of not clearly communicating these changes in policy directly to MacArthur, who continued to lobby for a wider war.

The President and his inner core of advisers—Marshall, Acheson, Bradley, Harriman and other members of the Joint Chiefs decided that no additional forces would be sent to Korea despite the fact that in the months both before and after the Chinese intervention, overall American defense spending quadrupled.

The new reality consisting of the dramatic rise in Communist aggression in both Europe and Asia in 1949 and 1950—vividly accentuated by the Russian detonation of an atomic bomb in August, 1949—had totally reversed the earlier return by the U.S. to a peacetime economy and the non-military posture of the late forties. NSC-68, a paper prepared by the National Security Council in 1950 called for a massive American re-armament program to enable the U.S. to better meet the challenges of the Cold War.

The Chinese intervention and resultant severe set-back for UN forces took its toll on more than the progress of the war. The two principal figures, Truman and MacArthur, both showed signs of the emotional strain which the military reverses had had upon them. The aging MacArthur, who had always been able to sleep no matter what

---

[140]   *MacArthur, A Biography*, op.cit., p. 159.

crisis confronted him, now suffered from insomnia. [141] His predictions of doom in Korea were greatly disproportionate to the true battlefield conditions of the forces under his command; and his call for UN troops to withdraw from Korea was a gross overreaction. It seemed that his remoteness from the beginning of the conflict from the actual theater of operations had in no small measure facilitated, first his supreme overconfidence in what he had accomplished in Korea with the Inchon landing, followed by his excessive pessimism concerning the UN Forces' strategic position after the Chinese Army had smashed his illusions. MacArthur's almost daily statements to the press and other media after things began to unravel during the last week in November, 1950, were defensive, self-serving and full of excuses. He took no responsibility for the disaster, but blamed it all on his superiors in Washington. The great hero of World War I, the stalwart of Bataan and Corregidor, the brilliant architect of the campaigns to liberate the Philippines and to storm the North Korean stronghold at Inchon, appeared to be in the midst of an intellectual and emotional melt-down in clear view of the eyes of the world.

Truman's reaction was vastly different. He remained calm but a seething anger was building up inside of him which would obtain its release only several months later.

As he assimilated the news of the overwhelming Chinese offensive and the retreat of MacArthur's armies, Truman ranted in a stream of consciousness to no one in particular as he signed documents in his White House office:

> The liars have accomplished their purpose. The whole campaign of lies we have been seeing in this country has brought about its result. I'm talking about the crowd of vilifiers who have been trying to tear us apart in this country. Pravda had an article just the other day crowing about how the American government is divided and how our people are divided, in hatred. Don't worry, they keep a close eye on our dissensions. [142]
> ...

Concerning MacArthur, Truman later spoke of his reaction upon learning of the accusatory statements the general was making to the press between November 28 and December 3:

---

[141] Ibid, p. 159.
[142] *Harry S. Truman*, op.cit., p. 493.

I should have fired MacArthur then and there. [143]

He did not fire MacArthur but rather, publicly supported him, while revealing to confidants that it would be bad for the war effort to fire him in the aftermath of a defeat.

At roughly the same time, General Matthew B. Ridgway, the Joint Chiefs' point man on Korean matters, pulled aside General Hoyt Vandenberg, Commander of the Air Force and pointedly asked him, "Why don't the Joint Chiefs send orders to MacArthur and tell him what to do?" "What good would that do? He wouldn't obey the orders. What can we do?," replied Vanderberg. Ridgway was not about to be put off that easily. His rejoinder and Vandenberg's reaction were a classic, which pretty much crystallized the bizarre dance in which MacArthur and the country's military leadership had been engaged since 1945:

> "You can relieve any commander who won't obey orders, can't you?," asked Ridgway. [144]

But Vandenberg just walked away without saying a word. His silence was eloquent testimony to the fact that Douglas MacArthur wasn't just any commander.

---

[143] Ibid, p. 494.
[144] Ibid, p. 492.

Chapter 9

The Ridgway Resurgence

War's a profanity, because let's face it, you've got two opposing sides trying to settle their differences by killing as many of each other as they can.

—General Norman H. Schwarzkopf

It should have been clear to anyone, that his [MacArthur's] refusal to accept the mounting evidence of massive Chinese intervention was largely responsible for the reckless scattering of our forces all over the map of Korea.

—Matthew B. Ridgway
1951 [145]

ON December 23, 1950, General Walton W. Walker was killed in Korea. He was on his way to inspect U.S. positions near Seoul when his jeep collided at full speed with a civilian truck. His son, Sam S. Walker, a Battalion Commander in Korea at the time, accompanied his father's body back to the United States for burial in Arlington National Cemetery. Walker had never held the confidence of MacArthur and his authority was greatly weakened by the creation of X Corps under General Almond. He had nevertheless, acquitted himself well in Korea under some of the most trying conditions ever faced by a commander, and was entitled to be well-remembered by his countrymen.

General Matthew B. Ridgway was the unanimous choice to replace Walker as Commander of Eighth Army. He was the bright shining star of the Army's hierarchy—liked by MacArthur but favored even more by the Joint Chiefs. MacArthur proposed Ridgway for the post and the Joint Chiefs readily endorsed his choice. Ridgway had become the benchmark by which other senior officers being considered for important command assignments were judged by the Pentagon's talent evaluators. "Is he as good as Ridgway?" was a commonly asked question.

---

[145] *Harry and Ike*, op.cit., p. 211.

Matthew Bunker Ridgway was a tough, decisive and aggressive commander who loved to attack and hated to retreat. He was a hawkish anti-Communist but a realist with a deep respect for the chain of command and the constitutional mandate of civilian leadership. The man's nature combined an uncompromising moral rectitude, an almost messianic fervor for the well-being of his troops and a supreme self-confidence which unerringly allowed him to speak truth to power in critical situations.

Born in Fort Monroe, Virginia, he graduated from West Point and was commissioned as a second lieutenant in 1917. Possessed of a facility with foreign languages, he returned to West Point in 1918 as an instructor in Spanish. Recognizing, however, his true calling as an infantry commander, Ridgway left West Point to attend the company officers' instructional course at Fort Benning, Georgia, after which he was given command of a company in the Fifteenth Infantry.

Ridgway received a prestigious position as an advisor to the Governor General of the Philippines in 1930 but was restive in such a tame position and longed to advance his career as a commander of troops. This quest landed him at the Command General Staff School at Fort Leavenworth, Kansas, followed immediately by his attendance at the Army War College at Carlisle Barracks, Pennsylvania, from which he graduated in 1937. Every academic course and most of Ridgway's duty assignments in the 1930s seemed to be designed to prepare him for the huge challenge to come—as a combat commander in World War II.

During the 1930s Ridgway caught the eye of the Army Chief of Staff, George C. Marshall, for his impressive performances as Assistant Chief of Staff of VI Corps, Deputy Chief of Staff of Second United States Army and Assistant Chief of Staff of the Fourth United States Army.

Ridgway combined intellect, character and decisiveness and Marshall knew that it was rare for an officer to be blessed with a high degree of all three qualities in equal measure. He may have lacked the charm and humor of an Eisenhower but Marshall was more interested in grooming Ridgway to lead large numbers of troops in battle. Accordingly, to help fill a vital national need for pre-war preparation and to burnish Ridgway's talents and reputation as a leader, Marshall assigned him in 1939, shortly after the outbreak in Europe of World War II, to the War Plans Division where he served until January, 1942. With America's entry into World War II, Ridgway's time had come. He was promoted to brigadier general about a month after the Japanese attack on Pearl Harbor of December 7, 1941; and to major general in August 1942.

Upon Ridgway's promotion to Major General, Marshall wasted no time in giving him command of the 82nd Infantry Division, which had been tapped to become one of the Army's five new airborne divisions.

Unlike the men who served under him in the 82nd Airborne, Ridgway had not gone to jump school. In the beginning, he was treated with derision by some of the paratroopers under his command who pinned on him the slang expression for a soldier not qualified to jump out of an airplane—"straight-legs." The derision, however, turned to admiration once the men saw how effectively he turned the 82nd into a first-rate airborne outfit. And Ridgway eventually did win his paratrooper wings.

When the 82nd Airborne was tasked with jumping into Sicily in July 1943 as part of the allies' invasion from North Africa, Ridgway played a major role in the planning and execution of the Airborne operation, including leading the 82nd in combat on the ground.

Next came the Allies' invasion of Italy. Part of the overall plan for the invasion and occupation was the audacious scheme to have the 82nd drop into Italy behind German lines on the outskirts of Rome and then take the city. The concept was to capture Rome without the heavy loss of life entailed in meeting the Germans head-on for weeks and perhaps months of deadly combat from the coast to the capital city.

Ridgway protested vociferously-considering it to be a hair-brained scheme dreamed up by some higher-ups who knew nothing of the realities of combat. For one thing, the 82nd would be dropped in the midst of two heavy German divisions and would be quickly surrounded. Secondly, there would be no sure method for re-supplying the 82nd once it was locked in combat on the ground. Amazingly, however, the operation was not cancelled until two hours before it was scheduled to launch. Echoes of the aborted Rome operation of 1943 were heard by Ridgway and others in their adamant opposition to MacArthur's poorly conceived rush to the Yalu River in October and November of 1950. To Ridgway it was déjà vu. As aggressive and attack-oriented as Ridgway was, his good common sense and innate realism militated against foolhardy operations which placed his troops at risk of being needlessly slaughtered.

In early 1944, Ridgway and the 82nd Airborne were pulled out of the Italian campaign and sent to England to become part of Operation

Overlord, the Allies' amphibious landing at Normandy on the French coast.

On June 6, 1944, Ridgway jumped into Normandy with his troops. At Normandy the 82nd Airborne distinguished itself during thirty three straight days of bloody fighting against the Germans. Their objective was St. Sauveur near Cherbourg in the middle of the Cotentin Peninsula, which they liberated in early July, 1944.

In September, 1944 Ridgway was given command of the XVIII Airborne Corps, which he led into Germany in 1945 and while there, was wounded in the shoulder by German grenade fragments on March 24, 1945. In June 1945, he was promoted to lieutenant general.

After World War II ended, Ridgway held several high-profile positions including Commander of U.S. forces in the Mediterranean Theater, U.S. Army Representative on the Military Staff Committee of the United Nations and Commander of U.S. Forces in the Caribbean. But it was his being named in 1949 as Deputy Chief of Staff for Operations and Administration under Army Chief of Staff, General J. Lawton Collins, which brought him to the seat of U.S. military power—Washington, D.C.—and then thrust him into the high command's nerve center following the North Korean invasion on June 24, 1950.

At the time of Walton Walker's death, Ridgway had already been sent by Collins at least once on an extensive fact-finding and evaluation mission to Korea and to meet with MacArthur in Tokyo. He was already deeply immersed in the Korean problem and highly knowledgeable of conditions there. With his no-nonsense attitude and dynamic personality he arrived in Tokyo to meet with MacArthur on Christmas Day, December 25, 1950 and took command at 8th Army Headquarters in Korea on December 26.

In his December 25 meeting with MacArthur, Ridgway informed him of his plan to stop retreating and start attacking. "The Eighth Army is yours, Matt. Do what you think is best," [146] replied MacArthur.

Ridgway wasted no time upon his arrival in Korea—he almost immediately began touring forward positions. Ridgway was "appalled by what he found; defeatist attitudes on the part of his commanders, low morale." [147] His first task was to evaluate his commanders. Anyone who showed hesitancy about going over to the offensive, was quickly replaced. He asked a regimental operations officer what his plan of of-

---

[146] *The Coldest Winter*, op.cit., p. 491.
[147] Ibid, p. 500.

fensive operations was. When the officer replied that he didn't have one, Ridgway replaced him the same day.

To many it looked like UN forces might have to evacuate Korea in order to protect Japan. But among those who believed that the UN position was better than it appeared on the surface were Army Chief of Staff Collins and Navy Chief of Staff Sherman. The U.S. still had control of the sea—thus holding out the prospect of another amphibious landing behind enemy lines. Bolstered by this fact, Ridgway was sanguine about the UN's situation.

Ridgway wanted Eighth Army to begin moving north again. He began the process in mid-January, 1951 at a time when the UN front ran west to east north of the Han River at some points but well south of Seoul, with a dangerous salient held by the Chinese Army—a bulge extending from Wonju in the north to a point close to the Han River in the south.

Directly west of Wonju and the western line of the Chinese salient was the village of Suwon, which was under assault by the CCF in mid-January. Ridgway called Colonel John Michaelis, commander of the 27th Regiment, known as the "Wolfhounds," to headquarters and without ceremony told him bluntly, "Take your tanks to Suwon." [148] Michaelis responded that he thought that getting to Suwon would be no problem but that the Chinese would probably cut the road behind him and prevent him from getting back. "Who said anything about coming back?" retorted Ridgway. "If you can stay up there for 24 hours, I'll send the division up. If the division can stay up there 24 hours, I'll send the corps up." [149] Michaelis later said that it was that pronouncement by Ridgway which let him know that the tide was turning and the days of retreat and defeatism were over. What became known as Operation Wolfhound was one of Ridgway's early successes.

Little by little, Ridgway restored Eighth Army's morale and fighting spirit. After being pushed back twice within a period of six months—in the summer of 1950 by the North Koreans and in November-December by the Chinese, Eighth Army was unraveling. Its confidence was at a low ebb. By the sheer force of his personality, Ridgway reconstituted battered units, such as the Second Infantry; required commanders to visit units on the front lines to show the troops their leaders cared about them; and removed commanders he believed were lacking in fighting spirit. Eighth Army underwent a transfor-

---

[148] Ibid, p. 501.
[149] Ibid.

mation in organization, effectiveness and morale within a matter of weeks.

Ridgway was in the words of David Halberstam, "fierce, purposeful, relentless—the perfect man to take command at a bad time in a bad place in a war that had suddenly gone from bad to worse..." [150] He was a warrior—a Spartan.

Ridgway also saw from his ideal vantage point at the front what the Joint Chiefs in Washington and MacArthur in Tokyo did not see—that the Chinese forces were overextended, seriously short of supplies and exhausted by many weeks of continuous combat. They had out-run their supply lines to a place too far. Despite their overwhelming numbers, skill at deception and ability to make a mountainous terrain their ally, Ridgway believed the Chinese forces were vulnerable to counter-punches. Those counter-thrusts would not be designed to capture territory but rather to kill as many Chinese as possible, to demonstrate to them that they could not conquer South Korea. In this regard, Ridgway asserted, "It would be a tremendous victory for the United Nations if the war ended with our forces in control of the 38th parallel." [151] On January 31, 1951, he had a long way to go. Seoul had fallen to the Chinese, and its Army had made incursions deep into South Korean territory. But Ridgway had just begun to engineer what in the words of a MacArthur biographer, was "the greatest performance of the twentieth century by an American field army. He displayed skill and charisma to resurrect the Eighth Army from its nadir ... During these same weeks, MacArthur immolated his position and inflicted devastation on his career and reputation." [152]

When the Chinese launched their third Korean Campaign on New Year's Eve 1950, their food supply trickling in along supply lines under relentless bombardment by United States war planes met only twenty-five percent of their needs, forcing them to forage the countryside and live off the land. By February 1, inadequate food and medical supplies, together with continuous fighting and U.S. airpower had left the Chinese forces exhausted.

By early February, the Chinese and United Nations Armies were careening towards a climactic confrontation in the region of the peninsula known as the "Central Corridor." By the end of February, two obscure Korean villages—Chip'yong-ni and Wonju—would have their

---

[150]   Ibid, pp. 486-487.
[151]   *Harry and Ike*, op.cit., p. 212.
[152]   *MacArthur, A Biography*, op.cit., p. 159.

names added to the lexicon of defining battles which had shifted the entire momentum of a war—Saratoga, Gettysburg and Stalingrad being prime examples.

Ridgway's influx of Intelligence was getting better and better each day. That, combined with the state of readiness of his troops, the geography of the Central Corridor and the vulnerability of the Chinese forces, caused Ridgway to seek a major squaring-off with the Chinese. He wanted to attack them head-on and hand them a decisive defeat.

The village of Chip'yong-ni was about fifty miles southeast of Seoul in the Central Corridor, towards the western side of the peninsula. As part of Ridgway's campaign to move north, elements of Eighth Army had established a defensive perimeter in and near the village. Ridgway was, in effect, inviting the Chinese to attack.

The Chinese forces considered Chip'yong-ni to be just one more obstacle in their inexorable march to the southern coast, the total conquest of South Korea and destruction of the UN armies. But they were about to encounter a very different American army than the one they had routed south of the Yalu. The difference lay not in the number of troops or sophistication of weaponry—but rather in its command structure.

At the top was Matthew B. Ridgway, given the nickname, "Old Iron Tits", for his custom of wearing two hand grenades on his chest (The truth is only one was a grenade. The other was a first-aid packet.). By mid-February, all of his hand-picked commanders bore the Ridgway brand—tough, aggressive, brave and with a burning passion for being in the thick of the action as they led their troops into battle.

One such officer was Colonel Paul L. Freeman, commanding officer of the 23rd Infantry Regimental Combat Team of the Second Infantry Division. Freeman established a strong defensive perimeter at Chip'yong-ni but the Chinese were unimpressed. By February 13, 1951, UN forces had abandoned Seoul, destroyed huge amounts of their own supplies to prevent their falling into enemy hands and had even prepared plans at headquarters in Tokyo for the total evacuation of the peninsula. Since the beating inflicted upon the UN armies in late November, the tactic most favored by the United Nations Command "was rolling with the punch." When attacked, a unit would engage in a strategic withdrawal to avoid encirclement instead of standing and fighting. This battlefield tactic was anathema to Ridgway and cut against the grain of everything he believed in. Freeman, selected in the image of Ridgway, felt the same. But the Chinese had no way of knowing that and expected little more from the Americans than they had shown for the last 2 ½ months.

One of the reasons, however, that U.S. forces had so much difficulty holding their ground was that more often than not on their left or right flank was a R.O.K. company or battalion. The South Korean units were notorious for collapsing at the first sign that the Chinese or North Korean units had gained the advantage in a battle. They would simply fold up their tents and exit the field of battle, leaving the American units in danger of being flanked and surrounded. So it was at Chip'yong-ni. Freeman's regiment was under attack and greatly outnumbered by the Chinese. True to their usual practice, the South Korean units on Freeman's flanks withdrew in the face of an ominous build-up of several Chinese divisions to Freeman's front, preparing to overrun his single regiment. Freeman radioed Second Division Commander Nick Ruffner for orders. To Freeman's surprise, Ruffner informed him that Ridgway wanted a test of strength. Chip'yong-ni and Wonju were to be defended at all costs and held. Ruffner ordered Freeman to form a tight pocket of defense and dig in deep. He was also to lay-in within the perimeter as much food, water, ammunition and medical supplies as he could. If supplies ran low, he would be resupplied by air. To greatly diminish the prospect of being overrun by the enemy, a column of the Fifth Cavalry Regiment of the First Cavalry Division which 15 years later distinguished itself in Vietnam at IaDrang, Khe-Sanh and A Shau Valley—was dispatched northward from Yoju to Chip'Yong-ni to come to the aid of the 23rd Infantry Regiment.

The 23rd Infantry was part of a resurrected and revitalized Second Infantry Division. That Ridgway was able to bring the Second Division back to life after the devastating losses it had suffered during Eighth Army's retreat from the Yalu, is a testament to his organizational skills; but even more so to his talent for inspiring those serving under him to meet even the most difficult challenges in the shortest amount of time possible. Only ten weeks after it had virtually ceased to exist as a viable fighting force, the Second Infantry Division was once again a force to be reckoned with and a key component in Ridgway's plans.

Freeman also embraced the challenge Ridgway had placed before him—promptly sending out patrols for up to three miles forward of every front line position. He configured his perimeter with First Battalion in the northern sector, Second Battalion at the southern rim of the perimeter, Third Battalion to the east and a French Battalion to the south and southwest. Two companies—B Company and a Ranger company were held in reserve.

The shelling of the UN perimeter began shortly after dusk on February 13. A shrill and raucous cascade of bugles and whistles signaled the beginning of the CCF infantry attack on the UN's First Battalion at around midnight. By daylight of February 14, the entire perimeter was under attack. Wave upon wave of CCF infantry assaulted the UN perimeter—a human tsunami of ferocious force and strength—threatening to smash and engulf the UN defenses at their weakest points. For most of the next three days the pounding continued with Chip'yong-ni in peril of being overrun. But Freeman's forward companies which had dug-in on elevated ground in classic text book fashion, held off the attackers and exacted a heavy tribute. Thousands of CCF troops lay dead on the frigid February ground.

Freeman was wounded in the leg by an enemy shell fragment but refused medical evacuation.

The UN perimeter, however, did not remain uniformly intact. Around 3:00 a.m. on February 14, the CCF breached the southern perimeter and seized the high ground after pushing Companies F and G back from their fixed positions. Freeman instantly recognized the gravity of the situation. If not immediately impeded, the CCF would flank the defenders of other areas on the perimeter and the whole UN line would be in jeopardy of collapse.

It was time for bold and decisive action. There would be no "rolling with the punch" this time. The gap had to be closed and closed fast. Freeman immediately counterattacked with his Ranger Company and the remaining elements of F and G Companies. And he wisely avoided over-committing his reserves. Knowing that the counterattack could fail, he held back B Company, his regimental reserve.

The counterattack kicked off at dawn on February 14 but after fierce fighting, was repulsed, and Freeman's men suffered heavy casualties. But on the next day, Freeman attacked again, this time using B Company, his regimental reserve. In executing B Company's assault, Freeman employed no stealth tactics. In almost a demonstration of disdain for his CCF foes, he attacked in broad daylight across wide-open ground. Again the attacking American troops were being battered and falling everywhere under withering mortar and machine-gun fire, but help was on the way. Freeman called for air support and soon U.S. fighter planes were raining napalm down on the Chinese positions. B Company rallied to push the CCF back off the original perimeter and closed the breach, but at the cost of fifty percent dead or wounded. These painful losses were in stark contrast to those of the units not called upon to counter-attack. Among the well-entrenched troops who remained strictly in a defensive posture, casualties were minimal—another of the countless examples of the capriciousness of war.

At about sunset of the third day of the battle, February 15, the Fifth Cavalry relief column from Yoju marched through the UN perimeter on the road separating the positions of the U.S. Second Battalion and the French Battalion. The perimeter was secured and the battle was over.

Although the hold of the surrounded 23rd Infantry Regiment and the French Battalion had been extremely tenuous for three days, in the end Ridgway got the big victory he was looking for in a direct confrontation with the Chinese. He had sought a test of strength, got it and prevailed. There were multiple reasons for the victory—the priority given by Ridgway to air power; the skill displayed by Freeman in erecting a solid and well-entrenched perimeter and then combining boldness with wisdom in his counter-attacks; Ridgway's impeccable timing in dispatching a relief force as soon as the heavy CCF assault began; the excellent U.S. leadership at the regimental, division and army levels; the poor state of the under-supplied and exhausted Chinese troops and the CCF's clear underestimation of the strength, spirit and resolve of the opposing UN force. The victory fashioned at Chip'yong-ni had the Ridgway brand name all over it. It "turned out to be the battle Matt Ridgway had wanted from the moment he arrived in-country." [153]

Without question, Chip'yong-ni was one of the decisive battles of the War. Another was soon to follow at a village southeast of Chip'yong-ni—a second classical test of strength, at the Battle of Wonju.

Dispatched to Wonju, the 9th and 38th Regiments of Second Division prepared for a major attack by the CCF in division strength. The independent-minded General George Stewart, an old artillery man, was placed in charge of the defense of the Town of Wonju. Stewart was advised by General Ned Almond, his commanding officer, that the attack would come from the right and to concentrate his fortifications accordingly. Stewart ignored that advice, convinced that the attack would come from the left. He was right.

---

[153] *The Coldest Winter*, op.cit., p. 541.

Stewart sent out artillery spotter planes to try to pinpoint the exact location of the advancing Chinese. The Som River winds its way through the mountains northwest of Wonju. An army spotter at perhaps five thousand feet scanned the landscape below along the sandy banks of the Som, observing the tree line at the edge. His intense gaze at first noted nothing unusual as the pilot prepared to head back to base. But something was not the way it should be—the tree line seemed to be moving. The spotter blinked his eyes and tried to concentrate his sights on the moving line below while the pilot lowered their altitude. Suddenly he realized it was not a tree line at all but a steadily moving mass of humanity. As the spotter plane descended, the amorphous mass began to take on more definition until its clear shape emerged as a long column of Chinese infantry—perhaps two full divisions—marching rapidly along the sandy river bank. The Chinese spotted the plane but took no obvious action to do anything about it. The Chinese almost never attacked in broad day-light but now here it was brazenly driving towards Wonju and displaying an assuredness that it was headed toward an overwhelming victory.

The pilot radioed the CCF position in to Stewart's headquarters. Stewart met the news with excitement—this was one of the few breaks the UN forces had had since Inchon. He immediately aimed virtually all of his artillery pieces in the direction of the approaching forces—130 big guns in all. Stewart may also have appreciated how Wonju could assume a significant place in history given its strategic location at an important road junction in the central corridor. It was critical to Ridgway and Eighth Army that its supply line and possible line of retreat to Pusan be kept open. If Wonju fell, these arteries could be cut off. Stewart knew that it wouldn't be enough simply to slow down or temporarily halt the southward advance of the CCF. He had the unprecedented opportunity to deal a devastating blow to a force of Chinese infantry numbering as many as 30,000—four divisions in all. He had no intention of letting such an opportunity slip by. With his mastery of artillery tactics, Stewart began a non-stop barrage of artillery fire on the advancing Chinese divisions. All of it was directed at their approach from the left and it continued for three hours. A nervous operations officer back at Division repeatedly requested that Stewart cease firing in order to save ammunition for possible attacks from the right. But Stewart refused to heed his warnings. He sensed that this was a pivotal engagement of the war and he would hold nothing back. In addition, Stewart had only a small force—two regiments against four divisions and believed that killing as many of the attackers as possible gave his units the best chance of survival.

The Division ops officer again urged him to cease firing. Stewart's response was to tell his teams to "keep firing until the gun barrels melt." Yet as many Chinese as went down, just as many kept coming. No amount of carnage and mayhem stopped their relentless advance. By the time the artillery barrage ceased, 5000 Chinese soldiers had been killed and thousands more wounded. Finally, faced with the prospect of suffering even greater losses, the Chinese assault force withdrew. It was a huge victory for Eighth Army and the UN forces in Korea; and George Stewart was the hero.

At the end of the day, Chinese losses in the Central Corridor were staggering—approximately 20,000 killed and wounded. General Almond decorated Stewart's counterpart at Division headquarters; but General George Stewart who had, contrary to Almond's advice, insisted the attack would come from the left, received not even a mention.

The battle at Wonju was referred to by some as the "Gettysburg" of the Korean War, after which the CCF never again was able to seize the initiative. The open question before the battles of the Central Corridor of whether United Nations forces could prevail against the CCF was resoundingly answered in the affirmative. Despite a successful counterattack by the Chinese at Hoengsong, the CCF clearly met its match at Chip'yong-ni and again at Wonju. The momentum of the War had swung once again back to the UN allies. Inspired by their victories in the Central Corridor, UN forces to the south blocked the CCF at several mountain passes, denying them access to the plains north of Pusan. Below Wonju, the U.S. Second Division together with French and Dutch battalions not only held on but mounted a counterattack into the town of Wonju. The fighting was fierce and several times Hill 247, a half-mile long crest two miles south of the town, changed hands. But, ultimately, UN forces held and dealt a major blow to the Chinese war effort. Ridgway was ready to move north to liberate Seoul once again.

History could not have produced a better leader for the dire circumstances in which America found itself at the end of December, 1950. Grave times, as it turned out, required a solemn leader. In 2009 America, the talking heads on cable television would describe him as a man of "gravitas." That he was—single-minded, determined, humorless, aggressive and totally focused on the job at hand. Those under his command were either inspired, or compelled, to emulate his intense ways. He drove everyone to improve and succeed—none more so than himself.

Ridgway knew that if he got the needed performance from his command, they would succeed. He had the Chinese at the end of a porous supply line extending about 260 miles from the Yalu River to the northern edge of the Central Corridor, which was under constant pounding by American war planes for its entire length. The flow of the staples of war—food, ammunition and medical supplies had been greatly obstructed. To add to the CCF's misery, an epidemic of Typhus, aggravated by the brutal Korean winter, decimated their ranks.

Ridgway relentlessly pushed his commanders to attack north—from the Naktong River to the plains north of the Pusan perimeter, to the Han River and then into major confrontations at Chip'Yong-ni, Twin Tunnels and Wonju. By the end of March 1951, Seoul was recaptured and UN Forces were back on the 38th Parallel.

Joint Chiefs Chairman, General Omar Bradley, was to say of Ridgway, "His brilliant, driving, uncompromising leadership turned the tide of battle as no other general in American Military history."

Chapter 10

The Crisis of Command

The die is cast.

—Julius Caesar

THE roots of the extraordinary confrontation between a United States president and his top commanding general in time of war, could be traced back to their beginnings. Harry S. Truman had received a powerful message during his formative and early-adult years that a man had to believe in himself completely without self-imposed limits on how far he could go; yet at the same time had to be wise and flexible enough to realize that he must accommodate reality when it interferes with one's plans. Because of family finances, some worthy individuals don't get to go to college. No matter how diligent a farmer is, one bad crop can wipe him out. Regardless of merit, a National Guard Captain will never achieve acceptance from the regular army officer corps. A small businessman may be smart, shrewd, tireless and popular with his customers yet still fail because of external economic forces or conditions. Of course, a person must be predisposed by DNA, genetics, environment, or a combination thereof, to accept such lessons of reality.

Life on the other hand, sent Douglas MacArthur a very different message with little ambiguity to it. In terms of the traditional aristocracy of the military, he was "to the manor born", harkening back to his Scottish ancestors. The MacArthur blood line included magnificent war heroes such as his father, as well as intellectually gifted men of public life like his grandfather. And nothing in his own development and accomplishments disabused him in any way of his core belief in his own exceptionalism. He knew with an immovable certainty that he had been called to be one of society's great leaders and to accomplish monumental things. Finishing number one in his graduating class at West Point, being the most decorated American officer of World War I, conceiving and executing a brilliant campaign against the Japanese in World War II, governing the defeated Japanese nation with wisdom and compassion and pulling off the audacious landing at Inchon, all simply reinforced what he already knew about himself. In many ways, his interior value system, unlike that of most people, contained its own self-justifying moral and intellectual scale, which weighed and judged his decisions and actions with simple clarity. If he believed it or did it, it was unassailably correct. Those who dissented from his convictions were automatically in error.

For most of his life, MacArthur had a grand vision of himself. Such grandiosity affected almost everything that he did, but sadly also stole away his objectivity. In an infamous disengagement from reality, MacArthur frequently made bitter reference to Dwight D. Eisenhower as "the best clerk I ever had and the apotheosis of mediocrity." [154]

The Chinese intervention shook Douglas MacArthur to his core. For probably the first time in his life, his self-justification impulse had failed him—leaving him reeling and bereft of the cool judgment a great leader so desperately needs. And at age 71, he simply no longer had the resources of strength and vitality needed to recover from such a staggering personal defeat.

Truman's problem was different but ultimately just as damaging to his political career. He had been one of MacArthur's many enablers but soon would be faced with the decision of whether to fire a legend. Truman had the internal strength to perform such a task but lacked the external reservoir of personal popularity to survive it politically.

Through January of 1951, as Ridgway was systematically laying the cornerstone for a great resurgence by Eighth Army and the rest of the UN force, MacArthur continued to inundate Washington with urgent missives demanding the right to widen the war by bombing Manchuria and taking the muzzle off Chiang Kai-Shek and his Nationalist Chinese Army.

In a dramatic counterpoint, the United Nations set off in the opposite direction. On January 13, 1951, it voted to hand over Formosa to Communist China if it would agree to a Korean settlement. No deal was struck but such a shameful display of spinelessness inflamed MacArthur's grandiose rhetoric even more.

Meanwhile Ridgway was not only firmly halting the 300 mile retreat of Eighth Army to below the 38th Parallel, but was doing what no one believed he could do: reversing the situations of the warring armies by leading Eighth Army over to the offensive around January 25. The same UN General Assembly, by a large majority, passed a resolution on February 1 branding Communist China as an aggressor in

---

[154] *Harry and Ike*, op.cit., p. 209.

Korea—apparently without embarrassment over its blatant inconsistency.

As Ridgway gave the performance of an impresario from mid-January to the end of March, MacArthur became more and more openly critical of the way the Truman Administration was conducting the war. Even in the face of Ridgway's spectacular reversal of the Chinese advances, and his counter-surge north, MacArthur voiced not a single word of praise for what Ridgway was accomplishing. Instead, he referred to the entire conflict as "an accordion war," in which all the UN was doing was advancing until its supply lines became overextended and then being forced to fall back until the enemy's lines were overextended, at which point, the process would again be reversed. MacArthur's characterization proved to be way off the mark. By March 20, 1951, the United Nations Army was solidly entrenched on the 38th Parallel, from where it was never again evicted. The Chinese Communist Army, contrariwise, was battered and on the brink of collapse. Confronted by the Eighth Army steam-roller which picked up speed and momentum as it approached Seoul and the regions beyond, Chinese soldiers were surrendering by the thousands.

In the post-Inchon euphoria, both the Truman Administration and the United Nations had given MacArthur the green light on October 7, 1950 to move north and unify Korea under Syngman Rhee. MacArthur still believed that he had such a mandate even after the Chinese intervention. Legally he was correct. But, United States policy was changing and Truman, although belatedly, made an earnest effort to explain the new policy to MacArthur.

His first step was to send MacArthur a long letter in which he stated among other things:

> Steps which might in themselves be fully justified and which might lend some assistance to the campaign in Korea would not be beneficial if they thereby involved Japan or Western Europe in large-scale hostilities.

Truman pointed out in the letter how much the United States would gain from a successful resistance in Korea—by deflating "the political and military prestige of Communist China." He expanded upon that premise with a more concrete and specific description of his vision:

We would make possible a far more satisfactory peace settlement for Japan. We would lend urgency to the rapid expansion of the defenses of the Western World.

If Truman's letter of January 13 contained more than a little wishful thinking, that was immaterial. All that was really relevant as far as MacArthur was concerned was that it was an explanation by the Chief of State to one of his important generals of the nation's policy as formulated by the Constitutional civilian authority. Truman was under no constitutional obligation to explain the government's policy to the military. MacArthur didn't have to like it, but since it came from the highest duly constituted civilian official of the country, he was legally bound not to contravene it.

To ensure that there would be no misunderstanding between himself and MacArthur, Truman then dispatched Army Chief of Staff Joe (J. Lawton) Collins and Air Force Chief of Staff Hoyt Vandenberg to Tokyo to meet with MacArthur and elaborate on the explanation provided in his letter.

Extraordinary deference had been given to MacArthur by his civilian and military bosses in order to achieve unity of civilian and military command. Over the next two months, a series of actions by MacArthur in response to the explanations and overtures made to him in good faith, would ignite the worst crisis of command in American history.

General MacArthur had an entirely different take on what Korean policy should be. In his memoirs, he wrote:

> It was my belief that if allowed to use my full military might, without artificial restrictions, I could not only save Korea, but also inflict such a destructive blow upon Red China's capacity to wage aggressive war, it would remove her as a further threat to peace in Asia for generations to come.

The die was cast. Truman wished to seek an armistice and MacArthur wanted to make war against China, presumably with nuclear weapons, if necessary.

MacArthur was certainly entitled to his opinion provided he did not voice it in such a way as to undermine official United States policy. The framers of the United States Constitution left no doubt about the strict subordination of the military to the executive branch. Otherwise, they would not have named the president as commander-in-chief of the armed forces. One hundred and twenty five years earlier, Lord Oliver Cromwell had been the virtual dictator of England by his iron-gripped control of the Parliamentary Army. With this example and others in mind, the founding fathers considered civilian control over the military to be a cornerstone of a democratic republic.

MacArthur was fully aware of this subordination of authority at an intellectual level, but his actions and words had ceased to signify that he believed it applied to him. He spoke and conducted himself like a head of state—a power unto himself—rather than as just one essential link in the chain of command. At some time during his string of un-paralleled successes, he had ceased to consider himself as answerable to a higher human authority.

It would be easy to blame the men who had appeased MacArthur for the last decade—Roosevelt, Marshall, Eisenhower, Truman, Collins, Bradley, etc.—for what MacArthur had become. But none of them were in positions of power in 1932 when MacArthur disobeyed Hoover's order not to take his troops across the Anacostia River; or when Pershing's senior staff ordered MacArthur in 1918 to carry a gas mask and a weapon when leading his troops into battle. His failure to obey this order almost cost MacArthur his life—but it didn't—perhaps one more affirmation to him that he transcended the ordinary rules which applied to other men. Was it a type of megalomania that drove MacArthur? The authoritative answer to that question could probably only come from a skilled mental health professional. Suffice it to say that by March of 1951, MacArthur had spun out of the control of any superior officer and of the dictates of his oath as a United States Army officer.

On March 15, 1951, he gave an extensive interview to Hugh Baille, the president of the United Press. In response to a Baille question, MacArthur accurately stated, "Our mission was the unification of Korea." By March, however, MacArthur had been repeatedly informed that U.S. and UN policy had changed. He exhibited no sense of restraint in the light of this policy change as he criticized the decision of the Truman Administration to stop at the 38th Parallel. By doing so, he specifically disobeyed his president's order of December 6, 1950 to refrain from commenting on U.S. policy to the press without first clearing it with Washington. This was a clear act of insubordination. Truman was on the cusp of sensitive negotiations to end the war and MacArthur's statement to Baille infuriated him.

The next escalation of tensions between MacArthur and Washington occurred on March 20, 1951. Truman had ordered the State Department to draft a carefully worded proposal to the Chinese containing the terms of a proposed armistice. The proposal would be circulated to all UN members with troops in Korea. To prevent MacArthur from sabotaging the negotiations, the Joint Chiefs called MacArthur, informing him of the plan and advising him that "strong United Nations feeling persists that further diplomatic efforts should be made before any advance with forces north of the 38th Parallel." The phraseology employed by the Joint Chiefs was typical of the way they had dealt with MacArthur all along. The selection of the wording, "strong United Nations feeling persists that further diplomatic efforts should be made" was a classic of tepid bureaucratize. If Ridgway had been made aware of the communiqué, he would likely have reacted with a few well chosen expletives.

The phrase "United Nations feeling persists" was at once an evasion of any responsibility to clearly articulate a directive from the Joint Chiefs in the matter; and an equivocation in the use of the word "persists", which managed to imply that the UN was imposing upon the Chiefs a policy they did not necessarily subscribe to. The door had been left wide open for MacArthur and he wasted no time in walking through it. He replied, "Recommend that no further military restrictions be imposed upon the United Nations Command in Korea. The inhibitions which already exist should not be increased."

With or without MacArthur on board, Truman pushed forward with his peace initiative. A presidential announcement was being prepared which would state that with the bulk of aggressors now cleared from South Korea, the United Nations was preparing to discuss conditions for peace in Korea. Time would be required to gauge diplomatic reactions and allow for new negotiations adapted to the reactions. An armistice would be particularly difficult to attain in view of the fact that the Ridgway resurgence had exacted heavy battlefield losses from the Chinese. Given the oriental mind, a way would have to be found to allow the Communist Chinese to save face while at the same time ensuring their total removal from all areas south of the 38th Parallel. The negotiations would be delicate and would require great finesse by all major figures.

It didn't take long for MacArthur to torpedo the incipient peace efforts.

On March 24, 1951, MacArthur issued a communiqué asserting that China's attempt to conquer South Korea had failed. "Within my authority as military commander" MacArthur declared,

I stand ready at any time to confer with the commander-in-chief of the enemy forces in an earnest attempt to find any military means whereby the realizations of the political objectives of the United Nations in Korea...might be accomplished without further bloodshed.

The communiqué, in asserting that the Chinese initiatives had failed, was tantamount to waving a red flag in front of Mao Tse-tung. And to exacerbate the situation even further, MacArthur "scoffed at Red China's vaunted military power and boastfully declared South Korea cleared of organized Communist forces." [155] MacArthur's statement "taunted the Chinese and undercut Truman's peace initiative." [156] Communist weakness, declared MacArthur, was "brilliantly exploited by our ground forces" and the enemy was showing "less stamina than our own troops under the rigors of climate, terrain and battle." [157]

MacArthur was a self-professed expert on the oriental mind. He had to know how inflammatory, dismissive and demeaning his remarks were to the proud Chinese.

The crusher, however, seemed to be aimed by MacArthur at both the American and the Communist Chinese governments:

The enemy, therefore, must by now be painfully aware that a decision of the United States to depart from its tolerant effort to contain the war to the areas of Korea through an expansion of our military operations to his coastal areas and interior bases, would doom Red China to the risk of imminent military collapse.

The Chinese "scornfully rejected MacArthur's ultimatum." [158]

MacArthur's blunt warning to China was at first met with incredulity in Washington. No one could quite believe that a commanding general of a theater of operations could be so contemptuous of his higher command. Acheson called MacArthur's statement "insubordination of the grossest sort." Omar Bradley called it an "unforgivable and irretrievable act."

---

[155] *Harry S. Truman*, op.cit., p. 512.
[156] Ibid, p. 512.
[157] Ibid.
[158] Ibid, p. 513.

Truman wasted no time in summoning his advisors to the White House for an emergency meeting and expressing his conviction that they were all in the midst of an unprecedented crisis of command. MacArthur had become a loose cannon on the deck and there was no telling what he would do next. For the time being Truman confined himself to a blunt cable to MacArthur reminding him of the presidential directive forbidding policy statements by military officers. But, without revealing his decision to his advisors, Truman had determined that MacArthur had to be fired. It was just a question of when.

In later years, Truman wrote expansively of the circumstances before and after MacArthur's ultimatum to Red China and how it placed America in a totally untenable diplomatic position:

> Dean Acheson and General Marshall and I decided we should send an ultimatum to the head of the Chinese government for a cease-fire in Korea. We sent the meat paragraphs to MacArthur for approval. Then he sent his own ultimatum to the Chinese. That is what he got fired for. I couldn't send a message to the Chinese after that. He prevented a cease fire proposition right there. I was ready to kick him into the North China Sea at that time. I was never so put out in my life. It's the lousiest trick a Commander in Chief can have done to him by an underling. MacArthur thought he was the proconsul for the government of the United States and could do as he damn pleased. [159]

Then Truman got even more to the point, but with words less expressive of his immense anger:

> It was an act totally disregarding all directives to abstain from any declaration on foreign policy. It was open defiance of my orders as President and Commander-in-Chief. This was a challenge to the authority of the President under the Constitution. It also flouted the policy of the United Nations. By this act MacArthur left me no choice—I could no longer tolerate his insubordination.

Yet, Truman still did not pull the trigger and recall General MacArthur. In the words of Dean Acheson, Truman continues to show

---

[159] See *Harry S. Truman*, op.cit., p. 513, quoting Truman's _Memoirs_.

"infinite patience" with MacArthur. In point of fact, Truman's "infinite patience" was exhausted but he still waited for MacArthur to engage in a further provocation. Truman was sure it would come because MacArthur's agenda to engage the White House in an ever escalating war of words was manifest.

Truman's calculation was correct. Joseph Martin, the Republican minority leader of the U.S. House of Representatives wrote a speech highly critical of Truman's foreign policy, referring to it as "defeatist," and sent it to MacArthur for his comments. MacArthur was only too glad to accommodate Martin and on March 20, 1951 wrote a letter to him containing his views. Martin made the letter public by reading it to the House of Representatives in public session on Thursday, April 5, 1951. Its text included an affirmation by MacArthur that Martin was right in calling for a decisive victory in Korea; in wanting to have nationalist Chinese forces from Formosa join the war against Communism; in stating that the real war was in Asia, not in Europe; in asserting that here [in Asia] we fight Europe's war with arms while the diplomats still fight it with words...and if we lose the war to Communism in Asia, the fall of Europe is inevitable, but if we win it, Europe would most probably avoid war and yet preserve freedom; and in declaring that "there is no substitute for victory."

The revelation of the MacArthur letter to Martin hit the AP and UP wires immediately and the reaction in Washington was instantaneous. At the Pentagon, General Bradley called an urgent meeting of the Joint Chiefs but they came to no conclusion as to what to do about MacArthur.

A new assistant press secretary, Roger Tubby, grabbed the ticker bulletin relating MacArthur's letter to Martin and breathlessly rushed into the Oval office to give it to the President. Tubby, according to Truman's biographer, David McCullough, found Truman "sitting quietly reading General Bradley's book, *A Soldier's Story*." [160] The following exchange between press secretary and president highlights the surface imperturbability which Truman was then displaying to virtually everyone:

> Mr. President, this man [MacArthur] is not only insubordinate, but he's insolent, and I think he ought to be fired.

---

[160] *Truman*, op.cit., pp. 146-147.

Truman after again looking at the ticker bulletin: "Well, I think they are maneuvering the general out of a job." [161]

Truman's cryptic response to Tubby typifies how close to the vest Truman was holding his cards when it came to MacArthur. On April 5 and the days which followed, General Bradley did not even know that Truman had already made up his mind to relieve MacArthur, but allowed that, "I thought it was a strong possibility." [162]

On Saturday, April 7, Truman called a meeting of his top advisors, Marshall, Bradley, Acheson and Harriman, to elicit their views as to what should be done about MacArthur. Truman's calm demeanor at the meeting seemed to convey that he had reached a decision and was very much at peace with what he had decided. But no one present could tell for sure and Truman revealed nothing about his own views. Marshall urged caution; Acheson, although clearly in favor of recalling MacArthur, warned, "If you relieve MacArthur, you will have the biggest fight of your administration." [163] Harriman stated that MacArthur had been a problem for far too long and should be dismissed at once. Bradley did not commit himself one way or the other.

For the next several days "an air of unnatural calm seemed to hang over the White House." [164] Truman was known to release passionate outbursts of anger from time to time but in times of crisis he was calm and steadfast—as he was upon making the decision to drop the A-bomb on Hiroshima in August, 1945 and to send troops to Korea in June, 1950.

The placid surface of the troubled waters surrounding Truman did not mean that he was not working on the MacArthur problem. Truman called Vice President Alben Barkley, and gave him a detailed briefing on the situation. Barkley reluctantly concluded that "a compromise was out of the question—MacArthur would have to go." [165] Truman also called Chief Justice Vinson of the United States Supreme Court and Speaker of the House Sam Rayburn to his office for a meeting on the situation. Vinson like Marshall, urged Truman to proceed cautiously. But Truman had moved farther out front of the problem than most of those whose counsel he sought. He knew without any

---

[161]   *Truman*, op.cit., pp. 146-147.
[162]   Ibid.
[163]   Ibid.
[164]   Ibid.
[165]   Ibid, p. 840.

doubt what had to be done. The following entry was written by him for April 6 in his diary:

> MacArthur shoots another political bomb through Joe Martin, leader of the Republican minority in the House ... This looks like the last straw. Rank insubordination ... I've come to the conclusion that our Big General in the Far East must be recalled. [166]

On April 9, 1951, he wrote in his diary, "recall orders" and in a separate entry wrote "He's going to be fired." [167]

To further bolster his case, Truman asked Marshall to review every single communiqué from and to MacArthur in the Department of Defense's MacArthur file. Marshall spent the night of April 8 reading the entire file. After doing so, he reported to Truman that "the S.O.B. should have been fired two years ago." [168]

On Sunday, April 8, the Joint Chiefs convened again for a lengthy meeting. They confined their evaluation of MacArthur to military grounds, believing correctly that matters of politics, legality and constitutionality were not within their province and were best left to the civilian leadership.

What emerged from the meeting was that the Chiefs were disenchanted with MacArthur. His decisions to split his forces in Korea and then to rashly launch the November, 1950 offensive to the Yalu without first gathering complete and reliable intelligence as to the strength and location of the Chinese forces were ill-advised strategy and tactics.

The Joint Chiefs also concluded that MacArthur, who after the Chinese intervention had expressed doom and gloom over the UN's military predicament, had lost confidence in himself. This in turn was eroding the confidence of his field officers and troops. When MacArthur by his communiqué of March 24, 1951 engaged in a flagrant act of insubordination to his commander-in-chief, that clinched it. Their unanimous opinion was that MacArthur should be relieved of his command. Bradley expressed his agreement with the decision, though as Chairman he had no vote.

Truman, still exhibiting rigid self-control, met with Marshall, Acheson, Bradley and Harriman on Monday, April 9 at Blair House.

---

[166] *Harry S. Truman*, op.cit., p. 516.
[167] Ibid, p. 516.
[168] Ibid, p. 515.

Perhaps buffeted by the unanimous conclusion of the Joint Chiefs, each of Truman's four key advisors now spoke in favor of relieving MacArthur. After quietly listening to their opinions, Truman for the first time voiced his own agreement with the proposal for an immediate recall. He ordered Bradley to prepare the necessary papers.

Truman and his key advisors, particularly Marshall and Acheson, had evidenced great moral courage by their action. They knew the calumny and abuse which would be hurled at them. At the end of long and distinguished careers, neither Marshall nor Acheson relished the thought of having their reputations sullied by a broadside of vituperation from their political foes. Just the previous fall, during the acrimonious Senate hearings over Marshall's confirmation as Secretary of Defense, Senator William E. Jenner of Indiana had called Marshall "a front man for traitors" and a "living lie." Then after the Chinese intervention, the House of Representatives passed a resolution calling for Acheson's impeachment.

On Tuesday, April 10, at 3:15 p.m., the same four top advisors reported to the Oval office where Truman signed the orders for MacArthur's recall. The orders were to be handed to MacArthur personally by Secretary of the Army, Frank Pace, in Tokyo. Pace, however, was with Ridgway in Korea and could not be quickly reached. The meticulously planned firing began to unravel.

Because of the delay in the transmittal of the orders, word of the firing was believed to have leaked out to the Press. The White House was worried that MacArthur would be tipped off by the Press and stage a grand resignation event before the orders reached him. As it turned out, MacArthur learned of his dismissal while having lunch in Tokyo on Wednesday, May 11, when his wife handed him a brown signal corps envelope containing the orders.

After the apparent press leak became known, Truman is reported to have said, "He's not going to be allowed to quit on me. He's going to be fired." [169] MacArthur is alleged to have said a few hours after receiving his recall orders that "if Truman had only let him know how he felt, he would have retired without difficulty." [170]

The order of April 10, 1951 relieved Douglas MacArthur of his command of all United Nations forces in Korea and named General Matthew B. Ridgway as his replacement. Accompanying the order was

---

[169] Ibid, p. 843.
[170] Ibid.

a terse message: "My reasons for your replacement will be made public concurrently with the delivery to you of the foregoing order."

Truman had seen a direct parallel between his intended recall of MacArthur and President Abraham Lincoln's removal of General George B. McClelland in 1862 as Commander-in-Chief of the Union Army of the Potomac. Before firing MacArthur, Truman had an aide bring him all available books and other research materials from the library on the Lincoln-McClelland affair.

Truman's research confirmed for him the key facts—that McClelland had shown no respect for Lincoln; that he openly spoke in a highly disparaging manner about the President; that he frequently snubbed him; that at times he refused to meet with him; that he disobeyed Lincoln's direct orders and that he made public statements on government policy directly opposed to the Administration's firm positions. After displaying great patience with McClelland, Lincoln finally felt that he had no choice other than to relieve him of his command.

Truman took solace from the fact that a great president, Abraham Lincoln, had handled a major conflict with his top general in the same manner as Truman had. Truman's inexhaustible patience gradually morphed into a hard resolve to do what was necessary in dealing with General MacArthur.

On April 11, 1951, the headline across the top of the front page of the *Washington Post* read, TRUMAN FIRES MACARTHUR. In one form or another, essentially the same headline appeared on page one of most daily newspapers across America and across the world. The Truman-MacArthur story would now enter its far more public and acrimonious stage.

The first phase of the crisis had coincided with a period in which Harry S. Truman had undergone some real emotional turmoil.

On December 4, 1950, Charlie Ross, Harry Truman's press secretary and life-long friend, had died suddenly and unexpectedly from a heart attack. The shock and grief sent Truman reeling. Shortly after Ross's death Truman wrote a belligerent letter to a music critic who had given a poor review to one of Margaret Truman's singing performances. There was little doubt that the combination of the shock of the Chinese intervention and his despondency over the death of Charlie Ross had left Truman in a depressed state. His bizarre reaction to his daughter's poor review did not go unnoticed by the press or public. A torrent of criticism over Truman's un-presidential behavior descended upon him, adding to the overall tension engendered by the war.

It was later suggested by Truman's critics that his state of mind in the wake of Charlie Ross's death and the Communist Chinese breakthrough had influenced his firing of MacArthur. The facts, however, simply do not support that theory. The recall of MacArthur was a process rather than a single incident—the culmination of a series of gradually escalating incidents which finally attained critical mass on April 10, 1951. It was also the unanimous decision of the President, Secretary of Defense, Secretary of State and Joint Chiefs of Staff. It was not an action which was the result of personal pique. Harry Truman endeavored mightily to remain calm and dispassionate and to discharge his constitutional duty, only after deep reflection and after an exhaustive study of the facts.

MacArthur's thoughts and feelings during the critical early months of 1951 are more difficult to read than Truman's. Truman left an extensive record through his letters to MacArthur and to the terminally ill Republican senator and statesman, Arthur Vandenberg; his diary entries; his remarks made during meetings with his top advisors and his contemporaneous conversations with his daughter, Margaret Truman, which were reported in her impressive biography of her father, entitled *Harry S. Truman*.

MacArthur left no such expansive contemporaneous record and his thought process is more opaque. But certain clear sign- posts do, to a certain extent, point the way to his state of mind. Ridgway's impressive progress in turning the tide in Korea did not seem to give MacArthur any satisfaction, but rather seemed to distress him even more. William Seybold, U.S. Ambassador to Japan, met with MacArthur frequently during the early months of 1951, finding him "tired and depressed"—voicing his distress over a "policy void" with respect to Communist aggression in Asia. MacArthur frequently expressed his wish for massive air attacks on Chinese transportation centers in Manchuria; and to sever Korea from Manchuria by laying down a field of radioactive waste all along the Yalu River. He also advocated a naval blockade of Chinese ports. These requests to Washington, like his other proposals to widen the war, were denied.

MacArthur-phobes have attributed shoddy motives to MacArthur for virtually everything he said during the incredible reversal of UN fortunes for the better from January through March, 1951. He was excoriated for being jealous of Ridgway's success, for wanting to upstage him, for wanting to undermine his efforts, plus other unflattering motives. Such criticism was and is based largely on circumstantial and non-conclusive evidence. It may or may not be true; or some of it may be true and the rest simply conjecture. What does seem clear, if for no other reason than its sheer consistency and repetition, was that MacArthur truly believed that it was necessary to widen the war with the Communists by exploiting America's one great advantage—its vastly superior air power and fire-power. His firmly-held views on global strategic policy were unalterably opposed to those of the White House. MacArthur's frame of mind would not allow him to even entertain the idea of an armistice in Korea. Inquiries by the President to MacArthur on the subject of possible peace talks during March of 1951 were simply ignored. MacArthur's grand strategic vision was leading him into one act of insubordination after another. Where his strategic concepts left off and his self-absorbed grandiosity took over is an interesting question for historians to ponder.

In briefing his White House staff that he might fire MacArthur, Truman added as almost an after-thought that he believed MacArthur wanted to be fired. Pure logic in a way seems to support this inference drawn by the President. MacArthur knew the rules of the game and how to shrewdly exploit them. His classic maneuver of President Herbert Hoover into a position in which he could not reprimand MacArthur over the 1932 Veterans' march debacle lest he contradict MacArthur's compliment of him as a savior of America, is one case in point. It strains credulity to think that MacArthur, brilliant in so many ways, did not realize that his constant tweaking of the nose of his Commander-in-Chief—his repeated insubordination—would not eventually get him fired. The only way he could not have known would have been if he had totally lost his grasp of reality—and if such were the case that alone would have required his dismissal.

What scant evidence there is, however, seems to lead to the conclusion that MacArthur had not completely lost touch with reality. He appears to have known the firing was coming. The day before his dismissal he met with General Ned Almond. As they parted MacArthur said, "I may not see you anymore, so good-bye Ned." Puzzled by this remark, Almond asked MacArthur what he meant. MacArthur's reply was, "I have become politically involved and may be relieved by the President." [171] Almond insisted that such a notion was absurd, but MacArthur was not dissuaded from his belief.

At about 1:00 a.m. on March 11, 1951, the following statement of the President was read to the assembled White House press corps:

---

[171] *The Coldest Winter*, op.cit., p. 606.

With deep regret, I have concluded that the General of the Army Douglas MacArthur is unable to give his wholehearted support to the policies of the United States government and of the United Nations in matters pertaining to his official duties. In view of the specific responsibilities imposed upon me by the Constitution of the United States and the added responsibility which has been entrusted to me by the United Nations, I have decided that I must make a change of command in the Far East. I have, therefore, relieved General MacArthur of his commands and have designated Lt. General Matthew B. Ridgway as his successor.

In Tokyo, MacArthur did not at first speak to the press about his recall. The first reaction from the Dai Ichi Building came from Major General Courtney Whitney, one of MacArthur's top aides, in a statement to the press, as follows:

I have just left him. He received the word of the president's dismissal from command magnificently. He never turned a hair. His soldierly qualities were never more pronounced—this has been his finest hour.

GENERAL HEADQUARTERS
FAR EAST COMMAND
OFFICE OF THE COMMANDER-IN-CHIEF

Tokyo, Japan

30 October 1950

Dear Mr. President:

I am most grateful for your kindly expressions which I have just received. Operations in Korea are proceeding according to plan and while as we draw close to the Manchurian border enemy resistance has somewhat stiffened, I do not think this represents a strong defense in depth such as would materially retard the achievement of our border objective. It is my current estimate that the next week or so should see us fairly well established in the border area, after which it shall be my purpose, as I outlined during the Wake Island conference, to withdraw American troops as rapidly as possible — this to the end that we may save our men from the rigors of winter climate at that northern latitude, and the Korean people from the undue impact of American troops upon the peaceful settlement of their internal affairs. For as you recognized during our conference on Wake, the political situation in Korea is both sensitive and explosive and calls for practical rather than idealistic diplomacy if our prestige and leadership gained through victory is to have a lasting hold upon the Oriental mind.

I left the Wake Island conference with a distinct sense of satisfaction that the country's interests had been well served through the better mutual understanding and exchange of views which it afforded. I hope that it will result in building a strong defense against future efforts of those who seek for one reason or another (none of them worthy) to breach the understanding between us.

With expressions of deep respect,

Most faithfully yours,

DOUGLAS MacARTHUR.

The Honorable Harry S. Truman
President, The United States of America
The White House
Washington 25, D.C.

Dear General MacArthur   The progress the forces under your command
have made since we met at Wake continues to be most
remarkable, and once again I offer you my hearty
congratulations. The military operations in Korea
under your command will have a most profound influence
for peace in the world.

                    Very sincerely yours,

                        Harry S. Truman"

                            Respectfully,

                        GEORGE M. ELSEY

PROPOSED MESSAGE FROM GENERAL MARSHALL TO SECRETARY PACE:

This message is in three parts.

Part I.   It is desired that you deliver in person, preferably at the Embassy, the following message to General MacArthur at 1000 hours, Thursday, Tokyo time. If on Thursday morning it appears that President's message cannot be delivered at that hour, you should send a flash message to the Secretary of Defense in order to control the release in Washington of the President's directive and statement:

Order to General MacArthur

"I deeply regret that it becomes my duty as President and Commander-in-Chief of the United States military forces to replace you as Supreme Commander Allied Powers; Commander-in-Chief, United Nations Command; Commander-in-Chief, Far East; and Commanding General, U. S. Army, Far East.

"You will turn over your commands, effective at once, to Lt. General Matthew B. Ridgway. You are authorized to have issued such orders as are necessary to complete desired travel to such place as you select.

"My reasons for your replacement, which will be made public concurrently with the delivery to you of the foregoing order, will be communicated to you by Secretary Pace."

Statement by the President

"With deep regret I have concluded that General of the Army Douglas MacArthur is unable to give his wholehearted support to the policies of the United States Government and of the United Nations in matters pertaining to his official duties. In view of the specific responsibilities imposed upon me by the Constitution of the United

States and the added responsibility which has been entrusted to
me by the United Nations, I have ~~completed~~ *decided* that I must make a
change of command in the Far East. I have, therefore, relieved
General MacArthur of his commands and have designated Lt. Gen.
Matthew B. Ridgway as his successor.

"Full and vigorous debate on matters of national policy
is a vital element in the constitutional system of our free democracy. It is fundamental, however, that military commanders ~~on
active duty~~ must be governed by the policies and directives issued
to them in the manner provided by our laws and Constitution. In
time of crisis, this consideration is particularly compelling.

"General MacArthur's place in history as one of our
greatest commanders is fully established. The nation owes him
a debt of gratitude for the distinguished and exceptional service
which he has rendered his country in posts of great responsibility.
For that reason I repeat my regret at the necessity for the action
I feel compelled to take in his case."

Part II. Deliver ~~in person and confidentially~~ *Have* the following ~~message~~ *order*
to General Ridgway ~~prior to your leaving Korea:~~ *as indicated
in part III following.*
"The President has decided to relieve General MacArthur
and appoint you as his successor as Supreme Commander, Allied
Powers; Commander-in-Chief, United Nations Command; Commander-in-Chief, Far East; and Commanding General, U.S. Army,
Far East.

"It is realized that your presence in Korea in the immediate
future is highly important, but we are sure you can make the proper

distribution of your time until you can turn over active command of the Eighth Army to its new commander. For this purpose, Lt. General James A. Van Fleet is enroute to report to you for such duties as you may direct."

Signed Marshall

Part III.   Leave Hull in Korea with arrangements for him to deliver orders to Ridgway immediately following your delivery of orders to General MacArthur.   Department of State desires that you deliver to General Ridgway, at time his orders are delivered to him, the copies of Mr. Foster Dulles' speeches which were furnished to you prior to leaving Washington.

DECLASSIFIED
E.O. 11652, Sec. 2(D) and 5(D)
WHITE HOUSE PRESS RELEASE 4/10/51
By NLT&C, NARS Date 3.7.75

PROPOSED ORDER TO GENERAL MacARTHUR TO BE SIGNED BY THE PRESIDENT

I deeply regret that it becomes my duty as President and Commander in Chief of the United States military forces to replace you as Supreme Commander, Allied Powers; Commander in Chief, United Nations Command; Commander in Chief, Far East; and Commanding General, U. S. Army, Far East.

You will turn over your commands, effective at once, to Lt. Gen. Matthew B. Ridgway. You are authorized to have issued such orders as are necessary to complete desired travel to such place as you select.

My reasons for your replacement, ~~which~~ will be made public concurrently with the delivery to you of the foregoing order, ~~will be communicated to you by Secretary Pace.~~ *and are contained in the next following message.*

Harry Truman

Chapter 11

The Aftermath

They have sown the wind, and they shall reap the whirlwind.
—Bible, Hosea 8;7

THE uproar triggered by MacArthur's dismissal was phenomenal, the public outcry unprecedented. The President and his inner circle of advisors knew they would face a storm of protest but no one could have anticipated the volcanic eruption of indignation which extended across the entire nation—much of it hysterical and even potentially violent.

April 12, 1951 was one of the bitterest days in the history of the United States Congress. Calls for the impeachment of the president were heard everywhere among Republican members of the House and Senate. Even the dignified and usually statesmanlike, Senator Robert Taft of Ohio, spoke with anger of impeaching President Truman.

At 9:30 a.m. an emergency meeting was held by the full Republican leadership, after which representative Joseph Martin of Massachusetts spoke to the press about impeachments, plural; and solemnly announced that General MacArthur would be invited to voice his views on the situation before a special joint session of Congress.

Senator Joseph McCarthy of Wisconsin accused Truman of being drunk when he decided to remove MacArthur; and Senator Richard M. Nixon of California demanded his immediate reinstatement.

Senator William E. Jenner of Indiana shouted on the floor of the Senate, "I charge that this country today is in the hands of a secret inner coterie which is directed by agents of the Soviet Union. Our only choice is to impeach President Truman and find out who is the secret invisible government which has so cleverly led our country down the road to destruction." Jenner's frenzied exhortation was greeted by tumultuous applause. Another legislator was so carried away with bombast that he declared the general's dismissal "another Pearl Harbor, a great day for the Russian Communists." MacArthur had been fired "because he told the truth" said Senator James P. Kerr, Republican of Missouri,—"God help the United States."

A Democrat from Oklahoma, however, Senator Robert Kerr, rose in defense of the President. "If the Republicans believed the nation's security depended on following the policy of General MacArthur,...they should call for the declaration of war against Red China. Otherwise Republican support of MacArthur was a mockery." [172] And some Republican senators reminded their colleagues that "Americans had always insisted on civilian control over the military. But such voices were lost in a tempest of Republican outrage." [173]

A Gallup Poll reported public opinion in favor of MacArthur over Truman, 69% to 29%.

Truman and Acheson were burned in effigy in towns and cities across the country and even on some college campuses.

In New York City, 2000 longshoremen walked off their jobs to protest the firing and enraged citizens lowered flags to half mast or flew them upside down.

Petitions condemning Truman's action were circulated and signed everywhere. The White House, the Pentagon, the State Department and Congress were bombarded with irate letters and telegrams. Western Union messengers made their deliveries in bushel baskets. Of the 44,358 telegrams received by Republicans during the first 48 hours following the announcement of the dismissal, all but 334 either condemned Truman or took MacArthur's side. The majority of the telegrams called for Truman's immediate removal from office.

Fights broke out "in bars between strangers and on commuter trains between friends." [174]

Former President Herbert Hoover exuberantly called MacArthur "the reincarnation of St. Paul into the persona of a great General of the Army who had come out of the east." [175]

The state legislatures of Florida, Illinois, California and Michigan passed resolutions condemning Truman's action. The Los Angeles City Council adjourned for a day of "sorrowful contemplation of the political assassination of General MacArthur."

"Impeach the Imbecile," "Impeach the Little Ward Politician from Kansas City" [176] were typical of telegrams inundating Washington.

---

172 *Truman*, op.cit., p. 844.
173 Ibid.
174 *The Coldest Winter*, op.cit., p. 608.
175 Ibid.
176 *Truman*, op.cit., p. 845.

In his calendar, President Truman laconically wrote, "Quite an explosion. Was expected but I had to act. Telegrams and letters of abuse by the dozens." [177]

Some newspapers and magazines were no less harsh. A front-page editorial of the *Chicago Tribune* read:

> President Truman must be impeached and convicted. His hasty and vindictive removal of General MacArthur is the culmination of a series of acts which have shown that he is unfit, morally and mentally, for his high office. The American nation has never been in greater danger. It is led by a fool surrounded by knaves...

Time Magazine reported that "seldom has a more unpopular man fired a more popular one ... the personification of the big man with the many admirers who look to a great man for leadership ... Truman was almost a professional little man."

MacArthur had been cast as both hero and martyr. Truman had been branded as the villain of the piece.

MacArthur said nothing at first. He never really expressed the full depth of his feeling about his dismissal until he finally gave voice to his ire in his memoirs, *Reminiscences*, writing that his firing was a vengeful reprisal by his enemies. "No office boy, no charwoman, no servant of any sort would have been dismissed with such callous disregard for the ordinary decencies," MacArthur wrote about the aborted attempt to have Army Secretary Pace deliver the recall order to him personally. "So drastic" was his dismissal wrote MacArthur, "as to prevent the usual amenities incident to a transfer of command and practically placed me under duress." [178]

Just as Truman and his advisers had underestimated the tumult MacArthur's firing would cause, the general greatly underestimated the extent to which he would be greeted as a conquering hero.

When he first read the order of his dismissal MacArthur said to his wife, "Jeannie, we're going home." [179] He had not been back to the United States since 1935 and was leery of the type of reception he would receive under the current circumstances. Believing that his fellow countrymen might receive him with indifference or even hostility,

---

[177] *Harry S. Truman*, op.cit., p. 515.
[178] *Reminiscences*, op.cit., p. 395.
[179] *Taking Command*, op.cit., p. 270.

MacArthur ordered his aides to schedule the flights home so that he would arrive in San Francisco at night. "We'll just slip into San Francisco after dark while everyone's at dinner or the movies," [180] said MacArthur. He clearly had no idea of the phenomenon which awaited him, in which he was about to play the central role. It started in Tokyo where 250,000 adoring Japanese, many of them in tears, most of them waving small American and Japanese flags, lined both sides of the street. [181]

It continued in Honolulu, Hawaii—where World War II started—after MacArthur's plane, "Bataan" touched down after midnight—there he was met by huge cheering crowds. The throngs were even greater in San Francisco when he again landed after midnight. So immense and tumultuous was the crowd that the security men could not contain it. Those gathered were unrestrained in their spontaneous outpouring of adulation.

In New York, seven million people turned out for a ticker-tape parade, stretching from the tip of the battery to mid-town, larger even than the one for General Dwight D. Eisenhower when he returned home after the Allies victory in World War II. Amid ticker-tape, confetti and flags, a nascent MacArthur for President movement began to stir, but never quite took hold across the country.

MacArthur had enthusiastically accepted Martin's invitation to address Congress. When he reached Washington, D.C., the hero's welcome continued unabated. Truman ordered the Joint Chiefs of Staff to give MacArthur full military honors and they were all on hand to meet him with salutes and handshakes. The President declared that all government employees were to have the day off. An enormous cheering crowd lined the way to the capitol building. In schools across the country, classes were suspended and students gathered in assembly halls to watch MacArthur's speech on television—a speech which would have the largest audience in television's short history. Television cameras of every network were on hand in the galleries above the House floor where a joint session of Congress would hear MacArthur's peroration.

Even before MacArthur's famous address to Congress, however, cracks in the wall of the nation-wide groundswell of support for MacArthur began to appear. It was true that Truman's firing of MacArthur was the most unpopular decision of his presidency—two-thirds of the

---

180 *War Letters*, op.cit., p. 50.
181 *The Coldest Winter*, op.cit., p. 607.

American public disapproved. But many influential voices, thus far muted, felt that Truman had done the right thing—and typical of those voices was that of General Eisenhower. [182]

Although Eisenhower greeted the news of MacArthur's dismissal with doubt, shock and dismay, he knew that Truman's decision was correct; but with one eye on the 1952 presidential election, "he refused to comment on the firing..." [183]

Equally significant was the fact that the majority of newspaper editorials in America supported Truman's discharge of MacArthur—even some staunch Republican papers such as the DesMoines Register and Tribune and the New York Herald Tribune. Notably, the Herald Tribune went out of its way to praise Truman for his strength of character; and added:

> The most obvious fact about the dismissal of General MacArthur is that he virtually forced his own removal...In high policy as in war there is no room for a divided command...he is the architect of a situation which really left the President with no other course.

But the political firestorm continued. In the first week after the dismissal of the iconic five star general, he pretty much had it his way. It was as if MacArthur had been lifted up by his countrymen and gently submerged in a luxuriant bath of praise and adoration, worthy of a triumphant Olympian of ancient Sparta. The culmination was the powerful speech MacArthur delivered to a packed joint session of Congress. MacArthur's impressive oratorical skills more than carried the day.

After first strongly defending his conviction that wars must be fought to win, that there was no substitute for victory and that he had been a bastion against those who would appease our enemies, he argued that defeatism and appeasement "but begets new and bloodier war."

MacArthur then elevated the emotional content of his rhetoric to a crescendo of bathos and drama seldom reached before in American political history. It was a virtuoso performance and earned him thunderous applause:

---

[182] *Harry and Ike*, op.cit., p. 214.
[183] *Ike*, by Michael Korda (Harper Collins, 2007) p. 629.

I am closing my fifty-two years of military service. When I joined the Army, even before the turn of the century, it was the fulfillment of all my boyish hopes and dreams. The world has turned over many times since I took the oath on the Plain at West Point, and the hopes and dreams have long since vanished. But I still remember the refrain of one of the more popular barrack ballads of the day, which proclaimed, most proudly, that Old ___ soldiers never die. They just fade away.

And like the old soldier of that ballad, I now close my military career and just fade away ____ an old soldier who tried to do his duty as God gave him the light to see that duty.

But MacArthur had no intention of fading away. He next embarked on a national speaking tour during which he became more and more critical of Truman's foreign policy with each stop. It had all the earmarks of a political campaign; and with the beginning of a presidential election year only eight months away, it may very well have been MacArthur's last gambit for the fulfillment of his presidential aspirations. His popularity was at its pinnacle; yet, still there were disquieting signs which rudely intruded upon the nation-wide celebration by MacArthur's supporters.

Truman had predicted before the firing that if his Administration could just ride out the storm, history would eventually vindicate him. Also, MacArthur's high-handed treatment of Dwight D. Eisenhower back in their pre-World War II Manila days ("the best damned clerk I ever had") certainly ensured that they would never be friends, even though on the surface they maintained a collegial relationship. The fact that they were also potential rivals for the 1952 Republican nomination for president further discouraged any support by Eisenhower for MacArthur. In most ways, Eisenhower was as big a hero in the eyes of the public as MacArthur, and a visible expression of support would have helped MacArthur maintain his aura. But Eisenhower was essentially an honest man and was not about to endorse something he thought was wrong. To an aide, he privately expressed his opinion with typical Eisenhower understatement and restraint:

You know when you put on a uniform, you impose certain restrictions on yourself. MacArthur may have forgotten them. [184]

---

[184] *Harry and Ike*, op.cit.

Eisenhower was disturbed by the shrill hyperbole being employed by MacArthur, believing it to be inappropriate for a five star general and a poor reflection on the U.S. military. He confided to a friend that MacArthur "now as always" was "an opportunist seeking to ride the crest of a wave." [185]

Then there was the question of America's NATO allies. Without exception, Europe considered MacArthur's dismissal as welcome news.

MacArthur's ardent supporters championed both their man and his cause with fervor and passion. But there was no lack of passion for the President by those who thought he was in the right—who believed that at stake was a bedrock principle. One of those persons was the Reverend Dr. Duncan E. Littlefair, the pastor of a Baptist church in Grand Rapids, Michigan, who delivered a sermon which cut through all the vitriol and overblown rhetoric to the heart of the matter:

> It makes not the slightest difference that we like him [MacArthur] better than we do Harry S. Truman. Principle, principle, must always be above personality and it must be above expediency. The principle here we recognize ... [is] that control of this country must come through the president and the departments that are organized under him through Congress ... nor is it to be overridden because we have a conquering hero.

From the moment MacArthur had touched down in Honolulu on his triumphant return to the United States, the Democrats in the White House and Congress had been on the defensive, simply trying to avoid being engulfed by the tidal wave of sentiment for MacArthur and against the President. But this was only temporary and soon they began to regroup and stage a counterattack. The first step by the White House was to release a transcript of the minutes taken of the Wake Island conference. At Wake Island, MacArthur had assured Truman and his party that Red China would not enter the war. Once back on American soil, MacArthur compounded his earlier rash prediction by denying that he ever said it in the first place. The reports of his prediction were, according to MacArthur, "Entirely without foundation." The White House, having caught MacArthur in an untruthful assertion, leaked the Wake Island transcript to Tony Leviero, a Washington beat reporter with the New York Times. The Times published it as an exposé and the following year Leviero won the Pulitzer Prize for his

---

[185]   Ibid, p. 215.

investigative reporting. Some of MacArthur's luster had been dulled by the revelations of his Wake Island predictions.

The tension engendered by the charges and counter-charges would build to a climactic showdown in the Senate hearings on MacArthur's dismissal.

No member of the Democratic majority wanted to preside over the hearings. The atmosphere promised to be super-charged with emotion, hype and controversy. The proceedings had the potential to be incendiary and politically dangerous for any politician too closely identified with them. It ultimately fell to Senator Richard Russell, the distinguished senior senator from Georgia and chairman of the Armed Services Committee, to chair the proceedings. Russell did not need to be concerned about the hearings killing any chance he might have in the future for the presidency because, as a staunch segregationist, he would never be able to secure the nomination of the Democratic party anyway.

Russell, as a man of old-fashioned rectitude and integrity, had the full respect of his peers in congress on both sides of the aisle. He was the logical choice for the unenviable position of chairman of the proceedings. The MacArthur Committee was a joint one which combined the Armed Services and Foreign Relations Committees.

Russell put his analytical mind and astute political instincts to work in devising a way of eliminating the circus atmosphere and sensationalism from the hearings. He wished "to marginalize the head-line hunting." [186] He solved that problem by decreeing that the hearings would not be covered live by radio or television. There would be no press or cameras in the hearing room either. He had the perfect rationale for his decision because the nation was at war and the testimony and evidence produced at the hearings would necessarily involve classified and other sensitive information concerning military operations and capabilities in Korea. Yet the hearings were of enormous interest to the public, who clearly had the right to know what was being said. Russell's solution was to have verbatim transcripts of the hearings prepared each day but then for reasons of national security, edited by a special military-civilian committee each night who would redact any sensitive material before their release to the public. It was an ingenious idea which allowed him to make the hearings both private and public at the same time.

---

[186] *The Coldest Winter*, op.cit., p. 611.

The next challenge Russell faced was the need to remove some of the passion from the deliberations so that a greater focus could be placed on the substance of the issues before the committee. To deal with this problem Russell decided to slow-down the entire process—by making it as deliberate and meticulously well-prepared as possible. The Republicans believed that Truman and his team were overmatched by MacArthur and wanted the hearings to be an extension of the momentum which MacArthur and his allies had created. They would serve as the ultimate forum for MacArthur to use his popularity and oratory to vanquish Truman and the Democrats—and thereby score a decisive triumph. But, Russell prevailed by delaying the commencement of the hearings and dictating a slow and deliberate pace. The hearings did not start until May 3, 1951 and continued for seven weeks.

MacArthur was the first witness and testified for three days. The committee, including the chairman, treated him with great deference and unfailing courtesy but the momentum of the "Old Soldiers Never Die" speech did not carry over into the hearing room. This was partly due to the procedural rules imposed by Russell but was mainly because of the formal and structured nature of the hearings themselves. The general had to sit and answer questions, not make speeches. It was a role he was totally unaccustomed to. He couldn't sit back as he did in unveiling the Inchon plan to Collins, Sherman and the staffers present, puff on his corn-cob pipe, listen to the naysayers calmly and then in a burst of brilliant oratory rebut all objections to carry the day. MacArthur found himself in an uncomfortable role. The general was used to asking questions, not answering them.

MacArthur brought with him into the hearings a major chink in his armor, of which few, if any, of his backers were aware. Upon returning home, he repeatedly claimed that he had the backing of the Joint Chiefs of Staff for the strategy he espoused and the decisions he had made. He may have actually thought that was the case but it was not. MacArthur had consistently throughout the Korean hostilities treated the Chiefs dismissively. He had disobeyed their directives and disrespected their authority. He also loudly and disdainfully criticized them to other military officials on many occasions. Like in most controlled institutions, in the military, gossip is the main source of information. The army was notorious for being a big gossip mill and the criticism got back to the Joint Chiefs. When the hearings started on May 3, MacArthur had burned his bridges behind him with the one group who should have been his supportive peer group—the military hierarchy. The Chiefs and their respective staffs believed that MacArthur had treated them with contempt and their resentment burned deep. Placing the unpopular General Edward Almond in charge of X Corps truly rankled and "symbolized his contempt for them." [187] MacArthur also had very little support among the younger group of officers in the Pentagon, many of whom had lost good friends at places like Kunuri and Chosin Reservoir. They were irate over the general's flouting of his orders and refusing to accept any responsibility for the unmitigated disaster of the Chinese intervention. This well-informed and technically knowledgeable group of officers willingly provided invaluable information to committee investigators.

MacArthur's charm and eloquence did not avail him during his testimony. The entire underlying premise for MacArthur's challenge to his superiors was that he was the vastly more knowledgeable and experienced military strategist and they were mere narrow-thinking second-raters. But unless that premise was rock-solid, MacArthur was in trouble. No man, and certainly no military man, could constantly buck the chain of command and be consistently insubordinate unless first, the issues concerned grave matters of life and death on a macro-scale and; second, he was completely right. The hearings, however, would demonstrate that MacArthur's aura of invincibility could not hold up under close scrutiny and that the underlying premise for his contrarian views contained a deep fault-line.

MacArthur didn't necessarily have to break new ground by his testimony but he at least had to maintain his credibility as a wise leader and an exceptional global strategist. Instead, he was the one who came across as pedestrian, disengaged and short-sighted.

When Democratic Senator Brien McMahon of Connecticut asked MacArthur about the risk a full-scale war against China would pose for the NATO countries under the threat of Russian aggression in Europe, MacArthur answered that he was only a theater commander and the Russian threat was not his responsibility. But wasn't that the crux of the problem? queried McMahon. The President had to carefully weigh how expanded military action in Asia might affect the entire world. He did have that responsibility. MacArthur answered McMahon's query by asserting that the Russians would not come in. But McMahon was not about to be put off. "But what if you are wrong?" [188] he pointedly asked MacArthur. Hadn't MacArthur also believed that Red China would not enter the war? "I doubted [their entry]," replied MacAr-

---

[187] *The Coldest Winter*, op.cit., p. 613.
[188] *The Coldest Winter*, op.cit., p. 614.

thur, [189] a damaging admission. Then he made it even worse by admonishing McMahon: "I have asked you several times not to involve me in anything except my own area... I don't pretend to be the authority now on those things." [190] MacArthur was almost making the President's case for him. Surely at this point the wily old general—the veteran of countless battles—knew that he had been forced over onto the defensive.

Momentum began to swing in favor of the Democrats. The major turning point was the testimony of Marshall, Bradley and the Joint Chiefs. Secretary of Defense Marshall was particularly impressive. He carefully made the case that the so-called dichotomy between MacArthur's and Truman's ideologies was greatly exaggerated. The differences between MacArthur and the Truman Administration were far more mundane than that—"a split between a theater commander with limited responsibilities" and a world leader with global responsibilities, whose orders were not those he would have written for himself if he were not so burdened by such broad obligations. Marshall testified that

> There is nothing new in this divergence in our military history. What is new and brought about the necessity for General MacArthur's removal is the wholly unprecedented situation of a local theater commander publicly expressing his displeasure at, and his disagreement with, the foreign policy of the United States.

Marshall had made a cogent point from the standpoint of both policy and politics. Like most human drama, the Truman-MacArthur controversy depended for its continued vitality on clearly defined heroes and villains—wrongheaded little man versus big man of great vision. Marshall had redefined the conflict. It wasn't really about ideology at all, but rather the encroachment of a military leader upon the constitutional prerogatives of the President. By altering the contours of the dispute, Marshall had drained it of much of its dramatic power.

Unlike Marshall and Acheson who had been targets for aspersions cast as a result of the gains of international Communism since the end of World War II, General Omar Bradley had managed to fly under the radar. But now as Chairman of the Joint Chiefs of Staff he was deeply immersed in the Truman-MacArthur controversy. His image had been

---

[189]   Ibid.

[190]   Ibid, p. 615.

that of a professional soldier and World War II hero above the fray of politics, and he could have simply rested on his laurels by giving innocuous testimony. Bradley, however, chose to voice his opinions without restraint. He testified before the joint committee that General MacArthur's "ideas on widening the [Korean] conflict would involve us in the wrong war, at the wrong place, at the wrong time and with the wrong enemy." [191]

And so it went. General Hoyt Vandenberg, Chief of Staff of the Air Force, told Congress that bombing Manchuria, as MacArthur advocated, would be no more than "pecking at the periphery" and that the losses the United States would sustain in men and planes would cripple the Air Force for years to come. U.S. airpower would be so depleted as to prevent us from meeting our defense imperatives at home and in other areas of the globe.

General J. Lawton Collins, was an under-rated World War II Commander, who had acquitted himself with great distinction at Guadalcanal, as Commander of VII Corps in Europe, as one of chief planners for D-Day, as commander of all American troops at Utah Beach, as a victorious American commander in Normandy and as a leader of the counterattack against the Germans at the Battle of the Bulge. He had been one rung above MacArthur in the chain of command during the Korean conflict, as Army Chief of Staff. This was a technicality to which MacArthur paid not even lip service. Collins testified in a soft Louisiana accent which made his testimony to the committee all the more damning. General MacArthur, said Collins, had violated almost every basic rule of military strategy by launching his entire army towards the Yalu River, knowing that the danger of massive Red Chinese intervention was very real.

Chief of Staff of the Navy, Admiral Forest Sherman "heaped scorn on MacArthur's proposal for a naval blockade of China, "unless the fleets of our allies joined us?" [192] The one ally whose participation in such a blockade would be absolutely essential to its success was Great Britain; and it was inconceivable that Britain would join the blockade since it would mean choking off the British crown colony of Hong Kong.

MacArthur had picked up no support from the Joint Chiefs of Staff and after seven weeks of hearings, the demythologizing of Douglas MacArthur was complete. The hearings had diminished MacAr-

---

[191]   *Harry S. Truman*, op.cit., p. 517.
[192]   *Harry S. Truman*, op.cit., p. 517.

thur's standing in the country and destroyed his chances of ever becoming President. The hearing's conclusion marked the end of both MacArthur's military and political careers.

The firing of MacArthur had also taken a heavy toll politically on Harry S. Truman. If he still entertained any thoughts of running for a second full term as President, he quickly banished such thoughts. There were great pockets of resentment and dislike for Truman all across America. With the 1952 presidential election only 16 months away, there was simply not enough time to rehabilitate his image. Truman, however, had accomplished a great deal. He had preserved for posterity the principle of civilian control over the military and had, in the process, added significantly to his legacy. Historians would be kind to Harry S. Truman and he is now recognized as one of America's greatest presidents.

With the overwhelming media attention given to the Truman-MacArthur story from April 11 until the end of July, it was too easy to forget that in Korea there were also momentous events occurring. Ridgway's all-out push to the 38th Parallel had once again liberated Seoul and inflicted heavy punishment on the Chinese. As Collins pointed out, Ridgway made no grandiose promises of conquering large swaths of territory. "He did not care about real estate," said Collins, "he wanted Chinese bodies." [193] Ridgway got them and by the time of MacArthur's dismissal on April 11, the Communist Chinese forces had suffered staggering losses. But, they were tough and resilient, and had an unlimited supply of reinforcements. Only 11 days later on April 22, Red China launched its "Spring Offensive."

Now, as the Commander of all United Nations forces in Korea, Ridgway wanted to establish a permanent line of defense just north of Seoul. A key aspect of his plan was to occupy only highly defensible positions—preferably on high ground. He did not want the North Koreans or Chinese to ever again be able to easily roll into South Korean territory.

Inspired by Ridgway's leadership and success, the morale of the troops was high, including those of some of our staunchest allies—Canada, Great Britain, Australia, the Netherlands, France and Turkey. All along the 38th Parallel the UN allies had dug into fixed positions. But as they soon learned, these positions were not impregnable.

On April 22, 1951 the Chinese Third Army, composed of hundreds of thousands of troops, attacked along the banks of the Imjin

---

[193] *Taking Command*, op.cit., p. 265.

River northwest of Seoul; their objective being, as always—demolish the United Nations Army.

In one of the most valiant defensive stands of the Korean War, the British 29th Brigade defended both the bridge over the Imjin and the thirty mile track from there to Seoul. They fought under the command of British General Tom Brodie who in turn fell under the overall command of the U.S. Third Army. The stand-off became known as the Battle of Imjin River.

The 29th Brigade heroically held back wave upon wave of attacking Chinese along the Imjin River; and particularly at the Battle of Gloster Hill where the Gloucestershire Regiment (750 strong) held off three Chinese Divisions (27,000 troops) for four days, until the Brits were so decimated that they were forced to abandon their position and withdraw. Outmanned by 27 to 1, they stubbornly held out for far longer than anyone could have expected and bought valuable time for central command and for many individual UN units, allowing them to reinforce and solidify their positions.

All along the 38th Parallel units of the Ridgway's forces repulsed one Chinese attack after another. The Spring Offensive soon ground to a halt and both armies settled into a stalemate along the same line of demarcation which separated North Korea from South Korea before the war began.

On June 23, Jacob Malik, the Soviet Union's Ambassador to the United Nations, announced that peace could be negotiated in Korea. Three days later the Communist Chinese government followed suit with an identical announcement.

The enemy had held out an olive branch and Truman, feeling that a fragile equilibrium had been restored on the battlefield, responded in kind by ordering General Ridgway to communicate with the high command of the Chinese forces in Korea to inform them that the United Nations would be willing to send envoys to Korea to begin discussions of an armistice. The Chinese accepted Truman's overture and both sides sent negotiating teams to open talks, which officially began on July 10, 1951 at Kaesong.

By the time peace talks got underway, Truman and MacArthur, who had at the start of the war been reluctant partners for a common cause, no longer spoke to one another. Their relationship, never more than a fragile one, was now hostile—a bitter estrangement which would continue for the remainder of their lives. Yet each of them had left his unique imprint on a period of world history when the tensions of the Cold War—a potentially cataclysmic global duel—flared into open and deadly hostilities. Over two million people were killed in the Korean War. It was part of a deadly and dangerous era, but one which might have been far, far worse had both Truman and MacArthur not been there.

Korea was the first conflict where a single misstep could have triggered a nuclear holocaust. The schism between Truman and MacArthur was more than a clash of personalities, egos and ideologies. It was also the opening round in a power-struggle between the civilian and military authorities of America which is still going on today. The nuclear age changed the rules. During the Cold War, the vast power which had been previously wielded by an Eisenhower in the Atlantic and by a MacArthur in the Pacific during World War II, was a thing of the past. When he left office as President, Eisenhower warned the nation to be careful to curb the power of what he referred to as the "military-industrial complex." The more deadly the weapon system, the more money there was to be made. The Pentagon-Defense Industry partnership required vigilant presidential oversight.

John F. Kennedy was fond of saying that war is too serious a business to leave to the generals. During the Cuban Missile crisis he preempted his generals and admirals and managed the nuclear show-down himself, mainly with the assistance of his brother, Robert Kennedy, the Attorney General at the time, and Secretary of Defense, Robert McNamara. President Lyndon Johnson seized full control of the conduct of the Vietnam War and rejected all suggestions by the military to employ tactical nuclear weapons. Equally firm control of the Vietnam War was later wielded by the tandem of Nixon and Kissinger.

The Korean War was one which could not be run by the generals, due to its potential for global nuclear war.

Of course, there have always been major policy and political influences in all wars but Korea was the first one where global political considerations took over completely and overrode all others.

U.S. negotiators were constrained in talking to their North Korean counterparts by the fact that those negotiators were receiving their orders from Peking, which at least to a certain extent was receiving directions from the Kremlin in Moscow. Ridgway's forces operated under the UN banner, another layer of constraint. The global political factors were further complicated by the nuclear dimension. No one wanted to trigger World War III, so caution ruled.

The battlefield settled into a stalemate which lasted for two years after the commencement of talks, during which time the parties dickered over the shape of the conference table, over which hill near the

38th Parallel would be Communist-controlled and which would be controlled by the U.S. They squabbled over how to release prisoners of war on both sides, particularly when thousands of Chinese and North Korean prisoners of war did not want to go home. Then there were South Korean president Syngman Rhee and North Korean president Kim Il-Sung, who often conducted themselves as if they didn't really want peace at all.

But, finally on July 25, 1953, after Truman was out of office, Stalin was dead, Dwight D. Eisenhower was the new American president and John Foster Dulles the new Secretary of State, a cease fire was attained ending all hostilities. A true peace treaty, however, was never achieved and today, sixty years after the North Koreans crossed the 38th Parallel into South Korea, a state of war still exists between the two nations; and United States troops still guard the 38th Parallel.

The Korean War has been referred to as "the forgotten war." It was fought at the beginning of a decade in which Americans turned their sights, perhaps as never before, to the acquisition of material goods, and the joys of peace and prosperity that only living in the richest nation on earth could provide. Americans were tired of war. They wanted to give their full attention to peaceful pursuits—even if that meant living in a state of mass denial of the nuclear cloud hanging over their heads. They hated the Korean War. It was an unwanted distraction in the quest for personal enrichment. It was also nasty, brutal, cruel, demoralizing, frustrating and incapable of being nicely wrapped in a neat abstraction, such as patriotism. It was emotionally unsatisfying in that it never produced the clear-cut victory Americans were so used to having.

Historically, the Korean War was of enormous significance. It was not an internal revolution in which the super-powers flocked to support opposite sides. North Korea was in every respect a satellite nation of the Soviet Union, and Kim Il-Sung was Stalin's hand-picked dictator. Even today, sixty years later, North Korea is a closed society with an extreme Marxist government. The Korean War, no matter what else it was, was truly a war between the super-powers—the United States and the Soviet Union. For three years, the Cold War turned hot and each super-power had enormous stakes in its outcome. The fact that it ended in a stalemate allowed each nation to turn its attention to other key battle grounds and conflicts of the Cold War—Berlin, Southeast Asia, NATO, the Warsaw Pact, the arms race, Hungary, Cuba, leftist insurgencies in Africa and the Americas, Poland, Czechoslovakia, sophisticated surveillance systems, the proliferation of offensive nuclear missiles and missile defense systems, including the uses of outer space to gain a military advantage.

The Korean War produced thousands of unsung heroes and one extraordinary military performance, Matthew B. Ridgway's turning of a massive retreat into a brilliant and inspired counter-offensive which propelled UN forces all the way from the Naktong River to north of the 38th Parallel in a period of two and a half months. It was a singular feat comparable to Grant's western campaign and Patton's drive to the Rhine; but today the mention of the name Matthew B. Ridgway evokes only a vague recollection from the same Americans who recognize Eisenhower, Patton and Grant as larger-than-life heroes. Ridgway's great misfortune was that he was an extraordinary hero of a forgotten war which ended in a stalemate.

Epilogue

The way to win an atomic war is to make certain it never starts.
—General Omar Bradley

STALEMATE (JULY 1951–JULY 1953)

WITH negotiations in full swing, the war continued with little new territory either won or lost. As the negotiators worked towards an armistice, both sides sought victories in the field which would strengthen the hand of their respective negotiating teams. If one side or the other could firmly secure a hill, a ridge or a river, they could then argue *fait accompli* at the bargaining table. Examples of such politically strategic battles included the Battle of Bloody Ridge (August 18—September 15, 1951), the Battle of Heartbreak Ridge (September 13—October 15, 1951), the Battle of Old Baldy (June 26 to August 4, 1952), the Battle of Triangle Hill (October 14 to November 25, 1952), the Battle of the Hook (May 28-29, 1953) and the Battle of Pork Chop Hill (March 23 to July 16, 1953).

The negotiations dragged on for two years—first at Kaesong in southern North Korea and eventually at Panmunjon on the border. A major stumbling block to an armistice was prisoner of war (P.O.W.) repatriation. Chinese, North Korean and UN negotiators agreed to "voluntary repatriation" conditional upon most POWs held by UN countries returning to either China or North Korea. The problem was that many Chinese and North Korean POWs refused repatriation. The hostilities continued until finally the Chinese and North Koreans dropped their demand and allowed their POWs the choice of whether or not to return.

The United States in October 1951 began operations to test the use of tactical nuclear weapons on the battlefield against the enemy's army. The conclusion drawn from the test bombing runs was that atomic bombs would be ineffective against massed infantry. What psychological impact, however, the testing had on the negotiations is another matter.

On November 29, 1952 U.S. President-elect Dwight D. Eisenhower went to Korea on a fact-finding trip to attempt to learn what might bring about an end to the Korean War. Anecdotal information exists that he let it be known to the Communists that if a negotiated peace could not be achieved, he would have to use his nuclear option.

Ultimately, the United Nations accepted India's proposal for an armistice. A cease fire was effected on July 27, 1953, with the line of demarcation between North Korea and South Korea drawn at about the 38th Parallel. A demilitarized zone was established located on both sides of the Parallel. The Armistice agreement was signed by the United States and North Korea. Syngman Rhee refused to sign it, thereby preventing South Korea from being a party to the armistice, even to this day.

Douglas MacArthur

"If Washington will not hobble me, I can handle it (the North Korean invasion of June, 1950) with one arm tied behind my back," boasted MacArthur shortly after the June 25, 1950 attack. Obviously, things did not work out for MacArthur the way he hoped. Korea humbled him greatly after first serving as the venue for one of his greatest triumphs—the Inchon Landing.

After the sobering Congressional hearings of May, 1951, talk of a MacArthur run for the presidency died down. He was 71 years old and would frequently tell friends that he was too old to run for president. In the 1952 Republican candidate-selection process, MacArthur did not put himself forth as a candidate and instead endorsed Senator Robert Taft of Ohio for President. MacArthur did deliver the key note speech at the Republican National Convention, which received mixed reviews. After Taft lost the nomination to Eisenhower, MacArthur sat out the election without publicly supporting Eisenhower. Eisenhower, however, is reported to have consulted with MacArthur on the Korean War and to have adopted his suggestion of threatening China and North Korea with the use of nuclear weapons if they would not agree to end the war.

During the Eisenhower years, MacArthur left Washington to head up the Remington Rand Corporation. He and his wife, Jean, moved into a penthouse of the Waldorf Towers in Manhattan, where they lived for the rest of their years together.

By his 80th birthday, MacArthur's health was deteriorating and he began to pay more attention to unfinished personal business. A visit to the White House for a reunion with Eisenhower was followed by a "sentimental journey" to the Philippines where he accepted the Philippine Legion of Honor rank of Chief Commander from President Carlos P. Garcia. Most notably he began writing his long overdue memoirs, which he entitled *Reminiscences*, after receiving a $900,000 advance from publisher, Henry Luce.

Following the fiasco of the Bay of Pigs invasion in early 1961, President John F. Kennedy held two meetings with MacArthur to seek his military counsel. Staying completely in character, the old general was extremely critical of the Pentagon and its military advice to the new president. MacArthur cautioned Kennedy to avoid a U.S. military build-up in Vietnam. There were far more urgent domestic problems which required the president's attention, said MacArthur. He later gave the same advice to President Lyndon B. Johnson.

In 1962, the U.S. Military Academy at West Point honored MacArthur with the Sylvanus Thayer Award for outstanding service to the nation. MacArthur made the trip to West Point in 1962 to accept the award, and addressed the corps of cadets on the plains of West Point with a speech which had as its theme, *Duty, Honor and Country*.

MacArthur's West Point speech proved once again his mastery of the spoken word. The speech soared on wings of eloquence and poetry—majestic in its power to touch the human heart with nostalgia while at the same time inspiring the young cadets to climb to new heights of duty and sacrifice. In its most memorable passage, the audience heard MacArthur intone these emotion-laden words:

> The shadows are lengthening for me. The twilight is here. My days of old have vanished, tone and tint. They have gone glimmering through the dreams of things that were. Their memory is one of wondrous beauty, watered by tears, and coaxed and caressed by the smiles of yesterday. I listen vainly, but with thirsty ears, for the witching melody of faint bugles blowing reveille, of far drums beating the long roll. In my dreams I hear again the crash of guns, the rattle of musketry, the strange, mournful mutter of the battlefield. But in the evening of my memory, always I come back to West Point. Always there echoes and re-echoes: Duty, Honor, Country. Today marks my final roll call with you, but I want you to know that when I cross the river my last conscious thoughts will be of The Corps, and The Corps, and The Corps. I bid you farewell.

Douglas MacArthur died on April 5, 1964 of biliary cirrhosis, shortly after completing his memoirs.

HARRY S. TRUMAN

Truman was saddled with the unpopular stalemate in Korea for the last year and a half of his presidency. His personal popularity continued to plummet, spurred on by relentless attacks by Senator Joseph McCarthy and his followers, in which they accused Truman and his State Department of being soft on Communism. Ironically, Truman had become more of a counter-force against the Soviet Union than ever—pushing back against the Kremlin's aggressive policies on many different fronts. The combination of the Soviets' acquiring the A-bomb in 1949 and their sponsorship of the attack on South Korea in 1950 had convinced Truman that only an all-out arms program would allow the U.S. to preserve its national security against the Soviet Union and Communist China, which had in early 1950 signed a mutual defense treaty.

Truman authorized the development of an even more powerful weapon—the Hydrogen Bomb; and the U.S. detonated the first one on November 1, 1952.

On October 10, 1951 Truman signed into law the Mutual Security Act authorizing more than seven billion dollars for economic and military development. A massive American military build-up followed and the nuclear arms race had begun.

Truman continued to strengthen NATO at the same time that the U.S. was unflagging in its efforts to keep the United Nations viable as a council of last resort for international peace and cooperation.

Truman's decision to stand up to the Soviets and Red China over Korea had an enormous impact. The United States economy which by the end of 1951 had entered a period of unprecedented growth lasting more than a decade, was stimulated further by the nuclear and conventional arms races. This growth in turn helped jump-start the economies of Western Europe and Japan.

Korea had militarized the Cold War and extended its geographic reach from Europe to the Far East. Later it was further extended to Africa, the Middle East and the Americas. And to make sure that the new extension of the Truman Doctrine to Asia would not come at the expense of Europe, American troop deployments to Europe were significantly increased. Truman had ushered in both the atomic age and the age of the United States as the world's predominant economic power. His successor, President Dwight D. Eisenhower, would consolidate those gains with his own under the slogan "peace and prosperity."

When Truman left the presidency in January 1953, he was one of the most unpopular politicians in America.

Yet Truman yielded power gracefully and seemingly without bitterness. An entry in his diary noted that one of his true heroes of history, Cincinnatus, knew not only when but how to lay down power. Harry and Bess Truman readapted to life in Independence almost immediately. With walking stick in hand, citizen Truman began brisk walks each morning which lasted for most of the remaining two decades of his life.

As President, Harry Truman received a salary of $100,000 per year which he and Bess lived quite well on; and they even managed to put a little aside for retirement. But earning a living was a challenge for him as an ex-president. The sole income the Trumans had was his Army pension which paid only $112.50 a month. And Truman was anxious to begin raising money for the construction of, the Truman Library and Museum—an estimated $1.5 million project.

As former president, Harry Truman had many job offers but none of them really interested him. He did, however, finally end his and Bess's financial problems by agreeing to write his memoirs. He sold the exclusive rights to his memoirs to *Life Magazine* for $600,000 to be paid over five years, a huge sum of money back in 1953.

Truman's real labor for the remainder of his working years was performed in his office at the Truman Presidential Library—collecting, organizing and editing his presidential papers. The library also gave him a comfortable and inspiring work place where he could read, write and attend to the multitude of small tasks required of an ex-president.

Margaret Truman married E. Clifton Daniel, a New York Times editor and eventually moved to Manhattan. The Daniels were blessed with four sons. When former president Truman paid one of his frequent visits to Margaret and her family at their Park Avenue residence, his daily walks on the streets of New York would attract a crowd, including many members of the press. Those reporters who were able to keep up with Truman's quick pace would pepper him with questions on current matters of state and politics. Truman was only too glad to accommodate them and without breaking stride would respond in typical Harry Truman feisty, folksy and sometimes blunt style. He enjoyed himself immensely—the walk and talk regimen providing him with a way to reach out to the public, an exercise he truly missed. The

Truman early morning walks became a major New York media event and introduced him to a whole new generation. Though his comments were sometimes acerbic and controversial, they did help restore some of the popularity and prestige which Truman had lost during the last couple of years of his presidency.

Truman wore the cloak of elder statesman of the Democratic Party comfortably and was even able to patch up the feud between himself and President Eisenhower dating back to when they were political rivals. His endorsements for the Democratic presidential nomination in 1952, '56 and '60 were eagerly sought by the candidates, among whom were two of his great favorites, Senators Lyndon B. Johnson and Stuart Symington.

Harry Truman was lucky to live long enough to witness his vindication by most historians for the firing of MacArthur. As he predicted, once enough time had elapsed for historians to revisit the Truman presidency and evaluate it in the light of his enduring accomplishments in foreign policy, national defense and domestic progress, a renaissance of scholarly thought concerning the Truman years occurred, which elevated him into the ranks of America's greatest presidents. Truman never spoke of himself as a great man but he did add George C. Marshall to his pantheon of the greatest Americans of all time, together with George Washington, Andrew Jackson, Abraham Lincoln and Robert E. Lee.

Harry S. Truman died on December 26, 1972, survived by his beloved Bess, Margaret and four grandsons. He was never a charismatic figure or a revered leader during his time as a public servant. He was never a rich man, had little formal education and was not a member of a learned profession. But like MacArthur, the whole man was greater than the sum of his parts. He was a public servant Cincinnatus would have been proud to know.

MATTHEW B. RIDGWAY

When NATO supreme commander Dwight D. Eisenhower resigned to run for president, there was only one logical successor. President Truman was fortunate to have a man of Matthew B. Ridgway's caliber waiting in the wings. In May of 1952, Ridgway became the second Supreme Allied Commander Europe. His tenure as NATO Chief was not without friction. The straight-forward, frequently blunt Ridgway, managed to ruffle the feathers of European military and civilian leaders alike with his irrepressible candor, which invariably caused him to say exactly what he thought. Lacking the skill for diplomacy and politics of Dwight D. Eisenhower, his relationships with the Europeans were frequently stormy. There was also resentment on their part that Ridgway's staff officers were mostly Americans.

Nevertheless, Ridgway oversaw the development of a coordinated command structure, significant growth in forces and facilities and improved training. As he had done with Eighth Army in Korea, Ridgway left NATO a far more effective military force when he moved on again on August 17, 1953 to replace General Collins as U.S. Army Chief of Staff. President Eisenhower promptly tasked Ridgway with assessing the pros and cons of United States intervention in Indochina, to come to the aid of the French. France was a major ally at that time and Eisenhower strongly supported the intervention. Ridgway's report detailed the necessity for a massive commitment of men and materiél in order for U.S. intervention to be effective. He also recommended against our involvement in Vietnam except in an advisory role; and Eisenhower reluctantly adopted his recommendation. A major U.S. military involvement in Southeast Asia was thus deferred for almost ten years until the Kennedy-Johnson years.

Ridgway's negative assessment of the prospect of a major United States role in Vietnam placed a considerable strain on the relationship between Ridgway and Eisenhower. It was no secret that Eisenhower had very much wanted to intervene. Their relationship was further tested by Ridgway's opposition to Eisenhower's proposal to significantly reduce the size of the army in favor of air power and nuclear weapons. Ridgway argued forcefully for a powerful, mobile ground force to counter the ongoing Soviet threat.

The continuing disagreements between Ridgway and the Eisenhower administration prevented his appointment to a second term as Army Chief of Staff, and Matthew B. Ridgway retired from the Army on June 30, 1955.

The remarkable military career of Matthew Bunker Ridgway had come to an end. It was only fitting that he went out the same way he had always conducted himself as an officer—respectfully assertive, strongly opinionated and unerringly forthright.

Ridgway was a great admirer of Harry S. Truman and it is not hard to understand why. In their outlooks—both on life and on the qualities of leadership—they were kindred spirits.

Even in retirement, Ridgway continued to advocate the need to maintain a strong military, but to be used judiciously. He expressed many of his ideas in two books, *Soldier: The Memoirs of Matthew B. Ridgway*, his autobiography; and *The Korean War*.

Ridgway stayed active in public and military affairs through his chairmanship of the Board of Trustees of the Mellon Institute, membership on multiple corporate boards and service on Pentagon strategic studies committees.

Tragedy struck the Ridgway family when his son was killed in a camping accident in 1971. Ridgway was said by friends to be never the same after that—suffering from a depression which made him morose a good deal of the time.

Matthew B. Ridgway died in July, 1993 at the age of 98. At his burial in Arlington National Cemetery, Chairman of the Joint Chiefs of Staff Colin Powell said about Ridgway, in a powerful eulogy, that "No soldier ever performed his duty better than this man. No soldier ever upheld his honor better than this man. No soldier ever loved his country better than this man did. Every American soldier owes a debt to this great man."

DEAN ACHESON

Acheson retired as Secretary of State on January 20, 1953 and returned to the practice of law at an office located only two blocks from the White House.

In retirement, the crusty Acheson crossed paths often with old adversaries. Notably, he served on the Yale University Board of Trustees with former Senator Robert Taft, his old nemesis. Even more surprising, he reconciled with his former political foe, Richard M. Nixon, and became a major advisor to President Nixon, although Acheson stayed strictly in the background and made a conscious effort to keep his influential status from being publicized.

During the "Cuban Missile Crisis" of October, 1962, Acheson was part of the inner group advising President Kennedy. He brought to the discussions the sobering point of view of a Cold War hard-liner, frequently expressing a deep skepticism over statements coming out of the Kremlin and urging extreme caution when judging the intentions of the Soviet Union. So valued was his role that President Kennedy dispatched Acheson to France to brief French president Charles DeGaulle on the crisis and secure his support for the U.S. blockade of Cuba.

Acheson remained, for more than two decades after leaving the State Department, an influential member of the foreign policy establishment, heading up Democratic policy groups and serving as a major adviser to Presidents Kennedy, Johnson and Nixon. In the 1960s he became a member of the bipartisan group called the *Wise Men* who initially supported the Vietnam War but later turned against it in March of 1968 during a pivotal meeting with President Johnson, which contributed to Johnson's decision not to run for another term as president.

In 1964, Acheson was awarded the Presidential Medal of Freedom and won the Pulitzer Prize for History for his memoirs of his time spent in the State Department.

Dean Acheson died following a massive stroke in 1971 at the age of 78, survived by a son, David C. Acheson, and daughter, Mrs. William P. Bundy.

GEORGE C. MARSHALL

President Truman fired Secretary of Defense Louis A. Johnson in September 1950, in the early days of the Korean War. The Defense Department had been poorly managed under Johnson's stewardship and was woefully unprepared for war. George C. Marshall had been retired for a couple of years, was aging and was not in robust health. Moreover, he had already achieved everything that could reasonably be expected of a man during one lifetime.

Truman, nevertheless, believed Marshall was the only man he could rely upon to rebuild the nation's defenses and bring the country back to a state of military readiness. After the post-World War II standdown, the nation needed to be put back on a war footing as quickly as possible. To meet what Truman considered to be the national imperative of putting Marshall in charge of the nation's defenses, he knew that only one thing would induce Marshall to return to government—his sense of patriotism and duty. When Truman approached Marshall, he did not beg, plead or cajole. He simply told him he had to take over at the Defense Department because his country needed him and his president needed him. Marshall's sense of duty compelled him to say yes, with the understanding that it would only be temporary. Marshall served as Secretary of Defense for one year only, from September of 1950 until September of 1951, but presided over the restoration of the nation's military might, including the kick-off of the nuclear arms race with the Soviet Union. By the time he retired from government for good in 1951, he had largely conducted the overall military operations of the U.S. during World War II as Army Chief of Staff; restored

Western Europe after the War through the Marshall Plan as Secretary of State; and brought the nation to full strength for the Cold War as Secretary of Defense.

In 1953, George C. Marshall became the only Army general in the history of the United States to be awarded the Nobel Peace Prize, for his work in planning and implementing the economic restoration of war-torn Europe through the Marshall Plan.

In a lengthy television interview on his years as president, former-president Harry S. Truman was asked who he thought was the American that made the greatest contribution to the world over the last three decades. Without hesitating for even a second, Truman replied, "George C. Marshall," adding "I don't think in this age in which I have lived, that there has been a man that has been a greater administrator; a man with a knowledge of military affairs equal to General Marshall."

George Catlett Marshall died on October 16, 1959 at the age of 79 and was buried in Arlington National Cemetery.

J. LAWTON COLLINS

His army colleagues preferred the nickname Lightning Joe Collins to the more formal J. Lawton Collins, which seemed a little too stuffy for a good 'ole Louisiana boy. Besides, Joe Collins's nickname was truly descriptive of his lightning-fast thrusts during World War II against the Germans as he led the charge in Normandy, at the Battle of the Bulge; and earlier against the Japanese at Guadalcanal.

After he completed a four year term as U.S. Army Chief of Staff on August 15, 1953, having held that position for the entire Korean War, Collins's new job, by its nature, could hardly be accomplished with lightning speed. As U.S. Representative to the *Standing Group of NATO*, his principle duty as prescribed by President Eisenhower was to visit the top military men and civilian defense officials of America's NATO allies in Europe, in an effort to persuade them in his soft southern drawl to meet their commitments of men and arms to NATO's forces. Having known many of the top European defense officials during his World War II days, Collins was always warmly received, but it was a receptiveness which did not translate into any kind of an enhanced contribution by the Europeans to NATO. The excuse was almost always the same—poor economic conditions in their countries would not permit it. The suspicion was that the real reason was that they were only too happy to rest under the huge protective umbrella of the United States.

But suddenly Collins was called to a new challenge under conditions of cloak and dagger-type secrecy which sent him halfway around the world. A mysterious phone call in October 1954 from an Eisenhower aide conveyed to Collins the President's order to return to Washington the very next day in order to meet with Secretary of State John Foster Dulles.

In May 1954 the French had fought and lost at Dien Bien Phu without receiving any U.S. assistance. Now Vietnam was divided at the 17th Parallel and the Communist Viet Minh was undermining the hold on South Vietnam of the U.S.—backed president, Ngo Dinh Diem. The President wanted Collins to leave immediately for Saigon as his personal ambassador, "to take a fresh look at the situation," to speak with full authority of the United States Government in its support of maintaining a non-Communist government in Vietnam and to assist President Diem in developing a strong internal security force. As President Eisenhower's man in Vietnam, Collins was to do everything he could to halt the progress of, in Eisenhower's words, "the dangerous forces threatening South Vietnam." Korea was frozen into stalemate and Vietnam was showing portents of becoming the next hot spot of a cold war. Collins got to know Diem well during his mission to Saigon and a mutual respect developed between them, but the seeds of the disaster which would occur in Vietnam in the '60s and '70s had already been planted. Eisenhower had sent Lt. General John W. "Iron Mike" O'Daniel to Vietnam as the head of an American military assistance group in Vietnam with a specific mission to develop an effective South Vietnamese Army. After a couple of months in Saigon, however, Collins had come to the conclusion that United States support for Diem was no longer a viable policy because he would never allow General O'Daniel to succeed in his mission. That success would mean Diem's giving up control of the armed services—something Collins was convinced Diem would never do.

On January 20, 1955 Collins reported to Dulles that South Vietnam could not match the military capability of the Viet Minh (later Viet Cong) and eventually it would overrun all of Vietnam. Collins was prescient in his prediction, although the heavy involvement of the North Vietnam regular army was required to complete the job after the massive U.S. intervention of 1965 through 1972.

Collins remained in Vietnam until May of 1954. Upon his return, he met with Eisenhower and Dulles and reportedly said to the President, "I hope, Mr. President, that you and Secretary Dulles do not feel that I have let you down in Vietnam." Collins could not, despite a good relationship with Diem, get him to do what had to be done; although during Collins's tenure as special ambassador, Diem did significantly strengthen South Vietnam's military. "By no means, Joe," answered Dulles, "when you went out, we thought there was a ten percent chance of saving Vietnam from Communism. You have raised that figure to at least fifty percent."

Collins returned the next day to his post as U.S. representative on the NATO Standing Group, a position in which he remained until 1960. He also found time to serve as Director of Hungarian refugee relief in 1956 through 1957. He served on the Board of Directors of Charles Pfizer and Company from 1957 to 1959. Collins wrote two books, *War in Peacetime*, in 1968, and his autobiography, *Lightning Joe*, in 1979.

J. Lawton Collins died on September 12, 1987 at the age of 92, survived by his wife, Gladys, his children, seventeen grandchildren and eight great-grandchildren. He was buried in Arlington Cemetery with the full military honors available to an American soldier buried at Arlington. Among his decorations were the Distinguished Service Medal, two Silver Stars, the Legion of Honor, the Croix de Guerre and the British Campaign of the Order of the Bath.

OMAR BRADLEY

General of the Army Omar Nelson Bradley was nearing the end of his illustrious military career as hostilities in Korea finally came to an end. As Commanding General of Field Forces, European Theater during World War II, Bradley had already achieved all he could have hoped for as a combat leader. After the war his sterling credentials were further burnished by a stint as Army Chief of Staff in 1948 and then as America's first Chairman of the Joint Chiefs of Staff from 1949 until his retirement from active service in 1953. Bradley had never been a flamboyant, or publicity-seeking, general and despite his many decorations, the appellation that he appreciated the most was the nickname he carried with him beginning with the end of World War II and for the rest of his life—"The GI's General."

After retirement from the military, Bradley reunited with his Truman Administration colleague, Dean Acheson, as a member of the "Wise Men," the think-tank created by President Lyndon B. Johnson, comprised by experts in their field, charged with recommending strategies for dealing with the nation's Cold War problems, particularly the Vietnam War.

Omar Bradley died on April 8, 1981 at the age of 88 and like most of the other giants of his era was buried at Arlington National Cemetery. Perhaps the most fitting epitaph for Omar Bradley were his own words spoken in 1949:

Ours is a world of nuclear giants and ethical infants. We know more about war than about peace, more about killing than we know about living.

OLIVER P. (O.P.) SMITH

After returning to the United States from Korea, General O.P. Smith became Commanding General of the Marine Corps Base at Camp Pendleton, California. He retired from the Marine Corps in 1955. So strong was the mutual loathing between Smith and Army General Edward Almond, that the controversy over Smith's role in the march to the Yalu continued to burn well-after the end of the War. In a book, General Almond attempted to blame X Corps' defeat on Smith's failure to obey his order to move with great speed north to the Yalu, after the First Marine Division's landing at Wonsan on the East coast. Smith's actions bordered on insubordination when instead he moved the Division at a deliberate pace north, establishing supply centers, garrisons and even an air field along the way. Knowing how well he had prepared his exit route from the Chosin Reservoir had undoubtedly given Smith the confidence to describe the First Marines' action not as a retreat but as an attack in the opposite direction. Military historians almost unanimously credit General O. P. Smith with having saved the First Marine Division on its long fighting retreat to Hungnam, where it was safely evacuated by sea.

Oliver P. Smith died in California on December 25, 1977 at the age of 84. Among the honors he received during his military career were the Korean Presidential Unit Citation, the Distinguished Service Medal, the Silver Star, the Bronze Star with valor and the Korean Service Medal with 5 Silver Stars.

LEWIS BURWELL "CHESTY" PULLER

Colonel Chesty Puller was the most decorated United States Marine in history. He is most famous for his quote during the withdrawal from the Chosin reservoir, "We've been looking for the enemy for some time now. We're surrounded. That simplifies things." After General O.P. Smith's return to the United States, Puller was thrilled to become temporary Commander-in-Chief of the First Marine Division in Korea until a permanent replacement was named.

After the Korean War, Puller's situation came to epitomize the worst in the inter-service rivalry between the Army and the Marine Corps. By Puller's scathing public criticisms of the performance of many Army units at Chosin, he burned his bridges behind him with the Army high command who now had one of its own, Dwight D. Eisenhower, in the White House.

To this day, Marines adamantly insist that Chesty Puller was never awarded the Medal of Honor because of pressure from senior army officers.

Nevertheless, Puller's career advancement was not impeded. In 1951 he became a Brigadier General, later a major general and retired at the rank of Lieutenant General.

In 1955 he collapsed from what he claimed was heat prostration but was diagnosed at Walter Reed Naval Hospital as a heart condition. Puller alleged that this was part of a conspiracy to force him out of the military. No proof of such a conspiracy was ever presented but General Puller was involuntarily retired for medical reasons in 1955. He died on October 11, 1971 at the age of 73. Few high military officers in America's history could match his record for personal bravery on the field of battle. Puller's actions along the retreat route from Chosin Reservoir were an inspiration to his fellow Marines and contributed immeasurably to their impressive performance.

Acknowledgments

THE historical and biographical sources which served as reference materials for this book are simply too numerous to mention. In any event, it was the many heroes of the early Korean War who are most deserving of acknowledgment. They were the co-authors of the Truman—MacArthur saga, the no-names who wrote their history in blood—the isolated units and individual soldiers who fought to the end in June, July and August of 1950 under Walton W. Walker, to keep the run-away train, which was the North Korean Army, from obliterating everything in its path until it reached the sea. That it was halted at the Naktong River is a testament only to the grit and courage of the men of the U.S. Eighth Army. The same can be said for the Marines who scaled the sea-walls at Inchon and those who attacked the Chinese positions at Chosin Reservoir head-on, in the middle of the night, in temperatures of thirty to forty below zero, while out-numbered ten to one. It is a tribute to the men of Fox Company who managed to keep Toktong Pass clear for four days while under unrelenting attack, thereby enabling the escape and survival of the First Marine Division; and to the cross-country warriors who in turn rescued Fox Company. It is the story of the men of the Second Infantry who ran the murderous gauntlet from Kunuri to Sunchon but still smashed through everything the Red Chinese Army could put in their way; and of the valiant Brits at Gloster Hill and the surrounded and vastly outnumbered U.S., Dutch and French units at Chip'yong-ni and Wonju who delivered such a smashing defeat to the Chinese Army. It goes on and on. They wrote the epic story of the early Korean War. Those of us who have chronicled their triumphs and tragedies are mere scriveners.

The story of Truman and MacArthur is both a metaphor for the danger, schisms and political polarization of their era and a prime example of how brave American patriots from Bunker Hill to Tora Bora were able to cast their deep differences aside in the pursuit of a vital common cause.

—Donald J. Farinacci

www.ingramcontent.com/pod-product-compliance
Lightning Source LLC
LaVergne TN
LVHW051623080426
835511LV00016B/2145